LIFE WITHOUT FATHER

LIFE
WITHOUT
FATHER

*Compelling new evidence that fatherhood and marriage are
indispensable for the good of children and society*

DAVID POPENOE

HARVARD UNIVERSITY PRESS

Cambridge, Massachusetts
London, England

First Harvard University Press paperback edition published in 1999 by arrangement with The Free Press, a Division of Simon & Schuster Inc.

Second printing, 2002

Library of Congress Cataloging-in-Publication Data

Popenoe, David, 1932–
    Life without father : compelling new evidence that fatherhood and marriage are
indispensable for the good of children and society / David Popenoe.
        p.   cm.
    Includes bibliographical references (p.   ) and index.
    ISBN 0-674-53260-0 (pbk.)
        1. Fatherless family—United States. 2. Fatherhood—United States. 3. Fathers—
United States. 4. Paternal deprivation—United States. 5. Children of single parents—
United States. 6. United States—Social conditions. I. Title.
HQ756.P65   1996
306.874´2—dc20   95-46233

Designed by Carla Bolte

Contents

Preface

The ideas in this book are an outgrowth of many years of thinking about family problems in a number of modern societies. The genesis of the book probably lies in Sweden, where I lived with my family for several years in the early 1970s and taught at the University of Stockholm. We loved our time in Sweden, and we highly value the progressive and enlightened character of Swedish society. But over the years it gradually became clear to me that, despite the benevolence of the welfare state which has largely removed from families economic pressures and uncertainties that loom so large in our country, childrearing couples in Sweden were breaking up at a remarkable rate, and children in great numbers were being separated from their biological fathers.

In America, the same trend exists in an even more flagrant form. The United States and Sweden, of course, stand at opposite political poles, one being the most laissez-faire of the industrialized societies and the other the most welfare-state oriented. In America, therefore, with the partial exception of the tiny percentage of families who actually are "on welfare," it can hardly be claimed that the welfare state is the main cause of the family problem. A more important cause here is an untrammeled market—the opposite of the welfare state. Yet a trend so powerful as to be found prominently in both of these nations must be generated largely by a culture that transcends all modern societies, and this thought was the basis of my first family book, *Disturbing the Nest: Family Change and Decline in Modern Societies* (1988). The book examined the family-related cultural trends—especially in Sweden but in comparison with Switzerland, New Zealand, and the United States—that are part of what we have come to label "modernization." It concluded that in each of these modernized nations the family has markedly declined as an institution.

Since then, in America, the "family values" debate has taken over the headlines. The present book is a contribution to that debate from the perspective of a social scientist. Some of the ideas in this book were first formulated at meetings of the Council on Families in America, an interdisciplinary group of family experts and scholars from across the political spectrum, of which I serve as cochairman. I owe a large debt of gratitude to the members and associates of the council, especially Jean Bethke Elshtain, Barbara Dafoe Whitehead, Don S. Browning, Leon R. Kass, Mary Ann Glendon, Sylvia Ann Hewlett, William A. Galston, David Blankenhorn, Allan C. Carlson, Norval D. Glenn, Judith Wallerstein, Judith Martin, Theodora Ooms, Steven Bayme, Gloria G. Rodriguez, and Vesna Neskow. Our deliberations over several years have been exceptionally stimulating. Conversations about fatherhood with Wade Horn and Don Eberle of the National Fatherhood Initiative, and the work of Amitai Etzioni, have also been particularly influential. The students in my family courses at Rutgers University have, over the years, been another major source of intellectual input.

I extend special thanks to Barbara D. Whitehead and Allan C. Carlson for reviewing portions of chapters 3 and 4; to Lionel Tiger and Helen Fisher for reviewing portions of chapter 6; and to Susan Repko for providing research assistance throughout. At the publisher's, Martin Kessler provided enormously helpful editorial assistance throughout the book writing process, and Abigail Strubel guided this book through production with a sure hand and continuous good cheer.

Undoubtedly, my greatest debt is owed to the members of my own family of marriage. It is from them that I learned firsthand how to be a father. My beloved wife of thirty-six years, Kate, has provided me with nothing less than a higher education in all matters of living. She also, with a wife's devotion for which I shall eternally be grateful, read and helped me to improve every page of this book. My two daughters, Rebecca and Julia, have made fathering the single most meaningful and worthwhile activity of my life. They have also enriched this book appreciably by reading and commenting on portions of it and by providing information from their areas of professional specialization as adults: anthropology and pediatrics, respectively.

This book is dedicated to the memory of my father, Paul Popenoe (1888–1979). He lived a long and immensely useful life, which included the raising of four sons. As but one small indicator of his many fatherly successes, he still exists as a brightly shining beacon in my own life.

Introduction

"Fathers should be neither seen nor heard," Oscar Wilde once wrote. "That is the only proper basis for family life." With each passing year, American society has increasingly become an immense social testing ground for this proposition. Unfortunately for Wilde's reputation as a social analyst, to say nothing about the health of our society, the results have proved highly unsupportive. American fathers are today more removed from family life than ever before in our history. And according to a growing body of evidence, this massive erosion of fatherhood contributes mightily to many of the major social problems of our time.

This book provides an analysis of the American experiment of fatherlessness. Drawing from the social sciences, history, and evolutionary psychology, it examines the nature and meaning of fatherhood and reviews the trend, the evidence, and the social consequences of the removal of fathers from families and the lives of their children. Regrettably, as I shall point out, America is at the vanguard of social trends and impulses that are affecting fatherhood and children in all modern societies.

The print pages and airwaves have been filled with discussions of fatherhood in recent decades. Yet most discussions have focused on just one issue—how to get fathers to share their traditional breadwinner role and take up a new (for them) child-care-provider role. The call from younger women has been loud and clear: We need a new conception of fatherhood, a "new father," one who will help equally in the home just as women now strive to help equally in the workplace; one who will share the "second shift" with his mate.

The father's role—what society expects of fathers—has indeed changed enormously in recent years. Fathers are expected to be more engaged with their children and involved with housework—if not nearly as much as most women would like, certainly far more than the past generation of fathers would have thought possible.

1

This role change has been highly positive in most respects. But with all the concentration on "role equality" in the home, the larger and more ominous trend of modern fatherhood has been mostly overlooked. We have been through many social revolutions in the past three decades—sex, women's liberation, divorce—but none more significant for society than the startling emergence of the absent father, a kind of pathological counterpart to the new father.

While the new father has been emerging gradually for most of this century, it is only in the past thirty years that we have witnessed the enormous increase in absent fathers. In times past, many children were left fatherless through his premature death. Today, the fathers are still alive and out there somewhere; the problem is that they seldom see much, if anything, of their children.

The main reason for contemporary father absence is the dramatic decline of marriage. Divorce rates have skyrocketed in the past thirty years, and even more recently we have seen a veritable explosion in the rate of unwed motherhood. What this means, in human terms, is that about half of today's children will spend at least a portion of their growing-up years living apart from their fathers.

As a society, we can respond to this new fatherlessness in several ways. We can, as more and more of us seem to be doing, simply declare fathers to be unnecessary, superfluous. This is the response of "single parents by choice." It is the response of those who say that if daddies and mommies are expected to do precisely the same things in the home, why do we need both? It is the response of those who declare that unwed motherhood is a woman's right, or that single-parent families are every bit as good as two-parent families, or that divorce is generally beneficial for children.

In my view, these responses represent a human tragedy—for children, for women, for men, and for our society as a whole. I am writing this book to tell you why. My main emphasis will be on children. I hope to convince you, especially those of you who rely on empirical evidence before you make up your mind, that the evidence is strong: Fathering is different from mothering; involved fathers are indispensable for the good of children and society; and our growing national fatherlessness is a disaster in the making.

THE DECLINE OF FATHERHOOD

The decline of fatherhood is one of the most basic, unexpected, and extraordinary social trends of our time. The trend can be captured in a single telling statistic: in just three decades, from 1960 to 1990, the percentage of children living apart from their biological fathers more than doubled, from 17 percent to 36 percent. If this rate continues, by the turn of the century nearly 50 percent of American children will be going to sleep each night without being able to say good night to their dads.

No one predicted this trend, few researchers or government agencies have monitored it, and it is not widely discussed, even today. But its importance to society is second to none. Father absence is a major force lying behind many of the attention-grabbing issues that dominate the news: crime and delinquency; premature sexuality and out-of-wedlock teen births; deteriorating educational achievement; depression, substance abuse, and alienation among teenagers; and the growing number of women and children in poverty. These issues all point to a profound deterioration in the well-being of children. Some experts have suggested, in fact, that the current generation of children and youth is the first in our nation's history to be less well-off—psychologically, socially, economically, and morally—than their parents were at the same age. Or as Senator Daniel Patrick Moynihan has observed, "the United States . . . may be the first society in history in which children are distinctly worse off than adults."[1]

Along with the growing father absence, our cultural view of fatherhood is changing. Few people have doubts about the fundamental importance of mothers. But fathers? More and more the question is being raised, are fathers really necessary? Many would answer no, or maybe not. And to the degree that fathers are still thought necessary, fatherhood is said by many to be merely a social role, as if men had no inherent biological predisposition whatsoever to acknowledge and to invest in their own offspring. If merely a social role, then perhaps anyone is capable of playing it. The implication is one of arbitrary substitutability. Not just biological fathers, but any competent actor who has studied the part can easily step in: mothers, partners, stepfathers, uncles and aunts, grandparents. Perhaps the script can even be rewritten and the role changed—or dropped.

FATHERS: ESSENTIAL BUT PROBLEMATIC

Across time and cultures, fathers have always been considered by societies to be essential—and not just for their sperm. Indeed, until today, no known society ever thought of fathers as potentially unnecessary. Biological fathers are everywhere identified, if possible, and play some role in their children's upbringing. Marriage and the nuclear family— mother, father, and children—are the most universal social institutions in existence. In no society has nonmarital childbirth been the cultural norm. To the contrary, a concern for the "legitimacy" of children is another cultural near universal: The mother of an illegitimate child virtually everywhere has been regarded as a social deviant, if not a social outcast, and her child has been stigmatized.

At the same time, being a father is universally problematic for men and for their societies in a way that being a mother is not. While mothers the world over bear and nurture their young with an intrinsic acknowledgment and, most commonly, acceptance of their role, taking on the role of father is often filled with conflict, tension, distance, and doubt. Across societies, fathers may or may not be closely engaged with their children, reside with the mother, or see their father role as highly important.

The source of this sex-role difference can be plainly stated. Men are not biologically as attuned to being committed fathers as women are to being committed mothers. Left culturally unregulated, men's sexual behavior can be promiscuous, their paternity casual, their commitment to families weak. Yet in virtually all societies, especially modern societies, both child and social well-being depend on high levels of paternal investment: the time, energy, and resources that fathers are willing to impart to their children.

That men are not perfectly attuned to fatherhood in biological terms is not to say that fathering behavior is foreign to the nature of men. Far from it. Evolutionary scientists tell us that the development of the fathering capacity and high paternal investments in offspring—features not common among our primate relatives—have been a source of enormous evolutionary advantage for human beings. Because human young are more dependent on adults for a longer period of their lives than any other species and human mothers require a great deal of help if their children are to survive, a key to human evolution was the capturing of male effort to the goal of childrearing. It is almost certainly the case that the human family is the oldest social institution, at heart a biological arrangement for raising children that has always involved fathers as well as mothers.

In recognition of the fatherhood problem—that fatherhood is essential but also somewhat problematic—human cultures have realized that sanctions are necessary if paternal investments are to be maximized. The main cultural carrier of sanctions is the institution of marriage, a major purpose of which is to hold men to the reproductive pair bond. Simply defined, marriage is a relationship within which a community socially approves and encourages sexual intercourse and the birth of children. It is society's way of signaling to would-be parents of children that their long-term relationship together is socially important.

As evidenced by the vows of fidelity and permanence that almost universally are part of the wedding ceremony, an important purpose of marriage is to hold the man to the union. Margaret Mead once said, with the fatherhood problem strongly in mind, that there is no society in the world where men will stay married for very long unless culturally required to do so.

FATHERHOOD AND MARRIAGE

Today, because the great social complexity of modern societies requires longer periods of socialization and dependency for children than ever before, the need for adult investments in children has reached new heights. In order to succeed economically in an increasingly technological society, children must be highly educated. In order to succeed socially and psychologically in an increasingly complex and heterogeneous culture, children must have strong and stable attachments to adults. Nonfamily institutions can help with education, but family and close-kin groups are essential for socioemotional success. Parents and other close relatives are still the persons most likely to have the motivational levels necessary to provide the time and attention that children need to feel loved and special.

Yet at the time when the childrearing task is ever more demanding and male assistance with the task is ever more important, cultural sanctions holding men to marriage and children have dramatically weakened. Marriage, once both sacred and economically essential for survival, is today based solely on the fragile tie of affection for one's mate. And whereas the institution of marriage once legally bound a couple with a high degree of permanence, marriages can now be broken unilaterally on a whim.

The United States has by far the highest divorce rate in the industrialized world. The chance that a first marriage occurring today will end in divorce stands at around 50 percent—by some estimates as high as 60 percent. The chance in the middle of the last century was around 5 percent. In the past three decades alone, the divorce rate has doubled or tripled, depending upon how one calculates it.

Marriages are not only breaking up in large numbers, but the institution itself is in decline. The marriage rate is dropping. In place of marriage we are witnessing the rapid rise of nonmarital cohabitation, which by its very nature implies a lower level of commitment. More problematic still is the increase in "single parenting by choice."

There has emerged in the last decade or two a tendency for women to go it alone. It would be nice, many of these women report, if the perfect man came into the picture. But he is not around, so I am going to have a child anyway. This phenomenon was made culturally memorable by the *Murphy Brown* television episode in which Murphy decided to have a nonmarital child and that fact was celebrated nationwide. Like Murphy, but typically without her level of economic resources, more and more women report with each passing year that they, too, might have a child if they are unable to find the right man.

The lifestyle of the single parent, rather than being eschewed, is becoming socially accepted as part of a new wave of tolerance befitting the contemporary celebration of diversity. Even marriage and family-relations professionals have come to extol "alternative lifestyles." Textbooks that used to be entitled *Marriage and the Family* (read: married-father-included) are now entitled *Intimate Relationships* or the all-inclusive *Families*. The growth of unmarried mothers on welfare has raised some national ire, but many on the Left believe that there is a new national "right" for such mothers to have as many children as they want and immediately receive support for those children from taxpayers.

With this kind of cultural acceptance, it is little wonder that the percentage of out-of-wedlock births in America has increased 600 percent in just three decades, from 5 percent of all births in 1960 to 30 percent in 1991.[2] If the percentage keeps climbing at its current rate, 40 percent of all births (and 80 percent of minority births) will take place out of wedlock by the turn of the century.[3]

THE SHRINKING FATHER

Contemporary fatherhood faces an additional challenge. The father's role has shrunk drastically over the years. American fathers have been losing authority within the family and psychologically withdrawing from a direct role in childrearing almost since colonial times.

The Puritan father was a domestic patriarch; he was not only the family's chief provider and protector but also the moral authority and chief educator, at least of his older children. In the last century, however, the focus of the family turned to mothers. With the rise of a major new family form—what historians label "the modern nuclear family" but what most people today know as "the traditional family"—the father's main role became family breadwinner. Legally and socially fathers became the second parent, and their direct role in the home increasingly was marginalized. Finally, with the waning of the modern nuclear family in this century, even the breadwinner role has eroded.

Today men are being asked to return to domestic roles. Fathers are badly needed as comprehensive childrearers on an equal basis with mothers. Not only does this represent a radical shift from recent history, but increasingly men are asked to become major caretakers for infants and toddlers, a role they never before in history have had to embrace.

THE FATHERHOOD DEBATE

Could it be that the era of fatherhood is at an end, that the fatherhood problem can be resolved by simply getting rid of fathers and perhaps substituting someone or something else in their stead? Is there something new and different about modern societies that makes single parenthood a reasonable option and makes these societies increasingly immune from the age-old proscription against illegitimacy? Have we become so free and individualized and prosperous that the traditional social structures surrounding family life no longer have the importance that they have had in all of human history to date?

Positive answers to these questions have been forcefully argued. The argument contains these key elements:

- Women no longer need men for provision or protection, the traditional male family roles. For provision, most women now have independent access to the labor market; and if they don't, they have access to government-supported welfare programs. For protection, women have the police, and in any event it is usually their male partner from whom they must be protected.
- Both single mothers and their children have been unfairly stigmatized over the generations. This has been grossly unfair to mothers as well as to the children who did absolutely nothing to bring about their plight. Societies today are able, thankfully, to correct this age-old injustice.
- Male-female family life is inherently inequitable, a patriarchal institution wherein men have always dominated women. Men are selfish, irresponsible, psychologically untrustworthy, even intractable. If women are to achieve true equality, therefore, we must find some alternative to the nuclear family.
- Men frequently leave their wives and children in the lurch, especially in times of crisis, either through psychological withdrawal or outright desertion. It is safer for a woman never to begin counting on a man.
- It is not clear that fathers any longer provide something unique to their children. There is not much they do that mothers do not, or cannot, do just as well.

There is some truth, of course, to each of these points. Many women today are perfectly capable, in economic and other terms, of raising children by themselves. The traditional stigma against illegitimacy is something that few people want to bring back. There does seem to be some kind of inherent inequality between men and women, if nothing more than that men are bigger and stronger and more aggressive. The selfish, irresponsible male is not uncommon. And since some fathers and mothers do carry out the same childrearing activities, the question of why we need both is a reasonable one to ask.

But the aim of this book is to try to convince you that this no-father argument is fundamentally wrong. If we continue down the path of fatherlessness, we are headed for social disaster.

FATHERS AND MOTHERS

It is the rare child who does not wish to grow up with both a father and a mother. We should ask the question, why do children have this desire? Despite their sometimes wanting candy for breakfast, children do have, after all, a certain wisdom about life. Is it simply that they don't want to be any different from their friends? Is it merely something they have been taught to say? I think not.

Every child comes into the world totally dependent upon adults, especially the parents to whom they were born. To a large extent children's life chances come from who cares for them and how they are cared for. Of course, children are surprisingly flexible and malleable; some can thrive in the most intolerable of circumstances. But this fact says nothing about the life chances for the multitude. I suspect that children instinctively realize that the world is made up almost equally of two sexes, that each sex possesses biological and psychological traits that balance and complement the other, and that each sex brings something unique and important to children's lives.

Whatever the basis for children's primal desire for a father and a mother, the weight of social science evidence strongly supports the rationality of their wish. In my many years as a functioning social scientist, I know of few other bodies of evidence whose weight leans so much in one direction as does the evidence about family structure: On the whole, two parents—a father and a mother—are better for the child than one parent.[4]

There are, to be sure, many complicating factors to the simple proposition that two parents are best. Family structure is only a gross approximation of what actually goes on within a family. We all know of a two-parent family that is the family from hell. A child can certainly be well-raised to adulthood by one loving parent who is wholly devoted to that child's well-being. But such problems and exceptions in no way deny the aggregate finding or generalization. After all, to take another much-publicized area of research, plenty of three-pack-a-day smokers live to a ripe old age and die of natural causes.

What does the social science evidence about family structure and child well-being actually show? Researchers Sara McLanahan and Gary Sandefur recently examined six nationally representative data sets containing over twenty-five thousand children from a variety of racial and social-class backgrounds. Their conclusion:

> Children who grow up with only one of their biological parents (nearly always the mother) are disadvantaged across a broad array of outcomes . . . they are twice as likely to drop out of high school, 2.5 times as likely to become teen mothers, and 1.4 times as likely to be idle—out of school and out of work—as children who grow up with both parents.[5]

Sure, you may say, that is because one-parent families are poorer. But here is the researchers' conclusion about the economic factor:

> Loss of economic resources accounts for about 50 percent of the disadvantages associated with single parenthood. Too little parental supervision and involvement and greater residential mobility account for most of the rest.[6]

Many other researchers, whose work is reviewed in this book, have come up with similar conclusions. The evidence covers the full range of possible effects, from crime to school achievement. Social analysts William A. Galston and Elaine Ciulla Kamark report, for example, that

> The relationship [between family structure and crime] is so strong that controlling for family configuration erases the relationship between race and crime and between low income and crime. This conclusion shows up again and again in the literature.[7]

Based on such evidence, a strong case can be made that paternal deprivation, in the form of the physical, economic, and emotional unavailability of fathers to their children, has become the most prevalent form of child maltreatment in America today.[8]

Is the missing ingredient in the single-parent family simply a second adult who can provide "parental supervision and involvement"? It is in part, but only in part. Consider this conclusion of McLanahan and Sandefur: "Children of stepfamilies don't do better than children of mothers who never remarry."[9]

The main missing ingredient in a growing number of families today, I shall argue, is the biological father. He can be replaced adequately here and there, and obviously not all biological fathers are good fathers, but in general males biologically unrelated to their children cannot be expected to have the same motivation and dedication to raising those children as males raising their own biological offspring. The incidence of sexual abuse among stepfathers, for example, is far higher than among biological fathers.

It is not my intent to stigmatize step- and adoptive parents. Those alternative family forms where parents are doing their job well deserve our deepest respect; those experiencing difficulties should be provided both compassion and tangible assistance. My point is this: Being a father is much more than merely fulfilling a social role. Engaged biological fathers care profoundly and selflessly about their own children; such fatherly love is not something that can easily be transferred or reduced to the learning of a script. Why many biological fathers themselves are now becoming disengaged from their children is, of course, a puzzling phenomenon and a focus of this book.

THE UNIQUENESS OF FATHERS

What is unique about fathers when compared to mothers? Studies show that virtually all children clearly distinguish a mother role from a father role, even if some contemporary adults do not seem to be able to.[10] Fathers and mothers differ, just as males and females differ. Part of the reason is cultural, to be sure, but only part. Inborn biology is also a major contributor.

You would never know it from reading today's typical social science textbook, but there is a large and growing body of biological evidence for an array of fundamental male-female differences. Indeed, this evidence has begun to dominate the science news. A recent cover story in *Time* magazine is typical. An article on "sizing up the sexes" began: "Scientists are discovering that gender differences have as much to do with the biology of the brain as with the way we are raised."[11] The time has come to view all human behavior as representing a combination of biological and sociocultural forces. It no longer makes sense to view these forces as, in the words of sociologist Alice Rossi, "separate domains contesting for election as primary causes."[12]

Across all cultures, the "natural and comfortable" way most males think, feel, and act is fundamentally different from the way most females think, feel, and act. Differences between men and women have been found universally with respect to four behavioral/psychological traits: aggression and general activity level; cognitive skills; sensory sensitivity; and sexual and reproductive behavior.[13] Perhaps the greatest difference is in aggression and activity level. Almost from the moment of birth, boys tend to be more aggressive and in general to have a somewhat higher activity level than girls. Differences in cognitive skills are less well understood and perhaps not as great. From early adolescence, females tend to have greater verbal ability than males, and males tend to have greater visual-spatial and mathematical ability than females. (Spatial ability refers to the ability to form a mental picture of the shape, position, geography, and proportion of physical objects.) Also, females tend to be more sensitive to all sensory stimuli. They typically receive a wider array of sensory information, are able to communicate it better, and place primacy on personal relationships within which such information is communicated.

While male proficiency rests with "things and theorems," female proficiency rests with personal relationships. Almost from birth, girls are more interested than boys in people and faces, whereas boys "just seem as happy with an object dangled in front of them."[14] The likely origin of sex differences in psychological and behavioral traits, as we shall see, is the differing male and female reproductive and productive roles found in early human evolution.

The stereotyping of such sex differences is easy, of course; we must not overlook the fact that within each sex a substantial range of traits can be found. It is important to realize that males are found at the extreme ends of the continuum with respect to several of these traits. Males, for example, disproportionately make up math geniuses, but also math dysfunctionals. Also, some cultures exaggerate these sex traits; others diminish them. Consider the difference in male and female gender roles between, for example, Sweden and Morocco. In Sweden, male aggression is discouraged, while the activity level of Swedish females is encouraged; in Morocco, just the opposite is the case. Still, the underlying sex-differentiated traits are present in each nation, if in somewhat different proportions.

How do the inherent male-female differences express themselves in dissimilar fathering and mothering behaviors? In dealing with infants, there is an enormous and obvious difference that stems from the woman's having carried the child in utero and from her ability to breast-feed. But beyond that, as Alice Rossi has noted based on an accumulating body of evidence, "In caring for a nonverbal, fragile infant, women have a head start." They are more able to read an infant's facial expressions, handle with tactile gentleness, and soothe with the use of voice.[15] With toddlers, while women provide comfort and emotional acceptance, men typically are more active and arousing in their nurturing activities, fostering certain physical skills and emphasizing autonomy and independence.

Even with older children the father's mode of parenting is not interchangeable with the mother's. Men typically emphasize play more than caretaking, and their play is more likely to involve a rough-and-tumble approach.[16] In attitude and behavior, mothers tend to be responsive and fathers firm; mothers stress emotional security and relationships, and fathers stress competition and risk taking; mothers typically express more concern for the child's immediate well-being, while fathers express more concern for the child's long-run autonomy and independence.

The importance of these different approaches for the growing child should not be underestimated. All children have the need for affiliation with others but also the drive to go off on their own, to be independent. They need both the personal security brought by strong social ties ("roots") and the push away from the group toward eventual autonomy ("wings"). They need a parent who says "strive, do better, challenge yourself," along with one who comforts them when they fall short.

For boys in modern societies, in order to counterbalance a common behavioral tendency, it is important, if they are to excel in life, to stress affiliation with family and community. For girls, for the same reason, it is important to stress independence. But for both sexes the resolution and balancing of these forces is one of the key components of maturation and personal achievement.

Certainly in a pinch, men and women, fathers and mothers, can play each other's parts in the script of life. Indeed, people can be taught to do almost anything. But most men and women are not predisposed or well-motivated to take on even temporarily the behavior and attitudes of the other sex. And most children want and need and can easily detect the real thing. Fatherless children are therefore at a distinct psychological disadvantage, as a growing body of evidence attests.

THE UNATTACHED MALE

Apart from enhancing children's lives, there are other good reasons why it is important for men to be engaged in parenting. One socially crucial reason is contained in this caveat: Every society must be wary of the unattached male, for he is universally the cause of numerous social ills. The good society is heavily dependent on men being attached to a strong moral order centered on families, not only to help raise children but to discipline their own sexual behavior and to reduce their competitive aggression.

Family life is a considerable civilizing force for men. It is not uncommon to hear men say, for example, that they will give up certain deviant or socially irresponsible behavior only when they have children, for then they feel the need to set a good example. Long ago the great sociologist Emile Durkheim noted that married men experience a "salutary discipline"; marriage forces men to master their passions, but it also encourages the regular work habits and self-sacrifice required to meet the family's material needs.[17]

A high proportion of male criminals are unattached. Unattached men are more likely to behave criminally and violently than attached men; they are also more likely to die prematurely through disease, accidents, or self-neglect. Men with various social and physical handicaps obviously find it more difficult to attract a spouse, and it is these same traits that may result in criminal behavior or shorter lives. Yet careful epidemiologic studies have shown that marriage has a protective effect for men independent of the "marriage-selection" factor.[18]

So even those who disagree that fathers are essential to sound child-rearing and feel sanguine about unmarried women taking on the task by themselves still should worry about how the men left out will be spending their time. Do we really want a society filled with single men, unattached to children, leading self-aggrandizing and often predatory lives?

FATHERHOOD, MARRIAGE, AND THE GOOD SOCIETY

Today in America the social order is fraying badly; we seem to be on a path of continuing social decline. The past three decades have seen steeply rising rates of crime, declining interpersonal and political trust, growing personal and corporate greed, deteriorating communities, and increasing confusion over moral issues.[19] I am referring not only to the situation of the inner city poor, with which most Americans have little contact, but to the overall quality of daily life. The average American seemingly has become more anxious, unsettled, and insecure.

Our societal decline can be phrased in terms of a failure of social values. People no longer conduct themselves, to the same extent as prior generations, according to the civic virtues of honesty, self-sacrifice, and personal responsibility. People have become strong on individual rights and weak on community obligations.[20] In our ever-growing pursuit of the self—self-expression, self-development, self-actualization, and self-fulfillment—the social has become increasingly problematic.

At the heart of the problem lies an erosion of personal relationships. People no longer trust others as they once did; they no longer feel the same sense of commitment and obligation to others. This is certainly not a new or original observation. The perceived erosion of "primary relationships" that is associated with modernity was one of the formative conceptions of the discipline of sociology in the last century.[21] But the early sociologists could not have known the great extent to which their conception would prove correct.

Fathers are one of the two most important role models in children's lives. Some children across America now go to bed each night worrying about whether their father will be there the next morning. Some wonder what ever happened to their father. Some think to themselves, who is my father? Is it a stretch to believe that the father-neglected or father-abandoned child is more likely to have a jaundiced view of such values as honesty, self-sacrifice, and personal responsibility, to say nothing of trust?

The decline of fatherhood and of marriage cuts at the heart of the kind of environment considered ideal for childrearing. Such an environment, according to a substantial body of knowledge, consists of an enduring two-parent family that engages regularly in activities together, has many of its own routines and traditions, and provides a great deal of quality contact time between adults and children. The children have frequent contact with relatives, active neighboring in a supportive setting, and contact with their parents' world of work. In addition, there is little concern on the part of children that their parents will break up. Finally, each of these ingredients comes together in the development of a rich family subculture that has lasting meaning and strongly promulgates such family values as responsibility, cooperation, and sharing.

In our society, as in all others so far as we know, the family is the seedbed of trusting and socially responsible personal relationships. The family is also, not coincidentally, the seedbed of those civic virtues that we are losing. Children do not hold such virtues as honesty and self-sacrifice at birth; these virtues must be purposefully taught and reinforced through close personal relationships and good example. Children learn many things, including values, through imitation or modeling. The more consistently caring and altruistic the parent is, the more likely it is the child will be so. If such virtues are not taught within the family, they normally are not taught at all.

What the decline of fatherhood and marriage in America really means, then, is that slowly, insidiously, and relentlessly our society has been moving in an ominous direction—toward the devaluation of children. There has been an alarming weakening of the fundamental assumption, long at the center of our culture, that children are to be loved and valued at the highest level of priority. Nothing could be more serious for our children or our future.

Our national response, therefore, should be the reestablishment of fatherhood and marriage as strong social and cultural realities. If we are to make progress toward a more just and humane society, a major national objective should be no less than this: To increase the proportion of children who are living with and cared for by their married, biological fathers and to decrease the proportion of children who are not.

PLAN OF THIS BOOK

Part One deals with fatherlessness and its effects. The remarkable decline of fatherhood and marriage in America over the past three decades is explored in depth, looking at symptoms and proximate causes. I show how the roots of the decline lie deep within contemporary culture. Drawing on a wide body of social science evidence, the tragic consequences of fatherlessness are described, indicating how the absence of fathers profoundly affects not only children but also women and men.

How did we get to our current situation? Part Two looks back at fatherhood, marriage, and family life in American history. It examines the trajectory of fatherhood through the rise and fall of the "modern nuclear family." This is the now-traditional family form that conservatives love and radicals hate; for better and for worse, it is also a family form whose era has ended. Over the course of the past two centuries, as we shall see, the father's role greatly narrowed. First men left the home, followed later by women.

Part Three is entitled "Why Fathers Matter." The social science evidence is analyzed to find out what fathers actually do that makes them so important and how they differ from mothers. Exactly how, for example, does a father's presence help to retard juvenile delinquency and teen pregnancies? Why are fathers—men—the way they are? In searching for the very essence of fatherhood, which is rooted in the biology of males, I turn to the evolutionary and anthropological record. It will be made clear why family-building fathers—especially biological fathers—are indispensable if society is to persevere.

The concluding Part Four summarizes the main thinking of the book and deals with how fatherhood and marriage can be reclaimed. I discuss strategies for reinvigorating the institution of marriage. Marriage, as we shall see, is more than a protective factor for men, encouraging responsible behavior and helping to curb antisocial tendencies; it is also strongly linked to men's overall happiness and subjective sense of well-being. And I present answers to one of the most important—and surprisingly controversial—questions of our time: Not what *do* fathers do, but what *should* they do? For make no mistake, in reclaiming fatherhood we must redefine what it means to be a father. It is imperative for the well-being of children and society that we retain the nuclear family—but not the nuclear family as it has existed in recent centuries.

Part One

Fatherlessness

1. The Remarkable Decline of Fatherhood and Marriage

It's very easy for a man to father a child. "To father a child," unlike "to mother a child," typically refers to a biological act, and men today do not seem to have much of a problem in that regard. But it is difficult for a man to be a father. To be a father, rather than merely to father, means to give a child guidance, instruction, encouragement, care, and love. Fatherhood—the state of being a father—is declining to a remarkable degree because so many fathers no longer live with their biological children.

Fathers in America today are living apart from their biological children more than ever before in our history. Close to 40 percent of all children do not live with their biological fathers, a percentage that is steadily climbing.[1] Of children born in the past decade, the chances that by age seventeen they will not be living with both biological parents stand at over 50 percent.[2] Many studies have shown that the typical nonresident father neither supports nor even sees his children on a regular basis. And, to make matters worse, many men who *do* live with their children are often removed from the day-to-day upbringing of those children. The new, nurturing fathers certainly exist, but in overall numbers they remain in short supply.

The widespread separation of fathers from their children in the late twentieth century is in many respects a surprising occurrence, something that no one anticipated. Thanks especially to the rise of modern contraceptives, men now have far fewer children needing their care; the average family size in America has dropped over the centuries from more than seven children to around two. Many fathers today, in fact, have only a single child, and that child has an excellent chance of living to adulthood. One would think that, with so few children, the responsibilities of fatherhood would be more readily accepted and more easily assumed.

At the same time, men are healthier, better educated, and better endowed materially than they have ever been. America is the wealthiest society in the history of the world in terms of material consumption, and much of that wealth is held by men. Most men not only have the means to invest heavily in their offspring, but they must know, given the recent advances in psychological awareness, how important parenting is for child well-being. Yet male investments in children are dropping.

So what has gone wrong? There are two proximate reasons for the contemporary outbreak of fatherlessness. The first is a very high rate of divorce: More than 50 percent of all first marriages today are expected to end in divorce. In the great majority of divorces, the children involved end up residing with their mothers and apart from their fathers.

The second is a very high rate of out-of-wedlock births, now more than 30 percent of all births. For most nonmarital births, unlike cases of divorce, the father is absent from the very beginning of the child's life. In only about a quarter of American nonmarital births is the father living with the mother, and in those cases the likelihood that the father will still be living with the mother when the child reaches adolescence is very low, considerably lower than for married-couple families.

Unfortunately, the statistical measures that indicate fatherlessness show little sign of diminishing. Divorce has leveled off from its peak in the early 1980s. But most of the leveling is due to an increase in nonmarital cohabitation. The marriage-wary and divorce-prone are now more likely to cohabit out of wedlock, and of course, those who don't marry can't divorce. The national nonmarital cohabitation rate *is* growing by leaps and bounds, and lamentably, cohabitation is a considerably less stable and committed relationship than marriage.[3] The estimated combined breakup rate of both married and unmarried unions, therefore, continues to escalate.

The increase of nonmarital births also continues at an alarming pace. Some predict that it could reach 40 percent of all births by the end of this century. Indeed, if present trends continue, nonmarital births will soon outpace divorce as a cause of fatherlessness.

Other father-absenting factors with potentially great impact loom on the horizon. Take the emergence of sperm-donor fathers, whose numbers are still small but rapidly growing. The sperm giving rise to their existence is the sole access most sperm-donor children will have to their fathers.

In each of these cases—divorce, nonmarital births, and sperm donations—the fatherlessness is voluntary. It could have been prevented if the adults in a child's life had made different decisions. There assuredly was a time in the past when the total amount of fatherlessness in society was higher than today, but it was involuntary father absence stemming from a high paternal death rate. In the early seventeenth century in colonial Virginia, for example, only an estimated 31 percent of white children reached age eighteen with both parents still alive.[4]

Yet rapidly lowering death rates have been one of the great achievements of the modern world, and that percentage climbed to 50 percent by the early eighteenth century and to 72 percent by the turn of the twentieth century. By 1940 most of the modern decline in parental death rate had occurred; about 88 percent of children born at that time still had two living parents when they finished childhood.[5] In recent decades, although the decline has slowed, the percentage of children who reach age eighteen with their parents still alive is well over 90 percent.

Contemporary fatherlessness is thus not only unexpected and mostly voluntary but also tragically ironic. It has taken thousands of human generations for the conditions to prevail whereby children could have confidence that their fathers would remain alive throughout their childhood and thus be able to help them through this critical stage of life. Almost all of today's fatherless children have fathers who are alive, well, and perfectly capable of shouldering the responsibilities of fatherhood. Who would ever have thought that, when such conditions finally were achieved, so many fathers would relinquish those responsibilities?[6]

We also could not have known what the evidence now suggests: that it is a decided disadvantage for a child to lose a father the modern, voluntary way rather than through death. It used to be said by many, including social scientists: What's the problem—children are merely losing their parents in a different way than they used to. You don't hear that so much anymore. A surprising finding of recent social science research is that the children of divorced and never-married mothers are less successful in life by almost every measure than the children of widowed mothers. In other words, the modern child is worse off, for reasons we shall explore in a later chapter, having a divorced father than a dead father! The replacement of death by divorce as the prime cause of fatherlessness, then, is a monumental setback in the history of childhood.

DIVORCE OVERTAKES DEATH

The year was 1974. That is when, as captured by official statistics, for the first time more marriages ended in divorce than in death.[7] But the date merely signifies the end of a long transition. The replacement of death by divorce had been quietly proceeding for more than a century.

Of children born in the first decade of the twentieth century (1901–1910), nearly 23 percent were in families disrupted during their childhood through a parental death versus only about 5 percent in families broken through divorce. Thus, the great majority of all single-parent children in 1900 lived with a widowed parent; only 2 percent lived with a divorced parent and 3.4 percent with a never-married parent. By 1960 death and divorce had already reached a parity among families with children. The percentage of children losing a parent through death had dropped from 23 percent to below 9 percent, while the percentage of children in families broken by divorce doubled, from 5 percent to over 10 percent.[8]

Up until the 1960s the lowering death rate and the increasing divorce rate neutralized each other as generators of single-parent families. In fact, the growth of single-parent families from 1900 to 1960 was so slight that few public concerns about it were raised. In 1900 the percentage of all American children living in single-parent families was 8.5 percent. By 1960 it had increased to just 9.1 percent.[9] Virtually no one at that time was writing or thinking about family breakdown, disintegration, or decline.

Indeed, what is most significant about the changing family demography of the first six decades of the twentieth century is this: Because the death rate was dropping faster than the divorce rate was rising, *by 1960 more children were living with both of their natural parents than at any other time in world history.*[10] Whereas at the turn of the century fewer than three quarters of all children were still living with their natural parents by age seventeen, this percentage went up to an all-time high of close to 80 percent for the generation born in the late 1940s and early 1950s.[11]

But then the death rate decline slowed, the divorce rate skyrocketed, and family structure went into a free fall. The nuclear family cracked. "The scale of marital breakdowns in the West since 1960 has no historical precedent that I know of, and seems unique," says Princeton University family historian Lawrence Stone. "There has been nothing like it for the last 2,000 years, and probably longer."[12]

Consider what happened to children. For the generation born during the 1970–1984 "baby bust" period, most estimates put the projected percentage of these children still living with their natural parents by age seventeen at only about 50 percent. This is a staggering drop from the nearly 80 percent figure of just three decades earlier.[13]

One estimate paints the current scene in even starker terms and also points up the enormous difference that exists between whites and blacks. By age seventeen, 19 percent of white children and 48 percent of black children born between 1950 and 1954 had lived part of their lives with only one parent. But for those born in 1980, 70 percent of white children and 94 percent of black children are projected to have lived with only one parent before they reach age eighteen.[14]

These are mostly fatherless children. In 86 percent of single-parent families today, the custodial parent is the mother.[15]

If one looks at the proportion of their childhoods children today will spend living with just one parent, the change is equally startling. White children born in the 1950–1954 period spent only 8 percent of their childhood with just one parent; black children spent 22 percent. Of those born in 1980, by one estimate, white children can be expected to spend 31 percent of their childhood years with one parent, and black children 59 percent.[16]

The picture grows worse. In addition to the rapid increase of divorce, what helped generate the family free fall is something new that came on the scene—nonmarital births. As late as 1965 only one out of every thirteen births took place out of wedlock. Today, nearly one out of every three does. And just as divorce has overtaken death, nonmarital births are expected to surpass divorce as the leading cause of single-parenthood and father absence later in the 1990s. Already today the proportions of single-parent children living with a divorced parent and with a never-married parent are almost identical.[17] And there is now substantial evidence that having an unmarried father is even worse for a child than having a divorced father!

The overtaking of death by divorce has had a remarkable impact on the family status of the male population.[18] At the beginning of the century, among those aged fifty-five to sixty-four, widowed men outnumbered divorced men by more than twenty to one. But when the divorced surpassed the widowed in the 1970s, the ratio reversed. By the year 2000, it is projected that there will be 3.7 divorced men for every widowed man in America.[19] The projections have yet to be made about the future numbers of never-married men.

MARRIAGE DECLINE

While the enormous increase in fatherlessness over the past three decades stems mainly from the two factors of divorce and nonmarital births, a single phenomenon underlies them both: a decline in the institution of marriage.[20] "At no time in history, with the possible exception of Imperial Rome," the eminent demographer Kingsley Davis has said, "has the institution of marriage been more problematic than it is today."[21] In addition to marital breakup, marriage rates have been dropping and marriages have become less satisfying.

Not so long ago, at mid-century, the United States was probably the most marrying society in the world. The effects of that era can still be seen in the older generation. In 1990 an almost unbelievable 94 percent of men (and 95 percent of women) aged forty-five to fifty-four either were or had been married.[22] But the marriage rate in recent decades has been steadily declining (despite the fact that in recent years the *number* of marriages has been at a record high because of large population cohorts at the most marriageable ages). In a little more than two decades, from 1970 to 1993, the percentage of never-married young men aged thirty to thirty-four increased from 9 percent to a staggering 30 percent.[23] To be sure, some of this new male singledom merely represents the delay of marriage, but a sizable portion of it almost certainly will become permanent.

A decline in the marriage rate might be good news if it meant that fewer couples would have to endure a bad marriage and go through a painful divorce. But this has not happened. While the marriage rate has declined, the divorce rate has climbed to an historically high level and stayed there. In raw terms, the divorce rate has merely doubled over the past three decades. Yet the probability that a marriage will end in divorce has gone through the roof. Only 14 percent of white women who married in the early 1940s eventually divorced, whereas almost half of white women who married in the late 1960s and early 1970s have already been divorced! For blacks the figures are 18 percent and nearly 60 percent.[24]

Apart from the high rate of marital dissolution, there is growing evidence that the quality of married life in America has taken a turn for the worse. Being married and being relatively happy in life have always been strongly associated statistically. But an analysis of survey data between 1972 and 1989 indicates that this association is weakening. An increasing proportion of never-married men and younger never-married women report that they are happy, along with a decreasing proportion of married women.[25]

Marriage has been losing its social purpose. In place of commitment and obligation to others, especially children, marriage has become mainly a vehicle for the emotional fulfillment of the adult partners. "Till death do us part" has been replaced by "so long as I am happy." Marriage is now less an institution that one belongs to and more a vehicle to be used to one's own advantage. Fewer than 50 percent of Americans today, for example, cite "being married" as part of their definition of "family values."[26]

This loss of social purpose is part of the broader cultural shift toward a radical form of individualism that accelerated rapidly beginning in the 1960s. With the rise of the "me generation," trust in all of our traditional social institutions waned. The legacy of this era remains firmly with us, with our attitude toward almost every social institution—government, religion, the law, the professions, education—now marked by a pervasive cynicism.

If present trends continue, the future of marriage does not appear bright. After all, if marriage is mainly for individual fulfillment, why marry just to be unhappy and eventually have to go through a painful divorce? Taking both childhood experiences and adult risks of marital disruption into account, only a minority of children born today are likely to grow up in an intact, two-parent family and also, as adults, form and maintain such a family. Because children from broken homes have a higher chance than those from intact families of forming unstable marriages of their own, the risks of family disruption are likely to accelerate.[27]

Marriage Decline and Fatherhood

The decline of marriage is a disaster for fatherhood. Women have always been able to view marriage and childrearing as somewhat distinct institutions. Whatever their marital state, when women bear children they generally assume responsibility for those children and continue to care for them over the course of their lives. For men, this is not the case. Men tend to view marriage and childrearing as a single package. If their marriage deteriorates, their fathering deteriorates.[28] If they are not married or are divorced, their interest in and sense of responsibility toward children greatly diminish.

That male interest in children has decreased is a fact verified by many public opinion polls and social surveys. Compared to their counterparts in 1957, fewer than half as many fathers in 1976 found children providing a major life goal.[29] In a recent nationwide poll of teenagers, the *New York Times* found that 52 percent of teenage boys answered "still happy" to the question "Could you have a happy life or would you feel you missed part of what you need to be happy if you don't have children?" Only 47 percent answered "missed."[30]

An especially troubling trend is that males today show a reluctance even to acknowledge children that they do not see or support. Sociologist Frank Furstenberg, Jr., reports, for example, that many males do not report their children in social surveys. "Fertility histories from males are notoriously unreliable," he says, "because many men simply 'forget' children living outside the household." And in his own studies of unmarried youth in Baltimore, he found "strikingly higher reports of offspring among females than males."[31]

Whereas men used to spend their entire lives residing in a family environment, today many do not. Partly due to the decline of marriage, there has been a marked reduction within the past few decades in the number of years men between the ages of twenty and fifty live in family environments where children are present.[32] For white males, time spent in a family environment including children decreased, between 1960 and 1980, from an average of 19.4 years to 15.7 years.[33] For black males, the change was even more dramatic: a decrease from 15.1 years to 11.6 years.

The Black-White Differential

Notice that the amount of time black males spent living in households with children in 1960, 15.1 years, was about what it was for white males in 1980, 15.7 years. Such a time and racial comparison yields similar results for many other family indicators, such as out-of-wedlock births, unmarried teen pregnancies, and percentage of single-parent families. Up to now at least, the characteristics of black families in America have anticipated the characteristics of white families by several decades. For example, 51 percent of black teenage mothers (12 percent of white teenage mothers) were unmarried in 1965; in 1990, among white teenage mothers, 55 percent were unmarried. In 1960, 22 percent of black children (7 percent of white children) were living with only one parent; in 1990, among white children, 20 percent were living with only one parent.[34]

Black family life, then, appears to be a precursor of what family life is likely to become for the rest of the population. While African-American families undoubtedly face some stresses that are unique to them, they are instructively viewed as prematurely suffering the negative consequences of an American family environment that all groups share.

THE DIVORCE REVOLUTION

The greatest cause of father absence today is divorce. Many divorced fathers say that they want to provide more care for their children from the broken marriage, but their wives won't let them. There is doubtless some truth to their plea. A visit to any so-called fathers' rights organization, where the more aggrieved men band together for support, yields abundant anecdotes of irate and punitive former wives lined up against innocent and well-meaning divorced dads.

Other divorced men deny that divorce has any ill effects on their children, apart from the effects of the conflict-ridden marriage that preceded the divorce. The children are better off, they claim, with the marital conflict diminished. There is also some truth to this belief. The divorce itself is by no means the only conflict generator. Some men even develop a better relationship with their children following the reduction of marital conflict that a divorce can bring.

But the larger truth is that most divorced fathers in America, for whatever reason, lose almost all contact with their children over time. They withdraw from their children's lives. They become terrible fathers. And for those noncustodial men who maintain some contact, the reality is that co-residence between father and child is usually a necessary, if not always a sufficient, basis for sound and effective fatherhood. Childrearing is one of the most time-intensive of all human activities, and it is very difficult to perform it well in absentia. Especially for men, "marriage and co-residence usually define responsibilities to children," concludes social researcher Judith Seltzer in her comprehensive research review of the topic.[35]

Divorce is a quintessential American problem; we have long had the highest divorce rate in the Western world. This is largely the result of our diversity, our mobility, and our individualism. In marriage, as in so many other spheres of life, Americans have been prone to pick up and move on when opportunity presents itself.

But yesteryear's scale of divorce was nothing like today's. In America's first few centuries divorce was all but forbidden in most states. The rate began to climb around the time of the Civil War, when several states changed their laws to make divorce possible on a limited basis. By the turn of the twentieth century, the divorce rate had climbed so far and so fast, especially during the period 1880–1900, that divorce had reached what to many Americans seemed a stage of crisis. In the first decade of the twentieth century, far more than today, public concern about the high rate of divorce was widespread. Newspapers took up the issue, churches became heavily engaged, and national commissions to investigate the problem were established. Yet the annual divorce rate in 1900 was still only six divorces per one thousand married couples.

Throughout most of the twentieth century the rate gradually climbed, reaching a peak of twenty-three divorces per one thousand married couples in 1980—a nearly fourfold increase from the turn of the century. Most of the climb took place after 1960, when the divorce rate was still a modest nine divorces per one thousand married couples. Today, with the divorce rate holding at a level slightly below its peak, the chances that a marriage will end in either divorce or permanent separation (counting both first and remarriages) stand, by one recent estimate, at a staggering 60 percent.[36]

As a classic example of what Senator Daniel Patrick Moynihan has called "defining deviance down," however, contemporary divorce is hardly recognized as a social problem. There seems to be an upper limit to how many things a society can consider to be deviant and problematic, and divorce has now dropped out of that category. Where is the government commission or even congressional hearing set up to investigate the divorce problem? The fact is, of course, that a great many of our public servants are themselves divorced and not eager to take up such a sensitive topic.

A Divorce Culture

Far from viewing divorce as deviant, we seem well on the way to developing what could be called a culture or climate of divorce. Once we were a nation in which a strong marriage was seen as the best route to achieving the American dream. Sadly, we have become a nation in which divorce is commonly seen as a path to that contemporary version of the American dream, personal liberation and self-fulfillment. Marriage, so we have been told in recent decades by a myriad of learned critics, is restrictive, confining, oppressive, and unliberating. The solution is the unattached and carefree life, the life without commitments, the life which can result from "the new beginning" that only divorce can bring.

Bookstores are flooded with publications that carry this message. One recent work entitled *Healthy Divorce* has the following publicity blurb: "It *is* possible for both parents and children to maintain emotional stability and a sense of security, find renewal, and ultimately flourish when emerging from a divorce—if the process has been conducted as a *healthy* divorce."[37] Stars of the entertainment industry, which now dominates popular culture to an unbelievable degree, are better known and even celebrated for their multiple divorces than for their good, monogamous marriages. Consider Elizabeth Taylor, Zsa Zsa Gabor, and Mickey Rooney, each with eight marriages. With his various wives Rooney has a total of nine children and two stepchildren. Or consider Glen Campbell, country music's golden boy in the late sixties and early seventies, who has eight children with four wives. This legacy is being emulated by the younger generation of celebrities.

Many family scholars and professionals argue that, because nothing can be done about it, we should accept the culture of divorce and adjust our institutions accordingly. The dean of American family sociologists, Harvard's William J. Goode, has said: "We should accept the fact that most developed nations can now be seen as high divorce rate systems, and we should *institutionalize* divorce—accept it as we do other institutions, and build adequate safeguards as well as social understandings and pressures to make it work reasonably well."[38] Frank F. Furstenberg, Jr., and Andrew J. Cherlin, in their influential recent book *Divided Families: What Happens to Children When Parents Part,* conclude: "We are inclined to accept the irreversibility of high levels of divorce as our starting point for thinking about changes in public policy."[39]

Some lawyers instruct people to prepare for divorce just as carefully as they prepare for marriage, including the use of a prenuptial agreement. Marriage therapists, in the name of "neutrality," often do less to promote marriages than to counsel individuals through a "good divorce." Family court judges typically are more interested in promoting divorce counseling than marriage counseling.

One indubitable effect of the widespread acceptance of divorce is its increase. Marriages *may* be more stressful today than ever before; that is debatable. But at the same time, divorce surely is taking place at ever lower levels of marital stress. Divorce was once limited to those marriages which had broken down irreparably, often because one spouse was seriously pathological, irresponsible, or incompetent. Today divorce may occur simply because a better partner has been located. And given the high rate of divorce, "better partners" in ever growing numbers are continually coming onto the market.

Changing Laws

The act of divorce has been made far easier in the past few decades by changes in the laws of divorce. Divorce law changes by themselves cannot bear too much scrutiny as the primary cause of the divorce revolution; changes in the law typically follow changes in values and behavior rather than vice versa. Yet some people doubtless decide what is right by seeing what is legal, and thus changes in the law have some behavioral effects. A worldwide analysis of divorce trends concluded that "the legal changes can certainly be said to have contributed to the increase in one-parent families, even if they did not cause it."[40]

Although they took place quietly, with little planning or public notice, little public discussion or input, and almost no controversy, the changes in divorce law represent one of the most radical legal transformations of recent years. One prominent book on the topic is entitled *Silent Revolution.*[41] Initiated and promoted by divorce lawyers through state legislatures, divorce law over a period of less than twenty years, from the late 1960s to the 1980s, shifted from being based on the principle of fault—requiring a finding that one party is guilty and the other is innocent—to the principle of no fault. Fault could be shown by such acts as adultery, cruelty, or desertion; the concept implies intentional harm or a breach of duty and has its roots in the view that marriage is a binding commitment in which society has a strong interest.

Under the new law, now in existence in almost every state, a marriage can be terminated unilaterally for almost any reason, regardless of who, if anyone, is "guilty." A principal reason for changing the old law was that it had become widely disregarded in the sense that many of the interested parties, along with the legal profession and the courts, openly colluded to get around it. Divorce law, in practice, had become a kind of legal scandal, a source of psychic warfare, dishonesty, and unfairness, and few people wish to return to those legally "messy" days of having to prove fault.

Yet the change virtually removed from the law all sense of personal commitment and social interest. In many ways marriage has become one of the least binding of legal contracts, a kind of temporary business partnership with an illusory contract in which neither party involved will be held liable for breaking any promises that are made. If a woman marries a man, for example, with his promise that he will "be there for the children," and then down the line he breaks his promise and deserts her for someone else, she has little legal recourse. She is simply out of luck.

Thus, in the eyes of the law and in the eyes of most citizens, the institution of marriage has shifted abruptly away from being a socially important relationship that involves a legally binding commitment. Marriage has become little more than a "notarized date," truly just the proverbial piece of paper.[42] Or as Robert Louis Stevenson once said about "marriage at its lowest," "We regard it as a sort of friendship recognized by the police."

Divorce and Children

The problem of divorce would surely be less serious if children were not involved. Divorces involving children used to be in the category of "unthinkable," and most divorces of earlier generations in fact did not involve children. In 1916 only three in eight couples divorcing reported that they had one or more children. Those days are gone. The proportion of divorcing couples with children crossed the 50 percent mark about 1957, reached 60 percent in 1963, and then leveled off.[43] Today more than three out of five divorcing couples have at least one child. The odds that a child today will witness the divorce of his or her parents are twice as great as a generation ago, climbing from about one in four to one in two.[44]

A careful analysis of divorce statistics shows that, beginning around 1975, the presence of children in a marriage has become only a very minor inhibitor of divorce (slightly more so when the child is male than female).[45] This is largely due to a new acceptance of divorce by childrearing couples. As one measure of such acceptance, the proportion of persons answering no to the question "Should a couple stay to-gether for the sake the children?" jumped from 51 percent to 82 per-cent between 1962 and 1985.[46] In other words, less than a fifth of the population believes that the presence of children should deter parents from breaking up.

One could conceive of a high-divorce society, with many children in-volved, in which the fathers merely moved into a separate household nearby and continued active childrearing. But that conception is far re-moved from present-day reality. For those fathers who divorce, the likeli-hood of remaining close to their children is strikingly low. According to data from the 1987–1988 National Survey of Families and Households, about one in five divorced fathers has not seen his children in the past year, and fewer than one out of every two fathers sees his children more than several times a year.[47] The 1981 National Survey of Children found an even more dismal picture; it focused on adolescents and included both children of divorce and those born to unmarried parents, a group that has even less frequent contact with fathers. Fifty-two percent of all adolescents aged twelve to sixteen who were living with separated, divorced, or remar-ried mothers had not seen their fathers at all in more than a year, and only 16 percent saw their fathers as often as once a week.[48]

As one might expect, contact with children drops off sharply with the length of time since the marital breakup and especially with the common occurrence that one or both of the former partners remarries. Among children from marriages that were disrupted ten or more years before, only one in ten had weekly contact with their fathers, and al-most two thirds had no contact during the past year. Almost 30 percent of remarried fathers *never* see their children who live in other house-holds, compared to only 13 percent of nonremarried fathers.

In their book *Divided Families* Furstenberg and Cherlin conclude, after a careful examination of the empirical studies, that "over time, the vast majority of children [of divorce] will have little or no contact with their fathers."[49] The outlook is even more grim if one considers that mere contact does not necessarily mean active involvement in the child's upbringing. Even those nonresident fathers who see their chil-dren may see them only briefly or engage with them in only superficial activities. Furstenberg and Cherlin continue:[50]

> This pattern of visitation actually overstates the involvement of nonresiden-tial fathers in raising their children. Even in the small number of families where children are seeing their fathers regularly, the dads assume a mini-mal role in the day-to-day care and supervision of their children. Children who saw their fathers at least fourteen days a year were asked how they spent time together. . . . Their replies indicated that most outside fathers

behaved more like close relatives than parents. They took their kids on shopping trips, out to dinner, and to the movies. Sometimes they played sports with them. But routine parent-child activities were less common. Only about one child in five stated that they had carried out some project with their father, and just one in ten had been helped with their school-work during the preceding week.

A reasonable conclusion from these data is that, unfortunately, if and when men are active parents, it is only to the children who live with them. This is largely because, as Furstenberg has stated elsewhere, "many men view marriage and childcare as an inseparable role-set. Accordingly, men often sever ties with their children in the course of establishing distance from their wives."[51]

The effect of this on children's feelings toward their fathers is predictable, and the feelings carry over into adulthood. A Gallup poll found that only 31 percent of adult children of divorced parents felt close to their fathers, compared to 77 percent of those whose parents are still married and live together.[52]

The lack of social contact between nonresident fathers and their children is only one of the problems. Many nonresident fathers fail to provide monetary child support, the now-familiar phenomenon of "deadbeat dads." For 1989 it was estimated that about half of previously married mothers did not receive any child support, and the amount of support received, averaging just $3,155 per year, was well below the costs associated with rearing children.[53] Despite recent federal legislation designed to insure that payments are made, there is no evidence that the number of deadbeat dads has diminished very much.

The problem of child support is two pronged. A substantial percentage of divorcing men with children—about 20 percent in 1988—leave marriage without a child-support requirement.[54] Of the divorced fathers interviewed in the National Survey of Households and Families, 35 percent did not have a child-support agreement (57 percent of minority nonresident fathers).[55] And for those who do have such an agreement, a majority fail to comply with it in part or in whole. A 1985 Bureau of the Census survey found that only 48 percent of mothers who were supposed to receive child-support payments reported receiving the full amount, 26 percent received partial payment, and 26 percent received nothing.[56] The likelihood of making payments and the size of the payments both drop off over time. To make matters worse, divorced fathers don't provide much financial support in ways apart from mandatory child-support payments. A recent study concluded: "Other than paying child support and buying gifts, the majority of [divorced] fathers have never provided assistance to their children."[57]

Stepfamilies

What a growing portion of divorced fathers do instead is transfer their parenting to stepchildren. Some 75 percent of divorced fathers remarry, and the percentage of children under age eighteen living with any step-parent jumped from 6.7 percent in 1960 to 11.3 percent in 1990.[58] More than nine out of ten stepchildren live with a stepfather and biological mother. The transfer of fathering to stepchildren has become so common that it has been described as a new "transient father syndrome," "serial parenting," or a system of "child swapping."[59] And, in another classic example of defining deviance down, some are calling the stepfamily the family of the future. As one social scientist put it, "if the nuclear family is suited to the needs of industrial society, by the same token, the stepfamily may be well suited to those of post-industrial society."[60]

Far from providing a solution to the erosion of fatherhood, however, stepfamilies are very much a part of the problem. While there are, of course, many caring and devoted stepfathers, transient child-swapping fathers in general, as one might suspect, leave much to be desired. Many studies have shown that stepfathering acts to diminish contact between original fathers and their biological children.[61] That cannot be news. Once stepchildren enter the picture, what little contact the father has had with his biological children typically goes by the wayside.

What is less widely known is that stepfathers, in their new families, take a considerably less active role in parenting than do typical custodial biological fathers.[62] The term often applied to the relationship between stepfathers and their stepchildren is *disengagement*. "Even after two years," it is reported, "disengagement by the stepparent is the most common parenting style."[63] This is "characterized by low levels of involvement and rapport, and a lack of control, discipline, and monitoring of the stepchild's behavior and activities."[64]

Another problematic aspect of stepfamilies is their high breakup rate, significantly higher than that of two-biological-parent families. According to the most recent census data, more than 62 percent of remarriages among women under age forty will eventually end in divorce, and the more that children are involved, the higher the redivorce rate. One study found that, while 10 percent of remarriages without stepchildren broke up within three years, the breakup rate for remarriages with stepchildren was 17 percent. Thus, not only is the quality of family life in stepfamilies typically inferior to that of biological-parent families, but the children of stepfamilies face a greater chance of family breakup than they did in their original families.[65] By one estimate, about 15 percent of all children born in recent decades will go through at least two family disruptions before coming of age.[66]

The social relationships within stepfamilies can become incredibly complex. Here is a description of a stepfamily by one of its members:

> Tim and Janet are my stepbrother and sister. Josh is my stepdad. Carin and Don are my real parents, who are divorced. And Don married Anna and together they had Ethan and Ellen, my half-sister and -brother. And Carin married Josh and had little Alice, my half-sister.[67]

Got it? In the words of a recent article in *Psychology Today,* stepfamilies "are such a minefield of divided loyalties, emotional traps, and management conflicts that they are the most fragile form of family in America."[68] If stepfamilies are being counted on to "meet the needs of postindustrial society," we had better brace ourselves for hard times ahead.

THE INCREASE OF NONMARITAL BIRTHS

The other major contributor to father absence, currently second only to divorce, is the startling growth of what in the social sciences now goes by the value-neutral term *nonmarital births.* The fastest growing group of single parents over the past two decades has been that of the never-married, especially in the black community.[69] Today nearly a third of all American births (70 percent of black births) occur outside of marriage, an increase from just 5.3 percent (22 percent of black births) in 1960.

This is an unprecedented phenomenon for America and perhaps for all of history. In the past, when an unmarried young woman became pregnant, family, kinship, religious, and community pressures—and often the desires of the father- and mother-to-be as well—generally led to a marriage at least by the time the child was born. But today, assuming the woman does not abort the child, she is twice as likely to remain unmarried as to get married by the time of the birth.[70]

Unlike those in European nations, where such births are typically to cohabiting couples, most nonmarital births in America are to unattached women. Only about 27 percent of American nonmarital births in recent decades have been to cohabiting couples, although the percentage varies greatly by race and ethnicity.[71] And for those children born to cohabiting parents, the advantage is not as great as one might suppose. One third of all cohabiting couples who have a child will never marry, and those who do marry have a far higher prospect of divorce than other couples. By one estimate only one quarter of all children born to unmarried but cohabiting couples will live into their teenage years with both parents.[72]

However one looks at the picture, as demographer Sandra Hofferth has put it, "A child born to a never-married mother has only a small probability of living with two natural parents. Thus, such a child's experience will be as different from that of a child who experiences a parental divorce as from a child who always lives with two natural parents."[73]

Culture of Nonmarriage

If there is a new culture of divorce, so does there also seem to be a growing culture of nonmarriage. Attitudes toward the unmarried adult have changed dramatically in recent decades. In 1957, 80 percent of the population believed that an unmarried woman was in some way deviant; by 1978 the proportion had dropped to 25 percent.[74] Traditional bachelors and spinsters, of course, hold an honorable status in many societies, more so in Europe than in the United States. They are not the problem. The problem is the growing acceptance of unmarried parents and of having children out of wedlock. Consider this enormous generational difference: Some 70 percent of young people between the ages of eighteen and thirty-four (and 79 percent of women in that age group) believe that people who generate a baby out of wedlock should not be subject to moral reproach of any sort, compared to only 29 percent of people over the age of fifty-five.

The group with the most dramatic increase in out-of-wedlock births over the past decade is college-educated women. The number of unmarried births to such women increased sixfold, from 18,000 in 1982 to 113,000 in 1992, with births to women in professional and managerial positions growing at a still faster rate. "She is not willing to settle for a man she doesn't love just to have his baby. Neither is she willing to forgo motherhood just because she is single," reports the *Philadelphia Inquirer.*

One can surely understand why an older and financially secure woman, her biological clock ticking and the right man not in sight, might decide to become a "single mother by choice." What is alarming is the meaning of this simple decision for society when it becomes widespread and accepted throughout our culture, as now appears to be the case. The implication is that fathers are unnecessary, superfluous, obsolete. A columnist in my local newspaper reported what is happening: "[Everywhere] I hear folks seriously claiming fathers aren't necessary to children's lives, beyond conception, of course."[75] The father's role has been stripped down to simple "conceiving."

In their widespread acceptance of fatherlessness at birth, modern societies are, to say the least, breaking new sociological ground. The celebrated anthropologist Bronislaw Malinowski once described what he referred to as the "principle of legitimacy:"[76]

The most important moral and legal rule concerning the physiological side of kinship is that no child should be brought into the world without a man—and one man at that—assuming the role of sociological father, that is, guardian and protector, the male link between the child and the rest of the community. . . . This is by no means only a European or Christian prejudice; it is the attitude found amongst most barbarous and savage people as well . . . I think that this generalization amounts to a universal sociological law.

Much evidence has been collected since Malinowski's time to support this principle. Virtually every known society has distinguished between legitimate and illegitimate births and favored the former.

THE SPERM-DONOR FATHER

The most male-abandoned children of all are those who have a sperm-donor, or "inseminator," father. Based on the biological fact that the mother as a living, functioning being is essential to reproduction but only the father's sperm is required, a whole new dimension of father-lessness has been generated in recent decades. Just as the technologies of birth control have made sex without reproduction possible, new technologies have now extended our options to reproduction without sex. The number of children born each year with donor sperm is still small—an estimated twenty to thirty thousand—and most of those children are in fathered families.[77] But artificial insemination with the use of donor sperm has become an important avenue to pregnancy for single women, although it currently takes place mostly outside the offi-cial medical establishment. In view of the growing cultural emphasis on "procreative liberty," the number of single women using this method to have a child will undoubtedly grow.

Often the sperm donor wishes to remain anonymous. Or the recipients intentionally pick unknown donors, for reasons that were sketched in a recent newspaper column:

They are concerned that a known donor may one day renege on his promise to stay uninvolved after conception. Moreover, there have been cases where men sue for custody after having a change of heart about being a father or after entering a new relationship where the wife or partner is un-able to conceive. Additionally, choosing D.I. [donor insemination] with an unknown usually shields you from legal issues complicating your life far into the future.[78]

Thus, we are seeing the emergence of an extreme form of fatherlessness in which the father is permanently absent, unknown, and often un-knowable from the moment of conception.

Some sperm-donor fathers, of course, do show love and concern—of a sort. On the Phil Donahue show, one such father read the letter that he had just sent to the parents of the five children whom he will never meet, to be given to those children at an appropriate time:

> I thought you might like to know a little bit about the man who assisted in bringing you into the world. I don't and won't take any credit for your birth. Your parents are the real heroes here. I can only imagine the sadness and doubt they went through to get you here. After you read this, I'd like for you to give them a big hug of thanks . . . I hope that your life goes well. I hope that your dreams come true. I hope that you are happy. I hope that you will love your children as much as your parents love you. We change the world for the better, one child at a time.[79]

Although little research on the topic has yet been conducted, much less completed, the negative consequences for children of sperm-donor fathers could be greater than for any other form of fatherlessness. How destructive to their self-esteem is it, as one expert witness testified at a New Jersey public hearing, for children "to find out their father sold the essence of his lineage for $40 or so, without ever intending to love or take responsibility for them?"[80] One Philadelphia psychiatrist, who has met with a few children born through donor insemination, suggests one answer:

> It is a big issue for the children. The way they came to be, with no passion, no intimacy, no affection, throws them into a turmoil about who they really are. There isn't even a good basis for fantasy. It is bound to affect their personality development and their sense of self-esteem.[81]

WHAT HAPPENED TO MARRIAGE?

Underlying virtually all contemporary fatherlessness, as we have seen, is the decline of marriage. Marriage is probably the world's oldest and most universal social institution; it has been a central feature of every known society to date. Through approving relationships involving sexual intercourse and the birth of children, it is society's way of signaling to would-be parents of children that their long-term relationship together is socially important. In the words of Kingsley Davis:[82]

> The genius of [marriage] is that, through it, the society normally holds the biological parents responsible for each other and for their offspring. By identifying children with their parents, and by penalizing people who do not have stable relationships, the social system powerfully motivates individuals to settle into a sexual union and take care of the ensuing offspring.

After millennia of human history in which marriage was so fundamental to every society, how and why did the decline of this once-powerful institution take place on such an unprecedented scale and with such rapidity in the late twentieth century?

The low marriage rates of recent years are by no means unprecedented. The rate of marriage has returned to the relatively low level, and the average age at first marriage has returned to the relatively high level, that prevailed at the turn of the twentieth century. But we are now rapidly surpassing those earlier levels and thus entering uncharted territory. And in nonmarital cohabitation, out-of-wedlock births, and marital dissolution, we are already well off the charts.

The extraordinary decline of marriage is reflected in a remarkable finding of several demographers. They concluded that, while the proportion of one's adult life spent living with spouse and children in 1960 was 62 percent, the highest in our history, in just twenty-five years it had dropped to 43 percent, the lowest in our history.[83] Any indicator that shifts in just twenty-five years from history's high point to its low point is surely pointing to a social fact of overriding importance.

The Fifties

One of the reasons why marriage decline (and family change in general) during recent decades has seemed so remarkable is surely because the era that preceded it, the so-called fifties, was unusual in its own right. Following World War II, the United States entered a two-decade period of extraordinary economic growth and material progress. It was the most sustained period of prosperity in American history. Together with most other industrially developed societies of the world, this nation saw improvements in the levels of health, material consumption, and economic security that had no historical precedent. For most Americans the improvements included striking increases in longevity, buying power, personal net worth, and government-sponsored economic security.

In association with this material affluence, the fifties were an era of remarkable familism and family togetherness. The family as an institution became the central focus of life for large segments of the middle and working classes. Home, motherhood, and child-centeredness reigned very high in the lexicon of American cultural values. The marriage rate reached an all-time high, the birthrate returned to the high levels of earlier in the century (generating the baby boom), and the divorce rate leveled off. Indeed, as we have already pointed out, a higher proportion of children in the fifties were growing up in stable, two-parent families than at any other time in American history.

Many observers have characterized this period as a time of crushing social conformity, stifling domesticity, egregious hypocrisy, and distressing female and racial oppression.[84] Often overlooked is the fact that it was also a time of widespread personal optimism, accompanied by a strong general sense that the "good society" was at hand. However one wishes to characterize the fifties, this was undoubtedly an unusual period in American history.

But even more unusual was what happened to marriage and the family in the following decades, and not just because the family was coming down from a fifties high. Beginning in the early 1960s, a series of mostly unanticipated social and cultural trends occurred that shook the family's very foundation. Some of the family changes, such as lower birthrates, higher divorce rates, and the shift of women into the labor force, were already underway well before World War II, but even for those changes the 1960s constituted a dramatic turning point.

The Sixties and Beyond

Let us look closely at what actually happened to the institution of marriage after 1960 by describing a sequence of marriage-related events, simplified of much of their complexity.[85] It is important to realize that, although the focus here is American, the cultural forces of change that have affected marriage and the family span the modernized nations of the world. There is no need to refer to specifically American events such as the civil rights revolution, the assassination of the Kennedy brothers, or the Vietnam War, which are often cited as being somehow influential for American social change. The trends to be described have taken place in every advanced society in roughly the same sequence, although at varying speeds and from different starting points.

We can start in the area of human sexuality, that fundamental life force. Premarital sexual intercourse (especially intercourse among "nonengaged" couples) became increasingly common, and the age of first sexual intercourse dropped. This was largely the result of a substantial change in sexual mores—the acceptance of more "permissive" sexual behavior—that is often referred to as the "sexual revolution."[86] The main impetus for the sexual revolution, as *Playboy*'s Hugh Hefner has constantly reminded us, was the belief that a main path to self-fulfillment lies through less inhibited sexuality.

Permissiveness in sexual matters, of course, had been gradually increasing in America for a hundred years or more. The sexual revolution of the 1960s was given a jump start by the new and widespread availability of contraceptive devices, especially the pill. One might also wish to add the new availability of abortions, partly due to changes in the laws. The availability of contraception and abortion greatly increased the possibilities for sex without procreation, for fewer unwanted children, and for fewer forced marriages. As a result, the average age at first marriage began to climb again following its very low level in the 1950s, and the average age of women at the birth of their first child also began to rise.

These trends toward later marriages and postponed first births were accelerated by the increased education of women and by the movement of women into the labor market. In unexpectedly large numbers, women were relinquishing their traditional mother/housewife roles. As we now know, this has been one of the most significant social trends of the century.

With childbearing and marriage no longer so closely linked and the birth of children postponed, marital dissolution began to occur earlier after marriages were formed. For one thing, with fewer children involved, there was less reason for concern about the adverse effects of marriage breakup. This helped to bring about a sharp rise in divorce rates among the childless, a trend that was accentuated by the easing of legal divorce restrictions. Later, as it became more generally accepted within the culture, divorce began to cut heavily into marriages with children.

Because a growing number of young people were marrying without procreation immediately in mind and with the intention of delaying childbearing, the legal seal of approval that marriage stands for no longer seemed as important. This led to a decline in the number of marriages, to a further increase in the average age at first marriage, and— importantly—to the widespread growth of nonmarital cohabitation.

Once cohabitation out of wedlock became widely practiced and accepted, the need to marry just to have children became less compelling. There were no longer legal penalties directed at the children of unmarried couples, and the social and religious stigma toward the practice diminished rapidly. In 1987, for example, a group within the Episcopal Diocese of Newark, N.J., issued this statement: "To minister to . . . those who choose to live together without marriage does not denigrate the institution of marriage and life-long commitments. Rather it is an effort to recognize and support those who choose, by virtue of the circumstances of their lives, not to marry but to live in alternative relationships enabling growth and love."[87]

The attitude toward formal marriage became: It is not really so important anymore. This attitude caused the age of first marriage to rise still further and also increased the percentage of couples who would never marry. In addition, over time, remarriages (as distinct from postmarital cohabitation) became less common. The drop in legal marriages naturally led to a tremendous increase in out-of-wedlock births and also to a leveling of the divorce rate.

Nonmarital Cohabitation

The rise of nonmarital cohabitation—two persons of the opposite sex living together in a marriagelike relationship—is a particularly noteworthy social phenomenon. While the average age of first marriage has returned to, and surpassed, the relatively high average age that existed at the turn of the twentieth century, the life situation of the late marriers is significantly different now from what it was then. At the turn of the century, most young people continued to live with their parents until marriage. They were surrounded by family members and family values. Today most leave their families prior to marriage and set up independent households, often in conjunction with a partner.[88] In 1960 and 1970 only 2 percent of all unmarried adults were cohabiting; by 1990 the figure had leaped to 8 percent for unmarried men and 7 percent for unmarried women.[89] The percentage is much higher today among young, single adults in the prime ages for marriage, an estimated 20 to 24 percent.[90] Higher still is the percentage of marriages that are preceded by cohabitation, an estimated 49 percent (in 1985–1986). This is a staggering increase from only 8 percent of all marriages in the late 1960s.[91]

In theory, nonmarital cohabitation could strengthen the institution of marriage. Acting as a "trial marriage," it provides a useful time for premarrieds to get to know one another and permits couples to choose their long-term mates more carefully. If they don't get along, they can easily break up. Many will thus be kept from rushing, out of loneliness or a need for sex, into ill-conceived matrimony. Those couples that survive the test will go on to strong marriages, and the divorce statistics will be lowered. The family life of the nation will be improved.

But, up to now at least, the rise of nonmarital cohabitation has hurt more than helped the institution of marriage. Perhaps as many as a quarter of cohabitors have no plans eventually to marry their partners; for them nonmarital cohabitation is not a trial marriage at all but merely an alternative to living on one's own.[92] Especially troublesome is the fact that over one half of all cohabiting couples have children present. Not only are these couples more likely than married couples to break up, but the obligations that go with legal marriage are more difficult to enforce in its absence, such as the claim children have to the resources of their fathers.[93]

A growing body of evidence indicates that living together before marriage is associated with proneness for later divorce. In large part this is probably due to the "selection factor"—the nonmarital cohabitation–prone and the divorce-prone are one and the same group of tradition challengers. Some hold, however, that nonmarital cohabitation may, in and of itself, actually increase the chances for eventual divorce.[94] One argument for this position is that nonmarital cohabitation, compared to marriage, represents a lowered level of commitment between two individuals, and over time one becomes adapted to low-commitment relationships. A lack of commitment in one's early relationships generates a lack of commitment in future relationships.

The trend toward nonmarital cohabitation is strong, and as it gains ascendancy within the population as a normal part of the life course, the selection factor will probably diminish and the association with divorce will dwindle. Nevertheless, the effects of nonmarital cohabitation on the institution of marriage will remain problematical.

Family Diversity

The sequence of events described above has had an enormous impact on the household composition of America, which shifted from a situation of relative uniformity to one of great variety. The age of family diversity had arrived. The percentage of single-person and other nonfamily households rapidly increased, as did households with cohabiting adults but no children and households with children but only one adult (each of which helped reduce dramatically the average household size, from 3.3 in 1960 to 2.6 in 1990). At the same time, households containing two married adults with children—the nuclear family with father—became only a small fraction of the total, 26 percent, down from 44 percent in 1960. Extended family households, those containing more than two generations or more than one nuclear family, diminished almost to the point of extinction.

In its celebratory mode, family diversity means that people have more freedom and choice in their private lives. What family diversity also means, however, is the decline of marriage—and the decline of child-centered family living in which fathers are involved.

SOME EXPLANATIONS

Scholars and social analysts have come up with a variety of causal explanations for what happened to marriage in the past three decades. In these explanations the big-three causes are economics, government, and culture.

Economics

Of all the explanations put forth to account for recent marriage decline, the economic factor has received the most attention. As economic conditions change, it is argued, so do the conditions of family life. Economic changes are believed to have affected the marriage attitudes and behavior of women more than men. During the past few decades, not only have women entered the labor market in vast numbers, but their actual wage rates relative to men's have increased substantially. By 1990, 59 percent of married women (husbands present) over the age of sixteen were in the labor force, compared to only about 15 percent in 1940.

The main argument for the importance of economic conditions in generating marriage decline is that this rise in women's employment opportunities and earning ability has reduced the benefits associated with sharing income and household costs with a man and also made divorce and the single life more attractive.[95] This argument is often labeled the "independence effect"—women's new economic independence enhances both their unwillingness to marry and their willingness to divorce. There is a substantial, although by no means conclusive, body of evidence to support it.[96]

A second economic explanation focuses more on men but still uses women as the reference point. The argument is that, as men's wages and job opportunities have declined relative to women's, the eligibility of men as potential marriage partners for women has dropped.[97] It may not be only a matter of female choice, of course; the economically disadvantaged men may not want to marry because they feel unable to support a family. The economic changes of recent decades lend themselves well to an interpretation of men's loss rather than women's gain. Since about 1970 the average real earnings position of young men at every educational level has deteriorated considerably, and the employment position of both high school dropouts and high school graduates with no college education has substantially worsened.[98]

This argument, applied to the extraordinarily low marriage rates found in inner-city black areas, was made quite persuasively by sociologist William Julius Wilson in his well-known books *The Declining Significance of Race* and *The Truly Disadvantaged*.[99] The deteriorating economic position of young men in general has been accentuated among young, poorly educated African-Americans. In the ghetto, not only are many men underpaid and out of work—partly due to economic restructuring and the shift of male work elsewhere—but the availability of eligible males is curtailed due to high homicide and incarceration rates.[100]

The economically-impaired-man explanation has garnered less empirical support than that of the economically independent woman. It probably applies more forcefully to the ghetto situation than elsewhere, but even there the evidence for it has not been strong.[101] Indeed, the decline of marriage has occurred up and down the class ladder, affecting the wealthiest to the most disadvantaged of men.

Government

Some observers believe it is the government more than the economy that has generated marriage decline. The government, as they see it, provides perverse economic incentives, incentives that reward people for being unmarried rather than married. The clearest case is in regard to our welfare programs. Welfare benefits—especially Aid to Families with Dependent Children (AFDC)—are said to reduce the costs of single motherhood and discourage young people from marrying.

Most, but not all, studies indicate that such a "welfare effect" exists, but it is relatively modest. A review of the data by William A. Galston, a former member of President Clinton's Domestic Policy Council, concluded that "a small but measurable fraction of family disintegration can be attributed to the effects of the welfare system. Perhaps as much as 15 or 20 percent."[102] Other scholars suggest that the effect is probably higher at the very bottom part of the income distribution, rising to as much as 30 percent.[103]

Yet the welfare population is only a tiny fraction of the total population; in 1993, 5.4 percent of the population were receiving subsidies through AFDC. As a general explanation for marriage decline in the population as a whole, it is hard to see that the American government has played much of a role.[104]

Culture

Both the economy and the government no doubt play some part in the marriage decline of the past three decades. But by far the most important factor, in my mind, is that invisible but powerful realm called culture. Culture consists of the values and beliefs that give coherence and meaning to life—our shared ideas about what is good and bad, right and wrong, desirable and undesirable, and the basic assumptions about reality that we take for granted. Although culture blends into the background of our lives, as does water in the lives of fish, it provides the justification for much of our behavior.

During this period there was an abrupt and extraordinary transformation of people's cultural values, worldview, and even self-definition, the ground rules by which we live. One conservative family scholar put it this way: "The social assumptions that had guided human conduct in this nation for centuries were tossed aside with a casualness and speed that were astonishing."[105] In a more academic tone, the liberal authors of a recent history of the American family similarly opined: "What Americans have witnessed since 1960 are fundamental challenges to the forms, ideals, and role expectations that have defined the family for the last century and a half."[106]

Large segments of the population came to regard self-fulfillment as their dominant life goal, pushing aside such traditional "Victorian" values as self-sacrifice, commitment to others, and institutional obligation.[107] This cultural shift has been widely documented by public opinion surveys. Pollster Daniel Yankelovich found, for example, that people today place a much lower value on what we owe others as a matter of moral obligation and a much higher value on self-realization and personal choice.[108]

One of the most important aspects of the rise of the self-fulfillment goal is that the traditional moral legitimacy and authority of almost all social institutions—education, religion, the professions, and government, as well as marriage—eroded. People lost trust and confidence in them. Confidence expressed toward organized religion, for example, declined from 42 percent to 16 percent between 1966 and 1989; that toward higher education from 61 percent to 32 percent.[109]

Marriage was particularly hard hit. Trust and confidence in marriage as a stable, lifelong social endeavor plummeted. Americans still believe strongly in "getting married someday." But marriage has become much less a social institution that expresses society's goals and more a personal, voluntary relationship which individuals can make or break at will in their search for self-fulfillment. The distinguished French sociologist Louis Roussel has suggested that marriage has undergone a "double deinstitutionalization": Individuals are more hesitant to enter or commit themselves to institutional marriage roles, and societies have weakened their normative sanctions over such roles.[110]

THE CULTURAL SHIFT

As the main underlying cause of the decline of marriage and fatherhood, the cultural shift toward self-fulfillment is worth considering in some detail. It represents the most serious threat to the restoration of marriage and fatherhood, to the social order, and even—ironically—to the goal of self-fulfillment itself.

America has long been known, and rightly so, as the land of individualism. We place a high value on human rights and the sanctity of the individual, on personal recognition and achievement. Yet this individualism has historically been tempered by a strong belief in the sanctity and importance of social units such as families, neighborhoods, schools, religious organizations, local communities, and the nation as a whole.[111] The identities of Americans were once strongly rooted in such social units, and their lives were directed toward the social goals these units espoused.

One can therefore speak of a "communitarian" individualism as the dominant value scheme of America in times past: The social and the personal were blended in a rather balanced way. "Doing one's duty" was clearly on a par with "personal choice." And as often as not, self-fulfillment meant self-improvement for the benefit of the group.

Today's radical, expressive, or unencumbered individualism is devoted much more to self-aggrandizement at the expense of the group. In place of group purposes serving as personal goals, self-expression, sexual freedom, and even impulsiveness have been substituted. "Do your own thing" and "get in touch with yourself" have become prevalent cultural themes.

One inevitable result is an anti-institutional frame of mind and a skepticism of authority. Social units of all types are seen to impinge on human behavior and increasingly are viewed as somewhat "illegitimate." Concern is shown for groups and for the public good only insofar as these directly advance personal well-being. Even informal relationships, social networks, and social supports are less prevalent. There has been a decline in visiting informally with others and belonging to voluntary associations, as well as an increase in living alone.[112]

Freedom and choice in our private lives would seem to be an essential condition for self-fulfillment. This is true, but only within limits. Any good thing can be carried too far. As the Latin poet Horace once wrote, "There is a proper measure in all things, certain limits beyond which . . . right is not to be found."[113] In almost every sphere of life the social has given way to the personal, the collective to the individual. No longer having a strong institutional repository, moral authority has become increasingly centered within the psyche of each individual. At the extreme, we are becoming a nation of asocial hedonists and narcissists.

The underlying purpose of all social institutions is to guide behavior in socially useful ways, toward the maintenance of an orderly social life in which citizens practice the social virtues of being kind and considerate, trusting and trustworthy, responsible and hardworking, honest and cooperative, and respectful of rules and legitimate authority. These virtues are essential underpinnings not only of social order but of civilization itself. They are the essence of the kind of society most people want and in which they thrive. Too seldom realized is the fact that only in such a society can true self-fulfillment be achieved.

Marriage and the family are the pivotal institutions in every society.

They are the seedbeds of social virtue. They teach, cajole, promote, and reinforce moral and civil behavior. Although families need outside help in this task, there really is no viable institutional alternative. An individualism unencumbered by families and other social institutions, then, brings personal freedom of a sort, but it also brings a high level of individual deviance and social disorder in which the social virtues are largely absent or are "used" cynically, as in financial scams and dishonest relationships.

The shift from a communitarian to a radical individualism has occurred to some degree in all urbanizing and industrializing societies; it seems to be an integral part of late-modernization.[114] Yet America has been in the vanguard of this trend because of two intrinsic features of our society: extreme cultural heterogeneity and great personal wealth.

America is undoubtedly the most culturally diverse society in the world. The nation has been built by bringing in people from diverse cultures worldwide and then assimilating them into a common culture through provision of employment, schooling, media, and residential living that are generally accessible to all. Ours is a grand social experiment, and cultural pluralism has enormously enriched American life. But it has also fostered over time, especially as the assimilationist impulse has weakened, an eroding sense of shared values and national identity that itself is a potent generator of radical individualism. When people cannot agree about what values they share and what social authorities they recognize, they naturally fall back onto more individualistic attitudes and patterns of living.

The shift toward radical individualism has also been strongly accentuated by our material affluence. We are no longer the world's wealthiest nation on a strictly per capita basis; several European nations (including Switzerland, Luxembourg, and the Scandinavian nations) and Japan have surpassed us in that respect. But we are still the wealthiest nation in terms of the private ownership of wealth, purchasing power, and average material level of living (such as size of housing units and ownership of consumer durables, including automobiles).

Such private, consumption-driven wealth provides the wherewithal to pursue an individualistic, privatized lifestyle apart from the larger community. To witness the apogee of this phenomenon, visit any of the walled-off suburban housing areas of the wealthy throughout the nation, protected round the clock by security gates and private security guards. Many American families, of course, are struggling economically just to get by. But even they are living at a material level virtually unheard of in times past.

Propelled by such enormous affluence and cultural diversity, America currently seems to be spiraling toward an ever more unencumbered individualism. A vicious circle has been established. As people become more individualistic in their thought and behavior, the authority of social institutions withers. And as institutional authority withers, people necessarily become still more individualistic.[115]

In short, America has become an overly individualistic society. Societies at the opposite extreme, collectivist and authoritarian societies, face problems of political or cultural tyranny, endless warfare with outgroups, and the suppression of individual rights and initiative. These problems have plagued most societies throughout history, and it is America's great achievement to have minimized them. But societies that have moved too far in the direction of unencumbered individualism face a new set of problems: personal alienation from the social order and a breakdown in the social control of individual behavior. America today has all the earmarks of this new set of problems: rising crime, declining interpersonal and political trust, growing personal and corporate greed, deteriorating communities, increasing confusion over moral issues, and not least, the decline of responsible fatherhood.

These are all dimensions of what is increasingly felt to be "social decline." The average American seemingly has become more fearful, anxious, and unsettled. Tempers have become shorter, life's little satisfactions less frequent, and the emotional feel of life less secure. The push for self-fulfillment, when carried to the extreme, leads not to personal freedom and happiness but to social breakdown and individual anguish.

FATHERHOOD IN CONTEMPORARY CULTURE

The end result of the many cultural, social, and economic trends we have discussed is a society surprisingly unsupportive of fatherhood. Indeed, if one were specifically to design a culture and a social system for the express purpose of undercutting fatherhood and men's contribution to family life, our current society would be close to what would result. Consider the following key elements one would want to incorporate:

1. Make marriage into a very weak institution. Say that marriage is just a piece of paper, little different from simply living with someone at your convenience. Replace the phrase "till death do us part" with "so long as I am happy." Indicate that single-parent families and other family forms where fathers are absent can be equally good at raising children as married-father families. Provide for easy divorce, whereby a man can simply walk out of a marriage at any time for any reason.

One of the principal social functions of marriage is to hold men to the mother-child bond. For men everywhere, marriage and parenthood are a package deal. In downgrading marriage, men will get the message that they are no longer needed, or even wanted, in family life.

2. Sexualize the society. Emphasize sex as often as possible in the media and popular culture. Stress that good sex lies at the root of personal fulfillment. Provide men with abundant opportunity to have as much sex as they want outside of the marital relationship.

Limiting sexuality and containing it within marriage is something that most men do with reluctance; male biology pushes them in quite another direction. Why resist temptation when it seems of little importance to do so?

3. Institute an educational system that disregards the fact that childrearing is a major adult responsibility and that marriage is important to childrearing. Pretend that the only adult role of importance is the work role; never mention that marriage and children may be a major part of a man's future life. Teach no "family values," for they are sure to be controversial if nothing else. Provide no skills or knowledge concerning how to care for a family. For sex education, assume that everyone is already having sex and mainly provide the knowledge and devices necessary for contraception.

The school system is an agent of child socialization second in importance only to the family. If men throughout their education never hear that family life and fatherhood are social concerns of the highest order, they will surely be less inclined to marry and to have children and more inclined to put their efforts into their work lives.

4. Have an economic system that does not recognize workers' family responsibilities and that stresses ever-increasing material consumption. Allow men little time off for family tasks and penalize them with lower salaries and slower job advancement when they take such time. Explain that doing their job is the main thing; what they do on their own time is their own concern. Move men around a lot from job to job, forcing them to change communities often.

A man can not pledge himself totally to the corporation and still have time properly to raise a family. What's important is to have the money to buy the products that the economic system provides. Money certainly doesn't come from having a family; on the contrary, one has much more disposable income as a single person. Men will quickly get the idea that it is better to remain single and childless.

5. Develop a culture that heavily stresses individualism. As the primary goals of life, promote individual freedom and self-fulfillment rather than social responsibility and obligation. Emphasize such slogans as "live and let live," "live free or die," and "do your own thing."

Men have always been somewhat more individualistic than women; they tend to strive more for risk taking, challenge, and independence. They are more likely than women to want society to "get off my back."

A strong cultural emphasis on individualism will help propel men even further in this direction, away from family life.

6. *In social discourse, through the media, and in the design of the built environment, deemphasize the importance of children to the continuation of society. Express no disapproval of men who have children and then abandon them. Feature in the media mostly adult situations in which children are not only absent but never mentioned. Design communities and shopping centers and transportation systems solely with adults in mind. Establish many adult-only communities in which resident children are not allowed.*

Many men find children to be an encumbrance to their worldly success and independence. Social and cultural expressions of childlessness will help justify their position.

7. *Overlook the importance of fathering when discussing male gender roles. Stress only that men must learn to be less aggressive, less competitive, and less interested in sports. Teach them to be less self-centered and better listeners on a date. Make them learn to cry in the movies.*

For those many men who don't want to become fathers anyway, at least they can be softened up a bit.

8. *When fathering is discussed, don't mention that fathers are unique and irreplaceable as protectors, challengers, disciplinarians, and guides. Explain that the goal is for fathers to become more like mothers; say that it is perfectly possible "for daddies to be good mommies."*

Since fathering is no different from mothering, males can easily (even preferably) be replaced in the home by females. The message is clear.

Is it not true that every one of these fatherhood-diminishing elements has become incorporated, to a large degree, into American culture today? From almost every social and cultural perspective, fatherhood has been made not only increasingly difficult but often seemingly superfluous and unnecessary. It is no wonder that fatherlessness is increasing so rapidly.

Some Advances

There have been, of course, a few offsetting advances in fathering in recent decades. Owing to more psychological sophistication and a more nurturing approach to childrearing, those fathers willing to stay married to the mothers of their children probably do a better job of fathering than their own fathers and grandfathers did. They are more sensitive to their children's needs, better companions to their children, and more helpful to their wives. And married fathers are increasingly involved in primary child care. Between 1988 and 1991 the percentage of preschool children (those under age five) who were cared for by their fathers while their mothers worked outside the home increased from about one in seven to one in five.[116] One reason for the increase is more dual-earner families where parents are working part-time or in non-day-shift jobs; another reason is male unemployment.

But empirical evidence for a major "new father" commitment to childrearing is, unfortunately, in scant supply. Furstenberg and Cherlin, for example, unexpectedly had to conclude from the National Survey of Children that children "who had at least some contact with their non-residential fathers were only slightly less likely than children from intact families to report that they frequently did things together with their fathers or that they spent as much time with them as they would like."[117]

The total time that parents spend with their children has decreased over the past few decades. This is mainly due to the entry of mothers into the labor force. But the time that fathers spend with their children apparently has changed little, if at all, despite the fact that mothers are spending less time with maternal and domestic tasks.[118]

CONCLUDING REMARKS

At one time in human history, cultural norms for sex, marriage, and family life were established and enforced by kinship groups. Recognizing that children's success in life was greatly improved by a father's presence, the kin group had a strong vested interest in having the man invest in his, and their, biological descendants. Tribal societies around the world still operate on this principle. With the arrival of complex societies, this function of the kinship group was taken over by organized religion and later by civil laws and their enforcement by government authority. Many societies have had a mixture of government, religious, and kinship enforcement.

In modern societies today the kinship group is mostly out of the picture, laws and the government take an increasingly hands-off policy, and organized religion is faltering. Sex, marriage, and the family fall almost entirely into the strictly private sphere. The private sphere has become ever more private, giving in to a radical form of individualism.

The end result is that fathers are vanishing from family life and only mothers are left to care about the children. And mothers, as we shall see when we look at the consequences of fatherlessness in the following chapter, are not enough.

2. The Human Carnage of Fatherlessness

The decline of fatherhood and marriage, discussed in the last chapter, has proved to be disastrous for children. One recent *New York Times* article is headlined "Study Confirms Worst Fears on U.S. Children"; another reports "Researchers Say U.S. Social Well-Being Is 'Awful.'"[1] The deteriorating condition of children—ranging from violent boys and promiscuous girls to abused children of both sexes—has become a regular feature of the daily news. As reviewed in this chapter, the linkage of these now-familiar conditions to fatherlessness is empirically verified by a voluminous body of social and behavioral research.

Because children represent the future of our society, these negative consequences are a social calamity in the making. But the perverse effects of fatherlessness extend well beyond children to include both women and the absent fathers themselves. As we shall see, fatherlessness impairs the lives of men and women in a number of important respects; it is a misfortune not just for those children affected by it but for every family member.

FATHERLESSNESS AND CHILDREN

By some measures—such as more years of education, more medical care, and more material affluence—the children of America have continued their gains of recent centuries.[2] In fact, by these measures the health and well-being of children should be much better today than they really are. Yet the American public is correct in its belief, documented by numerous public opinion polls, that child well-being over the past three decades has deteriorated markedly.

Juvenile violent crime has increased sixfold, from sixteen thousand arrests in 1960 to ninety-six thousand in 1992, a period in which the total number of juveniles in the population remained relatively stable. Reports of child neglect and abuse have quintupled since 1976, when data were first collected. The psychological pathology of children and youth has taken a drastic turn for the worse. Eating disorders and rates of unipolar depression have soared among adolescent girls. Teen suicide has tripled. Alcohol and drug abuse among teenagers, although leveling off in recent years, continues at a very high rate. SAT scores have declined nearly eighty points, and most of the decline cannot be accounted for by the increased academic diversity of students taking the test. Poverty has shifted from the elderly to the young. Since 1970 the percentage of children who are poor has increased from 15 percent to 22 percent. Of all the nation's poor today, 38 percent are children.

One can think of many reasons for such declining child well-being, including the growth of commercialism and consumerism, the influence of television and the mass media, the decline of religion, the widespread availability of guns and addictive drugs, and the decay of social order and community relationships in neighborhoods. None of these reasons should be dismissed. But the evidence is now strong that the loss of fathering from the lives of children is one of the most prominent reasons of all.

Surprisingly few studies have actually examined the effects on children of fatherlessness per se, independent of all other effects. The bulk of the studies have focused either on the effects of living in a single-parent family or of going through the divorce of one's parents. But in both cases the absence or loss of a father is a key factor. And in both cases the range of negative outcomes is extraordinary. Indeed, almost anything bad that can happen to a child occurs with much greater frequency to the children of divorce and those who live in single-parent families.

Economic Loss

The most tangible and immediate consequence of fatherlessness for children is the loss of economic resources. Take divorce. What happens to the income stream that had supported a child once a father leaves through divorce? By the best recent estimates, the income of the household in which the child remains instantly declines by about 21 percent per capita on average, a loss that remains stable at least through the first year.[3] And expenses go up. A new household must be set up, and thus the economies of scale gained from sharing expenses are lost. The childrearing household may face the necessity of moving, and moving is costly. New child-care expenses typically arise. To make matters worse, the social networks on which divorced single mothers might rely for financial aid shrink at the same time that these mothers experience difficulty obtaining commercial credit.

Over time, the economic situation for the child often deteriorates further. The child comes to rely primarily on the earnings of the mother, who typically earns considerably less than the father. As we now know, children cannot rely on their fathers to pay much in the way of child support. About half of previously married mothers receive no child support, and of those who receive it, both the reliability and the amount of child support drop over time. Fathers who live in separate households tend to become less economically altruistic toward their children or more distrustful of how their money is being spent or both.

Fatherlessness has led to a startling increase in child poverty. It is true that child poverty used to be rampant across America, far more so than today. Even in 1959, at the end of the prosperous 1950s, the percentage of children who were poor was 27 percent. But with continuing economic growth, the child poverty rate dropped to 14 percent in 1969 and remained relatively stable through the 1970s. Since then, it has been inching back up. Today more than 20 percent of the nation's children (and 25 percent of infants and toddlers) are again mired in poverty.[4] Unlike earlier child poverty, there is widespread agreement that the child poverty increase of recent years is due mainly to a single factor—the retreat of fathers from the lives of their children.

The loss of fathers' income, of course, is not the only reason for the recent growth of child poverty in America. But it is the predominant reason. By one estimate, 51 percent of the increase in child poverty observed during the 1980s (65 percent for blacks) can be attributed to changes in family structure.[5] Indeed, much of the income differential between whites and blacks today, perhaps as much as two thirds, can be attributed to the differences in family structure. It is no wonder that some are now saying that the best antipoverty program of all is an institution called marriage.

The proliferation of mother-headed families now constitutes something of a national economic emergency. About a quarter of all family groups with children are mother headed (for blacks, more than half), which is almost double the 11.5 percent figure in 1970.[6] No other group is so poor, and none stays poor longer. Poverty afflicts nearly one out of every two of these mother-only families (45 percent in 1992), whereas the income of fewer than one in ten married-couple families is below the government-set poverty line (8 percent in 1992). Ninety-four percent of the current caseload for Aid to Families with Dependent Children (AFDC) consists of single-parent families. Mother-only families even have lost ground in recent decades to other relatively poor groups, such as the disabled and the aged, because poverty rates for these groups have continued to decline.[7]

Poverty is much more severe among unmarried mothers than among divorced mothers, and unfortunately, never-married single mothers and their children make up the fasting-growing segment of the poverty population. Only 7 percent of single-parent children were with a never-married parent in 1970; today the figure has leaped to 31 percent. Having an out-of-wedlock birth as a teenager and not finishing high school is a particularly sure road to poverty for females. Eighty-eight percent of such women are living in poverty, compared to just 8 percent of women who finish school, marry, and have a baby after the age of twenty.

The children of mother-headed families are the very poorest of the poor. In 1991, 21 percent of all American children under age eighteen lived with their mother only (compared to 3 percent with father only, 3 percent with neither parent, and 73 percent with two parents).[8] Children in single-parent families have less than one third the median per capita income of children from two-parent families, and fully half of them fall below the poverty line in any given year. An estimated 73 percent of all single-parent children will have lived some period of time in poverty before they reach age eighteen, versus 20 percent of children in two-parent families. A sizable percentage of the poverty found in single-parent families is chronic: 22 percent of children from single-parent families will experience persistent poverty (of seven years or more), versus only 2 percent from two-parent families.[9]

Economic difficulties, such as the loss of the father's income following a divorce, ultimately account for a considerable portion of the negative social and behavioral outcomes found among children living in single-parent families. In education, for example, it is largely for economic reasons that children in single-parent families tend to go to lower-quality schools, to live in lower-income communities with fewer educational resources, to have fewer after-school lessons and extracurricular activities, and to have lower educational aspirations (due to an inability to afford the costs of a college education). In addition, it is quite common for absent fathers to refuse to pay for their children's higher education, even when they have been regularly paying child support. All of these income-related conditions, in turn, are strongly implicated in the significantly lower levels of school achievement and higher rates of school dropping out found among fatherless children.

By the best recent social science estimates, however, economic status accounts for no more than half of the negative social and behavioral outcomes of growing up in a single-parent family.[10] The other half of the problem outcomes under discussion stand in contradiction to the long-standing refrain of some social scientists that once economic status is adjusted for, the difference in child outcomes between nonintact and intact families all but disappears.[11] If this were the case, government employment and income-redistribution efforts could provide dependable remedies for our plight, and society would have no need to be concerned about absent fathers. Yet the evidence pouring in is powerful that father absence is an independent causative factor of major proportions in these negative outcomes. And these negative outcomes, it turns out, are remarkably large and pervasive.

Living in a Single-Parent Family

There has now been extensive research looking into the social and behavioral disadvantages to a child of growing up in a single-parent family. The latest and most authoritative review of this research is set forth by the prominent social scientists Sara McLanahan of Princeton University and Gary Sandefur of the University of Wisconsin in their new book *Growing Up with a Single Parent*.[12] The main source of their evidence is five nationally representative, large-scale social surveys.

McLanahan and Sandefur conclude that children who grow up with only one of their biological parents (nearly always the mother), compared to children who grow up with both parents, are three times more likely to have a child out of wedlock, 2.5 times more likely to become teen mothers, twice as likely to drop out of high school, and 1.4 times more likely to be idle (out of school and out of work). These are risk differentials of very substantial magnitude. The conclusions were reached, it is important to add, after adjusting for such income-related variables as race, sex, mother's education, father's education, number of siblings, and place of residence. In other words, the lower economic level of the children from single-parent families cannot account for their differential risks.

Another wide-ranging review of research, in this case on the relationship between fatherlessness and children's mental health, was recently completed by University of Texas sociologists Ronald J. Angel and Jacqueline L. Angel. They conclude "that father absence places children at elevated risk of impaired social development, that it hinders their school performance, and, ultimately, that it can limit their chances for optimal social mobility." They add, by way of summary, that "we can say with great confidence that father absence is, at least in the United States, a mental health risk factor for children."[13]

Similar conclusions have been reached by many other scholars. Research conducted by the National Center for Health Statistics, based on the 1988 National Health Interview Survey of Child Health, looked at a nationally representative sample of 17,110 children aged seventeen years and under. It found that "young people from single-parent families or step families were 2 to 3 times more likely to have had emotional or behavioral problems than those who had both of their biological parents present in the home."[14] Through this survey it was also determined that children living with single mothers or with mothers and stepfathers were more likely to have repeated a grade of school, to have been expelled, and to have elevated scores for health vulnerability.[15]

Another large scale study, the 1982 National Survey of Family Growth, focused on women aged fifteen to forty-four. It provided "strong evidence that women who spend part of their childhoods in one-parent families are more likely to marry and bear children early, to give birth before marriage, and to have their own marriages break up."[16]

Thus, we see that living in a single-parent family impacts negatively on almost all aspects of a child's life. The child is apt to have more emotional, behavioral, and physical health problems; he or she has more difficulties in school and drops out at a much higher rate. Girls are more likely to become unwed teen mothers. The problems linger into adulthood, with the children of single-parent families facing a much higher risk of difficulties in their own marriage and parenting experiences.

Children of Divorce

Evidence about the negative effects of divorce on the social and behavioral development of children is now legion in the social sciences. Although not always an intended measure of fatherlessness, divorce-effect studies provide in fact such a measure because most children of divorce end up living in single-parent families apart from their biological fathers. Indeed, the effects of divorce and living in a single-parent family are so closely intertwined that in many studies the two factors are combined or are virtually inseparable.

An example of the kind of research that has been done on divorce is the Kent State University Impact of Divorce Project. Six hundred ninety-nine elementary students nationwide were assessed over time by highly trained evaluators.[17] Children from two-parent situations (both biological parents present since the birth of the child) were compared with children from single-parent families resulting from divorce. The children from divorced homes performed more poorly on a wide range of assessments, such as: (1) parents' ratings of hostility toward adults, peer popularity, nightmares, and anxiety; (2) teachers' ratings of school-related behavior and mental health, including dependency, anxiety, aggression, withdrawal, inattention, peer popularity, and self-control; (3) scores in reading, spelling, and math; (4) school performance indices, including grades in reading and math as well as repeating a school grade; (5) physical health ratings; and (6) referral to the school psychologist. The researchers concluded that "the negative, differential effects of divorce on children and young adolescents were long term."[18]

One longitudinal study of the effects of divorce, a particularly sophisticated study in methodological terms, was done in Sweden. It followed into their teenage years *all* children born in Stockholm in 1953 (and still living there in 1963)—some 7,719 males and 7,398 females. Focusing on psychiatric disturbances, one investigator found that "the experience of family disruption involving parental separation or divorce has negative effects on later mental health whenever it occurs and regardless of the socioeconomic status of the household or of later changes in family structure."[19] Boys born to unmarried women, but whose subsequent life included living with a married and cohabiting couple at mid-childhood and with a separated or divorced parent at the age of seventeen (a not uncommon Swedish family life-course pattern), had an especially high rate of psychological impairment.

One of the first researchers to follow children of divorce over time and examine them clinically is the well-known social psychologist Judith Wallerstein. What she found in her California Children of Divorce Study was startling: "A significant number of children suffer long-term, perhaps permanent detrimental effects from divorce, and . . . others experience submerged effects that may appear years later." Five years after a divorce, over a third of the studied children had experienced moderate to severe depression. Ten years after divorce, a significant number of the (then) young men and women appeared troubled, adrift, and were achieving below expectations. Fifteen years after divorce, by which time the children had reached their thirties, many were having difficulty establishing their own love relationships. "What is clear," she wrote, "is that the multiple economic, social, and psychological life stresses of being a single or a visiting or a remarried parent, together with the unanticipated psychic reverberations of the broken marriage contract, have combined to weaken the family in its child-rearing and child protective functions."[20]

The number of studies reaching similar conclusions about the effects of divorce on young people as they reach adulthood is now nearly endless. Data from a national sample of 9,643 respondents collected through the 1987–1988 National Survey of Families and Households yielded this conclusion: "Family disruption during childhood has long-term consequences for the subjective well-being of both women and men."[21] Reviewing their own careful research that involved pooling data from eleven General Social Surveys conducted annually from 1973 to 1985 by the National Opinion Research Center, family scholars Norval Glenn and Kathryn D. Kramer of the University of Texas concluded: "The increase in the proportion of adults who are children of divorce in the next few decades will lead, in the absence of countervailing influences, to a steady and non-trivial decline in the overall level of well-being of the American adult population."[22]

One problematic aspect of much divorce-effects research, frequently discussed in both academic and popular media, is that of causation: Did the conflict leading to divorce generate the ensuing problems, or did the actual divorce and attending father absence create them? Short of running a massive social experiment and randomly assigning children to intact and nonintact families, there is no way to be certain about cause and effect on this issue. But based on the best information available, gleaned by adjusting for known differences between families that break up and those that stay together, by carefully studying children both before and after the divorce, and by applying various statistical controls, Sara McLanahan aptly summarized what is coming to be the prevailing view in the social sciences: "While some of the problems associated with single parenthood predate parents' separation, others do not. On balance, the average child does worse, not better, after a divorce."[23] Much of the "worse," it is fair to add, is caused by fatherlessness.

THE SOCIAL SCIENCE SHIFT

These research conclusions about the social and behavioral effects on children of divorce and single-parent families will no longer come as a surprise to many Americans. They have been widely reported in the media. Yet it was not so long ago that the divorce revolution was given a strangely positive cast in popular culture. If breaking up is better for parents, it was thought, it cannot be all that bad for children. What keeps parents happy should also keep children happy.

How can an idea so wrongheaded have been so pervasive? In part, of course, it was a convenient, guilt-retarding rationalization for parents who were breaking up. Unfortunately, however, it was a judgment put forth by many social scientists as well. At one time, the social sciences reached a quite different conclusion about these matters than they do today, and the earlier conclusion was influential in reinforcing the views of popular culture. Before we go on to explore in detail some of the most deleterious effects of fatherlessness—juvenile delinquency, teenage childbearing, child abuse, and violence against women—it is worth pausing briefly to examine what happened.

Back in the 1970s, at the height of the divorce revolution, the findings of many social scientists about the effects of divorce and resultant fatherlessness were remarkably sanguine. Typical was the work of Elizabeth Herzog and Cecelia Sudia. In a report written for the U.S. Children's Bureau (1973) entitled "Children in Fatherless Families," designed to "consider carefully what we do and do not know about the effects on children of growing up in fatherless homes," they concluded from a review of existing studies that the "evidence concerning [juvenile delinquency, school achievement, and masculine identity] is neither clear enough nor firm enough to demonstrate beyond doubt whether fatherless boys are or are not overrepresented."

Herzog and Sudia went so far as to discount any negative effects of divorce and fatherlessness, taking a position that resounded widely in the media of the time. They claimed that discord and conflict in the home prior to a divorce are more detrimental than a father's absence after the divorce and concluded that, therefore, "one is forced to prefer a 'good' one-parent [read: fatherless] home for a child." Here was their public-policy recommendation: Rather than "forestall the absence of fathers . . . it may be more feasible to reduce some unfounded anxieties of middle-class one-parent mothers and to offer them such community supports as can be developed."[24]

As Herzog and Sudia indicate, their recommendation is in the nature of a pragmatic forced-choice between two evils rather than a stamp of approval on divorce and father absence. Nevertheless, their underlying presumption—that divorce and fatherlessness are the better, "more feasible" option—has been translated in the minds of some social scientists into "divorce is for the best, and not to worry about fatherlessness." The authors of a recent work, *Mother-Headed Families,* for example, state: "The parent considering divorce may believe—and may be correct in believing—that the divorce will improve the children's lives."[25] It is inescapable that the presumptions about the benign nature of divorce and father absence on children have had a major impact on personal behavior across America by helping to legitimate family breakup and feeding the fantasy that whatever is good for the parents is good for the children. As *U.S. News & World Report* columnist John Leo once wrote: "If the father who runs out on his kids is merely creating another acceptable family form, how is he any better or worse than the father who stays committed to his 'double-parent' family?"[26]

A limitation of many of the early studies of divorce and fatherlessness on which Herzog and Sudia relied is that children were not followed over time (most of the fatherlessness in the early 1970s was due to divorce, not unwed births). The impacts investigated were short run and mostly involved children only in the youngest age groups. Rather than objectively measuring the children's condition, some studies relied on the questionable practice of asking parents to characterize the effects of the divorce on their own children—questionable because, as "interested parties" with the powerful divorce agenda of self-justification and self-fulfillment, they could not be expected to be objective informants.

It has to be supposed, in addition, that a little ideology crept into the research. Divorcing academics and antifamily feminists of the time were perhaps overeager to turn up minimal effects of divorce so that their own emotional lives would be spared or their negative views of the traditional nuclear family upheld.

At about the same time that Herzog and Sudia were making their pronouncements, however, a body of research was initiated that eventually led to a different empirical outcome. A number of longitudinal studies were launched that carefully and objectively followed the children of divorce into young adulthood to see how they fared. The targeted children in these studies—children from the peak years of the divorce revolution—are now young adults. Moreover, in the 1980s the unprecedented wave of children from broken families who were entering their teenage years generated an additional body of new research on the effects of divorce. It is the findings of these long-term studies that were reported above.

The more recent findings have changed the views of many social scientists. As an *Atlantic* cover-story article by Barbara Dafoe Whitehead, which reviewed the research, quite accurately began: "After decades of public dispute about so-called family diversity, the evidence from social science research is coming in: The dissolution of two-parent families, though it may benefit the adults involved, is harmful to many children, and dramatically undermines our society."[27]

JUVENILE DELINQUENCY AND VIOLENCE

Of all the negative consequences of fatherlessness, juvenile delinquency and violence probably loom largest in the public mind: There are too many little boys with guns. A 550 percent increase in reported violent crime has occurred since 1960, while the population has gone up by only 41 percent. The segment of the population with the fastest-growing crime rate is juveniles. Serious violent crime used to be an adult phenomenon, but arrests of juveniles for murder went up by 128 percent between 1983 and 1992. A study of the officially recorded criminality of two groups of Philadelphia boys, those born in 1945 and those born in 1958, found that the later group was three times more likely to commit violent crimes and five times more likely to commit robberies.[28] Killers and killed alike are younger than ever.

One can point to many recent changes in our society that have fed this outburst of violence among juveniles, including the lethal combination of guns and drugs in our inner cities, the decline of low-skilled jobs, and the violent themes of popular culture. But behind it all there lurks the strong probability that a key underlying cause is the rapid growth of fatherlessness. Many people have an intuitive presumption that fatherlessness must be related to delinquency and violence, and based on the research that has been conducted, the weight of evidence strongly buttresses that presumption. Juvenile delinquency and violence are clearly generated disproportionately by youths in mother-only households and in other households where the biological father is not present.[29]

What is the evidence? First, there are large-scale studies of statistical association. A statistical review of fifty major studies on the effects of family structure on delinquency concluded that "the effect of intact versus 'broken' families is a consistent and real pattern of association . . . the prevalence of delinquency in broken homes is 10–15 percent higher than in intact homes."[30] Similarly, a review of all significant studies of the impact of divorce on children conducted in the past few decades found that "research on antisocial behavior consistently illustrates that adolescents in mother-only households and in conflict-ridden families are more prone to commit delinquent acts."[31]

Comparable findings come from the National Surveys of Children, a major longitudinal study done in two waves.[32] The study found that family disruption "was associated with a higher incidence of several behavior problems, negative effects being greatest with multiple marital transitions."[33] The behavior problems included depression/withdrawal, antisocial behavior, impulsive/hyperactive behavior, and school behavior problems. One important finding was that a child living with a custodial parent of the opposite sex is especially prone to problem behavior. Given the makeup of most single-parent families, this applies mainly to boys living with their mothers.

Reviewing all such studies, criminologists Michael R. Gottfredson and Travis Hirschi concluded in their influential work *A General Theory of Crime* that "in most (but not all) studies that directly compare children living with both biological parents with children living in 'broken' or reconstituted homes, the children from intact homes have lower rates of crime."[34] The findings of the large-scale social surveys are corroborated by those of so-called ecological studies that examine the association of factors in particular areas of cities or geographic regions. From such studies, Gottfredson and Hirschi concluded that "such family measures as the percentage of the population divorced, the percentage of households headed by women, and the percentage of unattached individuals in the community are among the most powerful predictors of crime rates."[35]

Sixty percent of America's rapists, 72 percent of adolescent murderers, and 70 percent of long-term prison inmates come from fatherless homes.[36] As we shall see in chapter 5, this is no statistical artifact. Fathers are important to their sons as role models. They are important for maintaining authority and discipline. And they are important in helping their sons to develop both self-control and feelings of empathy toward others, character traits that are found to be lacking in violent youth.

Unfortunately, the die for the near future has already been cast. The teenage population is expected to rise in the next decade by as much as 20 percent, even more for minority teenagers, as the children of the baby boomers grow up. This has prompted criminologist James Fox to assert: "There is a tremendous crime wave coming in the next 10 years." It will be fueled not by old, hardened criminals but by what Fox calls "the young and the ruthless"—children in their early and mid-teens who are turning murderous. In 1993 there were 3,647 teenage killers; by 2005 he expects there will be 6,000 of them.[37] If fatherlessness continues to increase, we face even more dangerous times ahead.

TEENAGE SEXUALITY AND EARLY CHILDBEARING

The twin to the nightmare specter of "too many little boys with guns" is "too many little girls with babies." Again, fatherlessness is a major contributing factor to this serious domestic plight.

During the past three decades there has been a dramatic increase in the percentage of teenagers engaging in sexual activity. In the mid-1950s only 27 percent of girls had sexual intercourse by age eighteen (data unavailable for boys); in 1988, 56 percent of girls (and 73 percent of boys) had become sexually active by that age.[38] The largest relative increase in sexuality has occurred among younger teenage girls: 25.6 percent of fifteen-year-old girls had sexual intercourse in 1988, compared to just 4.6 percent in 1970.

The most obvious concern about teen sexuality is that it can lead to pregnancy. About one million teen pregnancies occur in the United States each year, giving this nation the highest teen-pregnancy rate in the industrialized world. Twelve percent of all women aged fifteen to nineteen and 21 percent of those who have had sexual intercourse become pregnant each year.[39] Fifty percent of these pregnancies end in births, 35 percent end in abortions, and about 14 percent end in miscarriages. The great majority of teenage births are unplanned and unintended.[40]

In most cultures around the world, teenage births are the norm. Even in the United States they were more common fifty years ago. But most of the teen births in the fifties took place within a marriage, as do

most teen births worldwide. Today, of all first births to women aged fifteen to seventeen, 81 percent are born out of wedlock, a startling increase from 33 percent in the early 1960s. (An additional 11 percent
today are conceived, although not born, out of wedlock.)[41]

Of all children born out of wedlock in America, most will grow up fatherless in single-parent households. Their chance of living in poverty is
five times greater than that of children growing up in intact families;
their chance of having socioemotional problems as adolescents is two to
three times greater; and their chance of generating additional problems
for all of us through their own antisocial behavior as teenagers and as
adults is difficult to estimate but probably great. Those children born to
teenagers who are unwed are even more at risk than these data suggest.

Teen pregnancy is not the only concern about the increase of
teenage sexuality. Early sexual activity poses a grave danger to adolescent health. An estimated three million teenagers (about a quarter of all
sexually experienced adolescents) annually contract a sexually trans-
mitted disease (STD), accounting for 25 percent of all new cases nationwide.[42] Because of anatomical differences, women are more susceptible to STDs than men. In a single act of unprotected intercourse with
an infected partner, for example, a woman is twice as likely as a man to
acquire gonorrhea, chlamydia, and hepatitis. Teenage girls are even
more susceptible to STDs due to immature biological development of
the genitals and the presence of fewer protective antibodies.[43] While
constituting serious health problems themselves, many STDs also generate increased risk of developing certain cancers, becoming infertile,
and contracting HIV on exposure. Moreover, many STDs tragically are
passed on by women to their children at birth.

Again, many factors can be cited to account for the new regime of
teenage sexuality and early childbearing, including a declining age at
first menarche, less parental supervision due to working parents, the
widespread availability of contraceptives, a heavy emphasis on sexual
themes by the organized entertainment industry and the media, and
the weakening of cultural norms governing teenage sexuality and especially the timing of sexual initiation. Yet as important as any of these, if
not more so, is fatherlessness. Fathers play a key role in the development of their daughters' sexual behavior.

The findings of large-scale studies lend strong support to the view
that the behavior of adolescent females, especially in their heterosexual
relationships, is markedly affected by father deprivation in childhood.
McLanahan and Sandefur, for example, concluded that "growing up in
a disrupted family increases the risk of becoming a teen mother by a
substantial amount."[44] Analyzing data from the National Child Development Study, a major British longitudinal study that followed the lives

of thousands of children born in 1958, social researcher Kathleen Kiernan found that young women with divorced or separated parents are "more likely to form unions in their teens, to have a child at an early age, and to bear children outside marriage."[45] Kiernan highlights one particular pattern of behavior that opens the door to other problems: Girls from single-parent families are more likely to leave home at an earlier age.

The presence of a surrogate father provides no respite. Other studies have found that early home leavers are even more commonly associated with stepfamilies. Indeed, one of the most well-established findings concerning the effects on children of living in stepfamilies is that "children in step family households—particularly girls—leave their households at an earlier age than do children in single-parent households or in two-parent households."[46]

If the growing problem of teenage sexuality and early childbearing can be resolved without bringing fathers back into the lives of their daughters, that way has not yet been found. And in view of the above findings, a good bet is that it will not likely be found.

CHILD ABUSE

Most serious child abuse, especially sexual abuse, is committed by men. The men who have greatest access to children are fathers. Since fathers participate less in the lives of their children today than ever before and children are more often under the sole care of their mothers, wouldn't you suppose that the rate of child abuse would have dropped? Unfortunately, quite the opposite has happened. As fathers have left home, the rates of child abuse have increased, and reported sexual abuse has increased at a faster rate than all other forms of child maltreatment.[47]

A major reason for the increase in child abuse is that unrelated men, surrogate fathers, are much more likely to abuse children than are natural fathers. And especially in single-parent and stepfamilies, such men have more access to children than ever before. Indeed, an important benefit of having a natural father in the home is precisely to protect against child abuse.

According to recent surveys, some 20 percent of adult women and 5 percent to 10 percent of adult men have experienced sexual abuse at some time during their childhood.[48] Physical abuse of children is more common still, being about twice as prevalent as sexual abuse.[49] Most evidence points to a real increase in both major forms of child abuse in recent decades. By 1990, when over two million combined cases of child abuse (including neglect and emotional maltreatment) were reported to social service agencies, the U.S. Advisory Board on Child

Abuse and Neglect pronounced that the amount of child maltreatment in the United States had reached the level of a "national emergency."[50]

One of the greatest risk factors in child abuse, found by virtually every investigation that has ever been conducted, is family disruption. And within the category of family disruption, living in a female-headed, single-parent household ranks as especially consequential. In 1981, 43 percent of children reported as having been abused were living in such households, compared to only 18 percent of children in the total population.[51]

Both sexual abuse and physical abuse are affected by single-parenthood, which of course means in most cases that children are living apart from their natural father. A 1985 national telephone survey that asked adult respondents about their childhoods found that those who grew up in a family form in which one or both natural parents were absent reported markedly higher incidents of sexual abuse. Another national survey, this time focused on physical abuse, found that "rates of severe and very severe violence toward children are substantially greater in single-parent households."[52]

Sexual Abuse

The most common victims of sexual abuse are girls; they make up 80 percent of cases reported to child protection authorities (a somewhat lower percentage is found in adult retrospective studies). The perpetrators of sex abuse, on the other hand, are almost all male: an estimated 95 percent of girl abusers and 80 percent of boy abusers.[53] Despite the fact that immediate family members have the most access to children, fewer than half of the sexual abuse perpetrators, it turns out, are actually family members and close relatives. And strangers make up only 10 percent to 30 percent of the cases. The remainder are acquaintances, including mothers' boyfriends, neighbors, teachers, coaches, religious leaders, and peers.[54]

Why does living in a female-headed, single-parent family have such an elevated risk for child sexual abuse? Two reasons have been put forth. First is a decrease in the quantity and quality of supervision and protection that children receive, thus leaving them more vulnerable. Second is that children from single-parent homes tend to be more emotionally deprived and needy and therefore "vulnerable to the ploys of sexual abusers, who commonly entrap children by offering affection, attention, and friendship."[55]

Fatherlessness is closely involved in both of these reasons. In most single-parent families fathers are not around to provide the supervision and protection that children need to avoid sexually-molesting acquaintances and strangers. Protecting daughters from the sexual overtures of other men has long been a major role of fathers. Fathers are also very important in providing models for the kinds of nonsexual relationships with men that daughters need to develop if they are to avoid the ploys of sexual abusers.

A special problem for children living with single mothers is that these mothers rely heavily on child-care providers who are not relatives, and much child abuse occurs when the child is under the care of such providers. The danger is greatest, of course, when the child-care provider is male. One study of sexual abuse in Iowa found that male sitters were responsible for almost five times as much sexual abuse as female sitters, even though they performed only a very small overall proportion of child care.[56]

By all accounts mothers' boyfriends are another serious problem, although the data are not available that would provide accurate information about prevalence.[57] Certainly, such predatory men are much in the news. One often hears, for example, of men who take up with a woman solely because they desire the possibility of sexual access to her daughter, and of women who urge their boyfriends to "play daddy" with their children, thus providing the boyfriend with an ease of access that can lead to inappropriate behavior.

Nevertheless—and although they represent a minority of all cases—those sexual abuse cases in which immediate family members and close relatives are involved certainly include some of the most serious and long lasting. They are also the most inexplicable because they violate the universal taboo against incest—forbidden sex among close relatives. The most lurid are those cases involving a father, such as this one recorded by researchers James Garbarino and Gwen Gilliam:

> If I was alone with my dad, he would touch and kiss me. I would try to please him in little ways because it was confusing to me. Then he came into my room one night. I was real scared, but he told me to relax and he wouldn't hurt me. It did hurt, but there were moments I remember enjoying. I mean, I was the ugly one and this was the closest thing I had ever experienced to love. The only affection I can remember were those times with my father. He told me he would kill me if I told, so I never told my mom. I still don't know if she knew.[58]

If cases of this kind were common, we could perhaps be more sanguine about growing fatherlessness. But they are not, despite the great attention they receive from the media. Among sexual abusers who are "blood relatives," only a small fraction are fathers. The great majority are uncles, grandfathers, brothers and stepbrothers, and male cousins.[59]

Indeed, it is reasonable to suppose that most fathers attempt to protect their daughters from abuse by relatives just as they do from abuse by acquaintances and strangers.

When a father is the perpetrator, it is typically not the natural father but a surrogate father, a man who is not genetically related. In a study conducted in San Francisco of a random sample of 930 adult women, for example, it was found that the chances of a daughter being abused by her stepfather are at least seven times higher than by her biological father.[60] Approximately one out of every six women who had a stepfather as a principal figure in her childhood years was sexually abused by him, compared to only one out of every forty women who had a biological father. The risk of abuse by stepfathers would be greater still if length of exposure were factored in, since girls tend to live many more years with biological fathers than with stepfathers.

To make matters worse, stepfathers commit abuses of a more serious nature. Forty-seven percent of the cases of sex abuse by stepfathers were classified as "very serious," versus only 26 percent of cases by the biological fathers.

Some biological fathers certainly are sexually abusive toward their daughters, however, and their numbers may be increasing. Paradoxically, this too may be related to growing fatherlessness or at least to the circumstances that surround the growth of father absence and family breakup. Here are some reasons.

• First, compared to abusing stepfathers, abusing biological fathers are more likely to live in circumstances of great personal and social disorganization.[61] They are more likely to have very bad marriages, to be suffering from alcohol and drug dependencies, and to be of extremely low income. In other words, they have been pushed over the edge.

• Second, a number of studies have found that children are at an especially high risk of sexual abuse in single-parent families in which the father is the single parent.[62] Just as fathers can protect their children from the abuse of outsiders, so mothers can protect their children from the abuse of fathers. The father-headed form of single-parent family is currently increasing.

• Third, a study comparing paternal sexual abusers and nonabusers was revealing. It found that, during their victims' first three years of life, the abusers were in the home much less and were less involved in nurturing activities.[63] Strong attachment and bonding between father and daughter in infancy, therefore, may be a critical ingredient for preventing later child abuse. In an increasingly fatherless society, especially with so many children born out of wedlock, intimate bonding is something that fewer natural fathers will experience. And, of course, it is something that surrogate fathers almost never experience; they come into the family at a later stage.

• Fourth, and perhaps most important of all, is a seldom discussed issue that relates to why a natural father would be willing to break the universal incest taboo, the taboo against having sex with people to whom one is closely related. There is evidence that the less confident a father is that a daughter is really his offspring, the more likely he is to have an incestuous relationship with her.[64] Societies in which fathers have low "paternity confidence," a term used by evolutionary psychologists, tend also to be societies with a high degree of incestuous relationships.

We know that paternity confidence must be dropping as a result of the sexual revolution. With so many people now sleeping around, how could it be otherwise? Indeed, declining confidence of paternity—and what it means for children—could be one of the big sleeper issues in the contemporary family debate.

All things considered, we can reasonably conclude that the daughter least likely to be sexually abused while growing up is one who lives in a stable family with both natural parents and whose father has paternity confidence and is closely involved in her nurturance during the early years of her life. The more that society departs from this ideal, the more likely it is that sexual abuse will occur.

Physical Abuse

An important difference between physical abuse and sexual abuse is that both women and men are heavily represented as abusers.[65] Yet even when women are the abusers, fatherlessness typically plays an important role. A mother is much more likely to be abusive and to allow others to mistreat her child when she does not have the support of an actively involved father. Another difference between the two forms of abuse is that preadolescent victims of physical abuse (and especially of more severe forms of abuse) are more often boys than girls.

Mothers in single-parent families have an understandably hard time raising boys. Not only is an adult male absent from the household, but the single mother often lacks the other supports that she needs for successful childrearing. In addition to economic deprivation, she may find herself living in a family-unfriendly neighborhood. The divorced mother typically has lost the potential support of relatives on the father's side of the family as well as the support of their common friends.

As one study concluded, "Assistance with children was the key form of support that appeared to decrease the incidence of unsupportive parental behavior."[66] It is no wonder, then, that single mothers "display more than two times more negative contact with their children than mothers in two-parent families," and are "significantly implicated in cases of child abuse."[67]

Moreover, single mothers tend to be more violent abusers than mothers in dual-parent households. In one national survey, single mothers reported a 71 percent greater rate of "very severe violence" toward their children than did dual-parent mothers. They were surpassed by single fathers, however, who tended to be even more violent.[68]

Probably the most serious threat to children in single-parent families is the mother's boyfriend. Mothers' boyfriends are overwhelmingly represented in physical-abuse statistics, especially for serious abuse. In a study of child abuse in single-mother households by educational expert Leslie Margolin, it was found that 64 percent of the nonparental abuse was committed by mothers' boyfriends. Nonrelatives such as day-care providers and adolescent baby-sitters were a distant second with 15 percent, followed by aunts and uncles (7 percent), grandparents (7 percent), siblings (4 percent) and other relatives (4 percent). This was especially surprising in view of the fact that these boyfriends were very infrequent caregivers; they performed only 1.75 percent of the nonparental care considered in the study. Margolin calculated that "mothers' boyfriends committed 27 times more child abuse than their hours in child care would lead us to predict."[69]

Why this tremendous overrepresentation of boyfriends? One explanation is drawn from evolutionary biology. These men are unrelated to the child, notes Margolin, and "a caregiver's level of protection and solicitude toward a child is directly proportional to the degree that the caregiver and child share the same genetic heritage."[70] Further support for this explanation was provided by the fact that, excluding boyfriends, all other male nonrelatives were significantly more abusive than male relatives.

But there are culturally-based explanations as well. Margolin offers this insight:

> Mothers' boyfriends have no predefined, culturally legitimate role vis-à-vis their partners' children. Like "marginal men" there are no norms to guide their actions in child care and also no norms informing children of their obligations toward them. Support for a mother's boyfriend is further limited by the perception that his relationship to his partner is illicit, indefinite, and extralegal, that his interests in her are often in conflict with her

children's, and that children's compliance with their mother's boyfriend could be seen as manifestation of disloyalty to their own father.[71]

In fact, Margolin found that children's disobedience or perceived disobedience was a common precursor to the violent abuse in which the boyfriends engaged.

Physical Abuse by Stepparents

The domestic threat posed by unrelated adult males reappears tragically in stepparent households, one of America's fastest growing family forms. Just as we saw above that stepfathers are disproportionately more involved than natural fathers in sexual abuse, so are they more involved in physical abuse.

Many studies have found that a child is far more likely to be physically abused by a stepfather than by a natural father. One investigation by Canadian evolutionary psychologists Margo Wilson and Martin Daly found that "preschoolers in Hamilton [Ontario] living with one natural parent and one stepparent in 1993 were 40 times as likely to become child abuse statistics as like-aged children living with two natural parents."[72] On the basis of this and other studies, these investigators concluded that "stepparenthood per se remains the single most powerful risk factor for child abuse that has yet been identified."[73] (It is probably the case, however, that stepfathers take second place to mothers' boyfriends.)

The high rate of child abuse in stepparent households is undoubtedly linked to the fact that many stepparents find their parenting roles stressful and unsatisfying. One researcher found, for example, that only 53 percent of stepfathers and 25 percent of stepmothers could claim to have "parental feelings" toward their stepchildren, and still fewer to "love" them.[74] Many explanations have been put forth to account for this stepparent phenomenon. Most revolve around such social issues as the "incomplete institutionalization" of stepfamilies and the "role ambiguity" which stepparents face.[75] Once stepfamilies are a fully accepted family institution, it is argued, and once the new family roles within stepfamilies are clearly worked out, the problems that stepfamilies encounter with parenting, including child abuse, should disappear.

The parenting problems that stepparents face may be eased by social change, but it is unlikely that they will disappear. They may to some extent, in fact, be inherent to stepparenthood. The reason why unrelated stepparents find their parenting roles more stressful and less satisfying than biological parents is probably due much less to social stigma and to the uncertainty of their obligations as to the fact that they gain fewer intrinsic emotional rewards from carrying out those obligations. This issue will be fully explored in chapters 5 and 6.

Adding fuel to this fire over stepparents is the fact that stepparents are discriminatory in their abusive behavior. When their household consists of both stepchildren and biologically related children, they are more abusive toward their stepchildren.[76] Even more tellingly, the physical abuse in which stepparents engage with their stepchildren is far more violent and lethal than that engaged in by biological parents with their natural children. In fact, compared to children in intact and single-parent households, Daly and Wilson assert, "stepchildren are not merely 'disadvantaged' but imperiled."[77]

They are not referring to any small difference. A look at U.S. data indicates that the youngest children (two years and under) have a hundred times greater risk of being killed at the hands of stepparents than of genetic parents; Canadian data put the risk factor at seventy times.[78] And statistical analysis has indicated that this greater risk cannot be attributed to reporting or detection biases, incidental traits of remarriage partners, differential poverty, maternal youth, family size, or other social factors that have been associated with child abuse.

Martin Daly and Margo Wilson make a strong and plausible case that the discriminatory and more lethal abuse patterns of stepparents are strong indicators that stepparents have fewer feelings of "parental solicitude" toward their children. Feelings of parental solicitude, in turn, are a universal impediment to child abuse.

> Stepparents do not, on average, love their children as much as genetic parents, and they are more likely than genetic parents to feel indifference or hostility instead. . . . Greater love motivates greater parental protection and vigilance against extrinsic threats, and it inhibits parents from damaging children recklessly or in anger."[79]

As further support for this theory of "differential parental solicitude" between natural fathers and surrogate fathers, Daly and Wilson provide substantial evidence that fathers of each type who kill their young children do so in strikingly different ways.[80] Beatings constitute a relatively large proportion of steppaternal homicides, either the result of a single burst of outrage ("the kid wouldn't stop crying") or incidentally as part of a prolonged cycle of regular abuse which eventually, accidentally, kills. Genetic fathers, on the other hand, are more likely to shoot or asphyxiate their victims, mitigating the duration of suffering. The killings by genetic fathers are often done "more in sorrow than in anger," perhaps reflecting some confused sense of "rescue" from a cruel world, and could be said to show less hostile resentment toward the victim. A surprisingly high percentage of these killings (but not killings by stepfathers) are followed by the fathers' suicide.

In conclusion, all of the above considerations point to the fact that physical abuse, like sexual abuse, is minimized in the situation where a child is raised continuously by the natural father and mother. The further removed children are from this family situation, the more they are imperiled.

VIOLENCE TOWARD WOMEN

In a now oft-quoted phrase, Gloria Steinem once said that "a woman without a man is like a fish without a bicycle." There is no doubt that many women get along very well without men in their lives and that the wrong men in their lives can be disastrous. Yet as fatherlessness overtakes the nation, the full importance of the loss of fathers in the lives of childrearing women is beginning to come clear. And it is hardly like a fish losing her bicycle. Fatherlessness appears to generate more violence toward women just as it increases violence toward children.

Violence toward women, especially the so-called family or domestic violence that is committed by intimates, has been common throughout history. Indeed, in many societies married women have been pretty much at the mercy of their husbands. The slogan of some feminists that "a marriage license is a hitting license," from this perspective, has some truth on its side. In times past, due to prevailing legal doctrines of "family privacy," a man could hit his own wife with impunity, but if he hit his neighbor's wife in the same manner, he could be arrested. He could also legally force his wife to have sex, an act which, if done with his neighbor's wife, would lead to the charge of rape.

Fortunately, this legal immunity that husbands have had is coming to an end. Because violent husbands now ordinarily are faced with legal restraint and because fewer women are married, one might suppose that violence against women would drop. But such a supposition is wrong. Modern family changes have not decreased violence against women, they have increased it.

Consider the fact that less than a third of violence (assault, robbery, and rape) toward women is committed by intimates and other relatives; most serious violence is committed by either unrelated acquaintances or strangers.[81] As the number of unattached males goes up, violence toward women increases. Or consider the fact that, of the violence toward women that is committed by intimates and other relatives, only 29 percent involves a current spouse, whereas 42 percent involves a close friend or partner and another 12 percent an ex-spouse.[82] As current spouses are replaced by nonspouses and exes, violence toward women increases.

In fact, marriage appears to be a strong safety factor for women. A satisfactory marriage between sexually faithful partners, especially when they are raising their own biological children, engenders fewer risks for violence than probably any other circumstance in which a woman could find herself. Recent surveys of violent crime victimization (1979–1987) have found that only 12.6 married women per 1000 fall victim to violence, compared to 43.9 never-married women per 1000 and 66.5 divorced or separated women per 1000.[83]

Underlying much and probably most domestic violence against women, ranging from beatings to homicide, is the proprietary nature of men with respect to their mates. The sexual possessiveness and sexual jealousy of men are legendary and well founded in evolutionary psychology, as will be discussed in chapter 6. Men are more deeply apprehensive than women about sexual infidelity (women's deepest concern is emotional faithlessness), and they more readily become enraged and violent over the perceived sexual misbehaviors of their mates. In spousal homicides, male sexual jealousy engendered by the wife's real or imagined infidelity or desertion is a primary cause, if not *the* primary cause. There is a remarkable prevalence of recently estranged wives as homicide victims.[84]

Being married and being a father are two different things, of course. The data do not exist whereby one could break down male perpetrators of family violence in terms of whether or not they have children. But it stands to reason that, because more is at stake, a married father will have an even lower propensity to spousal abuse than a childless married man. (This assumes that the children in question are biological offspring of the couple; some evidence exists that the presence of stepchildren is associated with increased spousal violence and homicide.)[85] Also, we know that, in general, married fathers have a very low rate of committing crimes of any kind.

FATHERLESSNESS AND MEN

The growth of fatherlessness has negative consequences not only for children and women but also for men. Men who do not father and who are not married can be a danger to themselves and to society.

The world over, young and unattached males have been a cause for social concern. It is well known that young men, compared to young women, tend to be more aggressive, violent, promiscuous, and substance-abuse prone and to die prematurely through disease, accidents, or self-neglect. They make up the majority of deviants, delinquents, criminals, killers, drug users, vice lords, and miscreants of every kind. By one recent count, only 21 percent of jail inmates are married, compared to about 64 percent of the general population.[86]

Wherever large numbers of young, unattached males are concentrated in one place, the probability of social disorder greatly increases. Two trenchant examples are the nineteenth-century American frontier West and the late twentieth-century inner-city ghetto.[87] As Senator Daniel Patrick Moynihan once observed, a society of unattached males "asks for and gets chaos."

Family life—marriage and childrearing—is an extremely important civilizing force for men. Control of the more unseemly male passions is a requisite for successful family living. Family men must develop those habits of character, including prudence, cooperativeness, honesty, trust, and self-sacrifice, that can lead to achievement as an economic provider. In addition, marriage notably focuses male sexual energy, and having children typically impresses on men the importance of setting a good example.

There is a civilizing effect for men in merely being in the company of women and children, an environment which typically promotes life-enhancing values. Association with single men, in contrast, tends to generate risk taking, aggression, and violence. The members of single-male peer groups are constantly challenging one another, and the jousting for position, honor, and esteem can become lethal.

It is not uncommon to hear young men say that they gave up certain deviant or socially irresponsible patterns of life only when they married and had children. At that point, based on the necessity to be a good provider and a good father, they developed a real stake in the system and felt the need to set a good example for their children. Empirical evidence exists to substantiate these reports. One longitudinal study of men's first two years of fatherhood found that prior to fatherhood, the men's identities centered on independence, aggressiveness, and self-concerns, whereas following fatherhood their identities included strong elements of caring and empathy.[88] Another longitudinal study of men found that fatherhood promoted male maturity, especially the ability of men to integrate their own feelings and to understand others' sympathetically.[89]

The civilizing effect of being a father is highlighted by a pathbreaking social-improvement endeavor in Cleveland. In Cleveland's tough, inner-city Hough neighborhood, social worker Charles Ballard has been turning around the lives of young black men through an organization he founded called the Institute for Responsible Fatherhood and Family Revitalization. Since 1982, using an intensive social-work approach that includes home visits, parenting programs, and group therapy sessions, he has reunited over two thousand absent, unwed fathers with their children.

The standard theory is that if you want these inner-city men to be responsible fathers, you first must find them a job. But Ballard has stood this theory on its head. His approach is that you first must convince the young men of the importance of being a good father, and then they will be motivated to finish school and find work.

An independent evaluation of his approach showed that it really works. Only 12 percent of the young men had full-time work when they entered his program, but 62 percent later found such work, and another 12 percent found part-time jobs. Ninety-seven percent of the men he dealt with began providing financial support for their children, and 71 percent had no additional children out of wedlock.[90]

It is difficult to disentangle the twin civilizing effects on men of marriage and of fathering. Few of Ballard's fathers married the mothers of their children. Yet, as we have noted, marriage and childrearing typically constitute for men a single package. Men's decision to marry is often linked to their desire for children, and their connection to children is normally through their wives. The childrearing participation of fathers, much more than of mothers, is contingent on the marital relationship.

Marriage by itself, without the presence of children, certainly constitutes one major civilizing force for men. As stated in the wedding vows, men are expected to remain faithful and responsible. There is no other institution save religion (and perhaps the military) which places such moral demands on men.

To be sure, there is a selection factor in marriage. Those men whom women would care to marry already have some of the civilized virtues.[91] And those men who are morally beyond the pale have difficulty in finding mates. Yet epidemiological studies and social surveys have shown that marriage has a civilizing effect independent of the selection factor. It is not just that particularly healthy and competent and morally upright persons are more likely to marry, but that marriage actually promotes health, competence, virtue, and personal well-being, as we shall see in the final chapter.[92]

With the continued growth of fatherlessness, however, we can expect to see a nation of men who are at worst morally out of control and at best unhappy, unhealthy, and unfulfilled.

CONCLUDING REMARKS

The negative consequences of fatherlessness are all around us. They affect children, women, and men. Evidence indicating damage to children has accumulated in near tidal-wave proportions. Fatherless children experience significantly more physical, emotional, and behavioral problems than do children growing up in intact families. Many of these problems continue into their adolescent and adult years, generating steeply elevated rates of juvenile delinquency, crime and violence, out-of-wedlock pregnancies, and substance abuse.

Fatherless children mostly grow up without a "protector"; without good role models (for sons) and male-relationship models (for girls); without positive models of mother-father interaction; without the kind of supervision that fathers can provide. Many have grown up lacking economic security. These children have been subject to much higher levels of physical and sexual abuse, to say nothing of neglect and emotional maltreatment.

The social damage done by fatherlessness has seriously frayed our social fabric. Attempting to undo the social damage is proving a costly and unyielding task. And although the rise of contemporary fatherlessness is associated with the revolution of self-fulfillment and its promise of greater adult happiness, no one, least of all men, seems to be any happier as a result. Women are at greater risk of violence and abuse.

Fathers are probably more important in childrearing today than ever before. Children are no longer raised by the whole village, most relatives have left the childrearing scene, and even mothers have relinquished a portion of their childrearing time to enter the workplace. The family has been reduced to a bare nucleus, and now that nucleus is splitting apart.

For successful childrearing, do modern societies have any alternatives other than strongly reinvolving males in fatherhood? The only alternative put forth with any seriousness is a system consisting of lone women (or groups of women) raising their children with economic support from the government rather than from fathers. This might theoretically be possible in purely economic terms, although taxpayer acquiescence—as we well know from recent political events in many modern nations—should hardly be taken for granted. But children need more than a father's money. They need a father's attention, care, and love. Moreover, we must ask, in such a society how are all the nonfathering men going to be spending their time? The prospect is frightening.

In order fully to understand the present and in order to plan for the future, we must look first to the past. Marriage has been changing, divorce has been rising, the father's role has been shrinking, and radical individualism has been growing for the past one hundred fifty years. The forces of change do not occur overnight. It is to the history of fatherhood and marriage in recent centuries, to the remarkable rise and fall of what historians call the "modern nuclear family," that we turn in the following two chapters.

Part Two

Fathers in History

3. Victorian Fathers and the Rise of the Modern Nuclear Family

"Paternal neglect," wrote the author of an article with that title in *Parents Magazine*, has become "epidemic."[1] The year was 1842. Although apprehension about the decline of fatherhood in America is widely perceived to be a recent phenomenon, largely a product of the past three decades, it has been evident for at least a century and a half.

The first serious concerns about "father loss" are typically dated to the decades of the 1830s and 1840s, when the migration of the American people from farm and rural village to town and city was getting underway. Associated with this migration and the accompanying economic and social shift to an urban-industrial way of life, fatherhood (and also motherhood) underwent a major transformation through the rise of a remarkable new family form. Historians call it the modern nuclear family. In this new family form—consisting of a married couple with children, living apart from other relatives—the productive work of men shifted from the home to an outside workplace, and fatherhood became a part-time activity.

The modern nuclear family, in the words of Princeton social historian Lawrence Stone, is "one of the most significant transformations that has ever taken place, not only in the most intimate aspects of human life, but also in the nature of social organization."[2] The marital union in this new family form was based on intimacy and companionship rather than joint economic function; the family unit was set up to achieve an intimate, protective environment for the nurture and care of its members rather than mere economic survival. And whereas husbands and wives had once shared both parenting and productive work activities, in the modern nuclear family women could leave productive (including farm) work—thanks to the men's outside income—to become full-time mothers and housewives. Mothers, not fathers, became the primary parents.

While the nuclear family is as old as humankind, the modern nuclear family held sway for only a relatively brief time, historically speaking. First evidenced in the upper classes in Britain in the mid to late 1700s, it became culturally predominant in the Victorian era as it spread to the new bourgeois middle class in both Europe and America, giving rise to the labels "Victorian" or "bourgeois" family. The modern nuclear family, including its 1950s-era version, was to dominate Western societies for the next 150 years before socially and culturally collapsing at the end of the twentieth century.

Just as the present decline of marriage is pivotal to a discussion of the faltering role of fathers in today's world, the rise of the modern nuclear family is pivotal to any discussion tracing the trends of fatherhood and marriage in American history. An awareness of issues attendant upon the modern nuclear family is also essential for comprehending the contemporary "family values" debate and for any serious discussion of the future of fatherhood and family life in modern societies. This is the family whose ideals shape the very language and values we use in thinking about what a family is, what "family" means, and what a father should do. It is the family that traditionalists love and many radicals hate.

Today, under the label "traditional nuclear family" or, popularly, the "Ozzie and Harriet family," this family form has become the object of scorn and ridicule in some circles. It is not hard to see why. By taking many women out of the workplace and keeping them out of public life, women were kept economically, socially, and politically powerless. It was this set of conditions that spawned modern feminism, and the nuclear family, by some alchemy, has come to represent them. "Far from being the basis of the good society," the prominent British anthropologist Edmund Leach said in 1967, "the family, with its narrow privacy and tawdry secrets, is the source of all our discontents."[3] This family form is said even to have generated contemporary women's studies, the academic discipline that has infused much of recent family history with a particular perspective. "The development of academic women's studies," wrote feminist Ann Oakley recently, "has very largely been the project of liberating women from the screen, I hesitate to say prison, of the family."[4]

The modern feminist perspective has contributed immensely to our historical understanding of family life in times past. Yet in its focus on the situation of women, this perspective unfortunately has clouded what an extraordinary achievement this new family form really was, especially for children. Part of the problem of contemporary interpretation lies in viewing past events with a hindsight shaped by current values. When this family form is compared instead with what preceded and gave rise to it, a different interpretation results, as we shall see.

Scholars also have neglected the situation of fathers in the modern nuclear family. In general, we know all too little about fatherhood in times past, although scholarly interest in the paternal dimension recently has been on the upswing.[5] As historian John Demos has said, "Fatherhood has a very long history, but virtually no historians."[6] What we do know, however, is that this new family form brought the age-old era of father rule, or patriarchy, nearly to an end and marked the beginning of the modern shrinkage of the father role. In the history of fatherhood, it is an immensely important chapter.

The modern nuclear family was not something that all segments of American society were able or willing to incorporate into their lives. In practice it was a middle-class phenomenon, and what follows deals mainly with the cultural center, not the periphery, omitting most regional, ethnic, and racial variations. But whether they could live that way or not, the modern nuclear family, as a national cultural ideal, was regarded in its day by almost all segments of the population as the best or right or preferable way to live.

THE PREMODERN FAMILY OF NORTHWESTERN EUROPE

The story of the modern nuclear family begins in northwestern Europe a few centuries prior to the Industrial Revolution of the late 1700s. In much of the rest of the world at that time, including other regions of Europe, complex, extended family systems prevailed; households were large and typically consisted of three generations, often including collateral relatives. But the societies of northwestern Europe, notably England, France, Belgium, and the Netherlands, were different. Although they had strong economic similarities with other parts of the world (being in the main rural societies based on subsistence agriculture, with productive activities customarily carried out in and by households rather than at separate, specialized workplaces), these European societies were made up largely of families living in the two-generation nuclear form—father, mother, and children without other relatives.

There did not exist in large numbers in northwestern Europe what has been called "the classical family of Western nostalgia": a large, rural, self-sufficient, patriarchal, extended household made up of many generations. Thus, the modern nuclear family did not emerge directly from some complex, kinship-dominated peasant family system.

Why this part of the world was unique and when it was that these societies broke away from the rest of the world to lead the trend toward the nuclear family are questions that have commanded a great deal of scholarly attention but remain largely unresolved.[7] There are some indications, indeed, that the peasant family steeped in extended-kinship ties may *never* have existed in northwestern Europe as it did in most other parts of the world during the preindustrial era and as it still does in most of the Third World today.[8] The family "exceptionalism" of northwestern Europe is typically attributed to unique cultural and geographic factors. For example, inheritance practices, typically primogeniture, forced all but the firstborn son, who inherited all property, to leave home. And intense cultivation and strict allocation of village lands made the coresidence of more than two generations very difficult for economic reasons.[9]

The sociocultural impact of the unique premodern nuclear family system of northwestern Europe was immense. In comparison to complex, extended family systems in most other parts of the world, these early nuclear families were associated with weak kinship authority, less rigid segregation of the sexes, greater equality for women, and more personal freedom. It is thought that through freeing individuals from primordial kinship ties and encouraging their creative and entrepreneurial impulses, the nuclear family played a significant role in the momentous historical changes pioneered by the nations of northwestern Europe: the break away from feudalism and the generation of capital and capitalism that led to the Industrial Revolution, and the development of political democracy and egalitarianism that is associated with the French and American revolutions.

In its basic demographic structure the preindustrial nuclear family was not very different from the modern nuclear family of the industrial era that was to come. According to Peter Laslett, the scholar who played the leading role in the development of "the new demographic history," the main characteristics of this family system were a large percentage of households consisting of a married couple and their offspring without the addition of other relatives; a relatively late age for marriage and childbirth, with a significant percentage of the population not marrying at all; and only a few years separating the ages of husband and wife.[10] As today, newly married couples then tended to take charge of their own households rather than become a part of households in which older couples were in charge, which was the normal pattern in extended family systems around the world.[11]

In nondemographic respects, however, the preindustrial nuclear family was a world apart from its modern nuclear successor. The quality of family experience in the two family forms bore little similarity. Marriage in the preindustrial family was primarily an economic arrangement, not the strongly emotional connection based on romantic love that it was later to become; the purpose of the marriage was not so much affection and companionship, although those traits certainly must have existed in many marriages, as it was economic survival in tough times.

Particularly lacking in this family form was any sense of familial privacy. Although premodern nuclear families in northwestern Europe were much less kinship-bound than is the case in extended family systems, they nevertheless were deeply imbedded socially in the surrounding community. The families existed in small, close-knit communities, and the family-community boundary was highly permeable. Childrearing was a community phenomenon, for example, and many adults outside the immediate family were involved in the task. It was the whole village that raised the child, to paraphrase the oft-quoted African proverb.

Lawrence Stone has described the English family as it existed before the late sixteenth century as

> an open-ended, low-keyed, unemotional, authoritarian institution . . . it was neither very durable nor emotionally or sexually very demanding. . . . Lacking firm boundaries [it] was open to support, advice, investigation and interference from outside, from neighbors and kin, and internal privacy was nonexistent.[12]

The community culture, one must add, was a deeply religious one, with religious precepts guiding virtually all aspects of daily life.

Fatherhood in the Premodern Family

The father, as designated head of the premodern European family and household, was a powerful figure. Father power rested on the ownership of land, the primary basis of production, and was fully enshrined in law. In addition, most important kinship relationships were formed around the man and not the woman, as is the case today.

Patriarchal power, however, had become a pale shadow of what it had been in some earlier times, such as the Roman era. Some traditional family functions had weakened or been lost over the millennia through a shift to new and larger institutions outside the family, notably the religious, the protective, and the governmental. These functions formerly had provided a compelling reason for all-powerful male authority in the home.

In the age-old struggle for survival (in which the family was the key and sometimes the only social unit), patriarchy arose, as historians Michael Mitterauer and Reinhard Seider have noted, "from the need to secure the family's existence by concentrating tasks and duties in the family, which in turn required a strongly hierarchical organization."[13] Although the struggle for existence was attenuating, one remaining function of the premodern family did provide an enduring reason for male dominance—economic production. The family was a work unit, and even today the efficiency of most work units requires a hierarchical organization with a clearly recognized leader at the top.

A clear standard of manhood prevailed. To be fulfilled as a man, an adult male, if firstborn, took ownership of land from his father, successfully headed a household, and carefully guided the destiny of his progeny. The husband role was considered to be less important than the father role; manhood was achieved not so much by taking a wife, although that was important, as by becoming a father. This patriarchal life mission is still imprinted in the minds of many a Western man today.

FATHERHOOD AND FAMILY IN THE AMERICAN COLONIAL ERA

The premodern family of northwestern Europe—a nuclear, father-dominated, community-imbedded, economic production unit—was the family that, by and large, was transferred to America by the early English colonists. It became the founding family form in America.

The colonial family remained a unit of economic production and the home a place of work, as had been the case for most families throughout history. Almost all families were engaged in farming or craft work. The family was relatively unstable in terms of membership turnover, not because of divorce but because of premature deaths. In the early colonial period in Virginia, fewer than half the children reached age eighteen with both parents still living.[14] Also, each household had a high membership turnover due to the fluctuating presence of non–nuclear family members such as relatives and servants.

Because it was based largely on economic considerations, the marriage bond in the colonial family was more functional than romantic. Most marriages of the time were thought to have been relatively cold and unemotional, certainly by today's standards, although such subjective qualities are notoriously difficult to assess.[15]

The Puritan Experience

It was the New England Puritan experience that most influenced the new American culture and became the measure of comparison for family life in the new United States to come. In the nineteenth century the "Yankee" descendants of the Puritans were highly influential in spreading across America the family ideology that accompanied the rise of the modern nuclear family. And it is the Puritan experience, fortunately, for which we have the most historical data and analysis.[16]

The Puritan, preindustrial family was a more important as well as more cohesive unit than its counterpart in England and continental Europe, partly due to its new environment, an unsettled wilderness with a virtual absence of surrounding institutions. The Puritans generally arrived in family groups and lived in small communities. The family was nuclear, consisting of one adult couple and their own children with the occasional addition of an aged grandparent or a domestic helper.

Despite the nuclear character of the family, the Puritan household was highly multifunctional and relatively self-sufficient, serving as a workshop and business, school, vocational institute, church, welfare institution, and even "house of correction," as well as the seat of all domestic activities. Indeed, as the core multipurpose institution in Puritan society, each family household has been called a "little commonwealth" because it catered to almost all the needs of its members.[17] Unlike today's situation, the family and not the individual was the major unit of society. Each household, for example, not each individual, had a vote at the town meetings.

At the same time, in line with its European roots, the Puritan family was still heavily entrenched in the life of the surrounding community. The boundary between family and community was highly permeable, and private and public life were often indistinguishable. It was thought to be perfectly appropriate for the community to intervene in the life of a particular family should a family falter in its duties—for instance, in the raising of its children. Yale historian John Demos, one of the leading scholars of that era, characterizes the early Puritan family setting as follows:

> The family and the wider community are joined in a relation of profound reciprocity; one might almost say they are continuous with one another. . . . Families and churches, families and governments, belong to the same world of experience. Individual people move back and forth between these settings with little effort or sense of difficulty. . . . Family relationships were effectively discounted, or at least submerged, in this particular context.[18]

Puritan Patriarchy and Fatherhood

Puritan families also remained relatively patriarchal and authoritarian—even more so, perhaps, than their English predecessors. The male head of household was the towering figure and unquestioned ruler, and by today's standards, his authority was stern and rigid. It was believed that men were endowed with more "reason" than women and thus were born to rule in both domestic and public affairs. Women were regarded as intellectually inferior, morally less virtuous, and emotionally fragile. Puritan wives were expected at all times to be submissive and obedient. Puritan children were at all times to show honor and respect for their fathers. Such unquestioned patriarchy was strongly upheld as the will of God by the Christianity of the day.[19] Nevertheless, the Puritan father/husband was expected to treat his dependents with respect and restraint, and male gentleness in social relations was admired.

Male household heads controlled all property, and they had to give specific approval (or disapproval) to the courtship and marriage making of both sons and daughters. Kinship authority was also still fairly important, with the eldest male relative serving as the overall family patriarch. Elaborate kinship networks in some local areas were common, and kinship ties were very important in market and political as well as family exchanges.

Fatherhood was remarkably strong among the Puritans, much as it is today among such traditional religious groups as the Amish and Orthodox Jews. It was a substantial part of the Puritan man's deeply felt sense of duty toward others. All adult men were expected to become fathers, and there was a large father presence in the lives of children. John Demos detects a particularly high level of devotion to their children among Puritan fathers, one that he believes has not been equaled on a large scale since.[20]

Because the home was an economic production unit in which both fathers and mothers participated, fathering was an extension, if not a part of, the routine activities of daily life; domestic and productive life were often one and the same. Sons, especially, worked side by side with their fathers from their earliest years until their own marriages. Sons were often close replicas of their fathers, and generational continuity from father to son was relatively smooth.

Puritan fathers could be harsh disciplinarians, however, and the administration of physical punishment was customary. Such discipline doubtless led to frequent conflict and tension within the home. Some colonies even had laws calling for stern penalties, including death, for children who cursed or struck their fathers, although such penalties were seldom if ever enforced. Many Puritan families continued the European practice of life-cycle servanthood, sending their teenaged children for a period of years to work in the homes of other families, where they were subject to even stricter discipline than they might receive in their own homes.

Most direct care of infants and young children was performed by women; but in a childrearing regime that stressed authority, control, deportment, and morality, the father was considered the primary parent. The childrearing prescriptions of the time, for example, were addressed almost entirely to fathers. And, certainly unlike present practice, societal praise or blame for the child's outcome was typically bestowed on the father, not the mother. Where schools existed, the teachers were always men. Yet most of the formal teaching was done by fathers in the home, where the emphasis was on the teaching of moral and religious matters.

The wife/mother was regarded as an essential part of the family unit but essential as an assistant to the father rather than his equal. Her special realm was that of affection and nurturance, and her "maternal indulgence" had always to be counterbalanced by strong paternal governance. Within the home she carried out a range of domestic duties necessary to the maintenance of the household, but her other roles were highly circumscribed. Legally, for example, a married woman had no separate identity apart from her husband, according to the principle of "coverture." At marriage, unless specifically excluded by prenuptial agreements, all property she owned became her husband's, and her rights to it were forfeited.

The situation of children in the Puritan family was much different from that in modern times. Puritans were devoted to their children and dedicated to assuring their children's well-being. Yet childrearing was not seen to be the most important function of the family but something subordinate to larger family interests. And childhood did not last very long. By around age six or seven children were expected to wear adult clothing and seriously undertake the family's productive work activities.

It was believed by the Puritans that children come into the world inherently "stained" with sinful urges, so-called natural depravity, and the father's job was to restrain these urges through strict discipline and moral teaching.[21] As the more evangelical among the Puritans saw the matter, if the child's autonomous will and self-assertiveness were not stamped out entirely, the child would ultimately be damned for eternity. "Better whipt, than damned" was Cotton Mather's advice to parents.[22] Moderates maintained that the child's will, at the very least, had to be strongly bent in the direction of piety and virtue. Given this view of child development, it is little wonder that in later times when fathers left the home and many of their governance and teaching roles were taken over by women, conservative analysts grew deeply concerned about "paternal neglect."

Fatherhood may have reached its apogee among the Puritans, at least for the time span of recent centuries, as an all-powerful, self-consuming, fully engaging activity for men. In what historian E. Anthony Rotundo has called "communal manhood," the Puritan man's sense of identity was inseparable from his family and community obligations. "Through his role as head of the household, a man expressed his value to his community and provided his wife and children with their social identity."[23] Since Puritan times, one could say, it has been all downhill for fathers. They have lost power, authority, control, and status. Yet in many respects life has improved for women, for children, for society as a whole, and even for men. The all-powerful father is obviously not an unmitigated good.

The Dawn of Democratic Individualism

By the 1700s the stern, authoritarian patriarchy of most colonial American families was beginning to weaken. Women's roles, abilities, and accomplishments were accorded more respect, and the paternal control of courtship and arrangement of marriages declined. As one measure of the father's loss of control over his children, the number of brides who were pregnant when they got married increased enormously, from an estimated 10 percent in the early Puritan years to 40 percent by the middle of the eighteenth century.[24] In a shift of symbolic importance, a matrilineal pattern of naming emerged, at least in New England; the primary responsibility for naming children passed from the father to the mother. As historian David Hackett Fischer notes, this shift "was a loss not of family consciousness, but the growth of a new ideal that was less patriarchal and more matrifocal, less hierarchical and more egalitarian."[25]

The gradual rise of individualism and enlightened political and economic ideas that took place during the eighteenth century brought the autonomous citizen—mainly, of course, the white male citizen—to the fore as the constituent unit of society and ultimate source of cultural value. He was to engage in the competitive pursuit of self-interest. Yet an unrestrained individualism was greatly feared; so a companion cultural emphasis emerged which focused on the family as the seedbed of civic virtue, a place where the right kind of individual could be produced. Thinkers like Jean-Jacques Rousseau envisioned a family that could become an almost self-sufficient moral institution, capable of sustaining republican or democratic regimes apart from the authoritative and coercive state and religious structures that were being overthrown.

As part of this new cultural emphasis much was written, especially during the American revolutionary period, about a new family role for mothers. Their emerging task, thought of as a crucially important new "public" role that theretofore had been played mainly by fathers, was to rear children to have those civic and moral virtues necessary to develop and sustain the emerging democratic republic.[26]

The family grew more private and personal in nature. A greater emphasis was placed on trying to build the family into an affective unit, one based more on open warmth and intimacy that would enable the family to stand on its own against the travails of the weakening community and the emerging urban-industrial order. To leading French thinkers and later to New England intellectuals, the Quaker experience in the middle colonies of the Delaware Valley proved to be an admirable model for the ideal family. The Quakers eschewed all formal institutions and sought to develop a strong, relatively egalitarian family that could be morally self-sufficient. They were highly successful in economic terms, thanks in part to the rich land they had settled on, which reinforced in the eyes of the world the validity of the new social forms which they pioneered.[27]

The Enlightenment brought new ideas of freedom and personal happiness for children as well as adults. The Quaker belief summed up the new view: "God's truth dwells not within institutions but within individuals, including young children." A new concern for parental responsibilities and the proper care and nurture of children arose; childrearing began to emerge as the family's central function. Indicative of the new way of thinking, the practice of sending teenagers away from the family to work as servants was on the wane.

In religion a fundamental reevaluation of children occurred. The Calvinist notion of innate child depravity gave way to the belief that children were "innocent" little beings whose character would blossom with proper care and nurturance; the child's will was to be shaped, not broken. Following John Locke's view of the infant's mind as a blank slate (*tabula rasa*), environmental influences, especially during the first few years in the life of a child, came to be regarded as central to the determination of individual conscience and character.

Fathers were advised to become more tender with their children and sensitive to their children's needs and wishes, and in a break from the harsh practices of their own fathers, a growing number of men sought to limit their use of physical punishment. The new perspective is summed up in what the French businessman J. P. Brissot de Warville, a devoted follower of Rousseau, wrote about the Quaker father following his American visit in 1788: "If he has many children, he loves them and sees ways of planning for their future. Such a man is a good husband, for putting his whole happiness in his family life, he is forced to be good in order to be loved, and he can be happy only by making those around him happy."[28]

This was the dawn of democratic individualism. With these changes gradually entering the culture of British North America, the climate was set for the great family transformation—and the quiet decline of the man as head of family and primary parent.

FATHERHOOD AND FAMILY
IN THE VICTORIAN ERA

The Rise of the Modern Nuclear Family

With the industrialization and urbanization of the early nineteenth century, "family life," in the words of John Demos, "was wrenched apart from the world of work."[29] For the first time in human history on a large scale, the family lost its status as a unit of economic production, and the small community and its social solidarity withered. The family grew more private, and family life and community life became increasingly separate. By the time Alexis de Tocqueville arrived in America in the 1830s, he found a privatized and individualized family, one already set quite apart from the surrounding social order. Far from being imbedded in the community, the family was eventually to become a kind of refuge from it, what the late Christopher Lasch called a "haven in a heartless [read: urban-industrial] world."[30]

The modern nuclear family was smaller than its preindustrial predecessor, not because of fewer servants and unattached relatives, but because of fewer children.[31] It was even more nuclear, in the sense of being further split off from relatives, and more stable because early deaths of husbands and wives were less common. But the feature that made the modern family truly unique was the character of family life. Marriage partners were freely chosen, based on romantic love rather than economics or parental concerns, and the marriage relationship changed from being relatively unemotional and functional to warm and companionate. Life in the family became emotionally intense, more nurturant, and highly protective. In authority structure, the family became relatively egalitarian. Most important of all, the family came to focus primarily on the needs and care of its children.

The Victorian era, like perhaps none prior to it, was preoccupied with home, family, and domesticity. As the values of the new industrial order became dominated by mobility and materialism, the values of the family stressed cooperation and self-sacrifice. As the outside world became more and more impersonal, the inside world of the family became more personal, based on love and affection between husband and wife and between parents and children. The middle-class home became a peaceful retreat from an increasingly industrialized, market-dominated, and morally suspect world.[32]

Mrs. E. B. Duffey in *What Women Should Know* (1873) characterized the "cult of domesticity" that became a sort of secular religion for Americans:[33]

The true home is a world within a world. It is the central point of the universe around which all things revolve. It is the treasure-house of the affections, the one serenely bright spot in all the world, toward which its absent members always look with hope and anticipation.

Of course, this was the ideal. It was certainly not a realistic characterization of the homes of the poor and downtrodden, recent immigrants, or even the working class. Working-class families, for example, were less individualistic, more kinship-oriented, and had higher rates of family failure. Still, it was an image indelibly stamped on the minds of most Americans of the time. They did not all live that way, but they wished that they did. And by the late nineteenth century, according to historian Carl Degler, an estimated three fifths of the nation's population had made it to the middle class, assuming that commercial farm families were so designated.[34]

Changing Roles

As income-producing work left the home, so—during the weekday— did the men. Men increasingly withdrew from direct-care parenting and specialized in the provider or breadwinner role. The man's prime responsibility was to take care of his family's economic needs, both when he was living and after he died. Thanks to growing affluence, many families were able to make do on the outside incomes of their male wage earners. Unmarried women typically were in the labor force, but at time of marriage they were expected to leave and become full-time mothers and housewives. If a married woman was in the labor force, it reflected badly on the adequacy of her husband and took a job away from a man (a view that prevailed well into the twentieth century).

For the first time in history on a large scale, women filled the roles of mother and housewife full-time and over the course of their adult lives remained outside of the productive economy. The new ideal wife and mother "was expected to run an efficient household, provide a cultured atmosphere within the home, rear moral sons and daughters, display social grace on public occasions, and offer her husband emotional support."[35]

The Victorian era has often been described in terms of strong gender-role contrasts and "separate spheres," in which men and women came to inhabit quite distinct worlds of culture and behavior.[36] Men dominated the public sphere, and women came to dominate the private, family sphere and to claim it as their own. That men are best suited to life outside the home and women are best suited to the life of a homemaker was believed at the time to be entirely normal and natural. The division was enhanced by the rapidly changing social order of early urban-industrialism. Men became the spearhead of competitive capitalism, expressing through the marketplace an ever-growing individualism, while women, left at home, became the bearers of traditional moral values. Women were the essential providers of moral and psychological checks needed to keep the new social order in some kind of balance and especially to keep men's aggressive impulses and passions under control.

Romantic Love and Sex

The modern nuclear family was the first large-scale family system that was based mainly on romantic love.[37] From the 1830s until the end of the nineteenth century, as historian Karen Lystra indicates, romantic love became for middle-class men as well as women "an intellectual and social force of premier significance."[38] Romantic love became a necessary precondition for marriage; more than anything else, it enabled couples to bridge their separate spheres and create a relatively egalitarian unity of opposites based on emotional collaboration and mutual respect.

"True love," some combination of intimate self-expression and self-disclosure and ultimately shared identity with an individual of the opposite sex, was thought to be a divinely endowed gift, and it was considered to be both the fundamental basis for a good marriage and the one best path to self-fulfillment. Indeed, at least during the courtship period when it was at its peak, according to Lystra, "romantic love contributed to the displacement of God by the lover as the central symbol of ultimate significance."[39] Having been pushed out of the home and into the cold and impersonal world of the marketplace, many men sought after and treasured the intense, emotional world of women and family, based on romantic love, which brought them some assurances of a meaningful private life.[40]

It has been posited that romantic love, at least its more heady and ethereal aspects, "is based at least 95 percent on unrequited sex." The Victorians' suppression of sexuality has often been wildly exaggerated. As Karen Lystra has stressed, "Victorians did not denigrate sex, they *guarded* it."[41] Nevertheless, their preoccupation with romantic love may well have been stimulated by the restrictive sexual codes of the time, which morally eschewed premarital sex.

An important cultural prescription of the Victorian era was for men to marry late. Many engagements lasted two years or more, and we have only recently returned to the older average age of marriage that prevailed in the late nineteenth century, which for middle-class men was nearly thirty. This late age was to allow men to have time to garner the economic means to support a wife and also to reach a level of psychological and sexual maturity necessary to be a good husband and father. It was the very clear expectation of the time that a man was not to marry until he was financially able to do so.

During this long waiting period of young adulthood, male sexual self-control was thought to be of the essence. Men were expected to have sexual self-mastery to the nth degree. Premarital sex was considered morally wrong in the extreme, and men were taught that masturbation, the "solitary vice," would lead to effeminacy, insanity, and ill health. The view was widely circulated that "storing semen" in their bodies was a medical benefit. Needless to say, not all Victorian men were able to live up to this high expectation. In the mid-nineteenth century as many as one in four brides went to the altar pregnant, and many men turned to the services of a burgeoning urban prostitution industry.[42] Bachelors were regarded as slightly inferior beings, in part because it was thought that they fell prey more easily to the temptations of masturbation and prostitution.

Fathers and Mothers in the Victorian Family

It was still clearly expected that men should be in charge at home, and most fathers clung to their authority role of family patriarch and head of household. The cultural expectation of male leadership in the Victorian family, showing its strong religious underpinnings, was stated unmistakably by Catherine E. Beecher and her sister Harriet Beecher Stowe in their widely read 1869 book *The American Woman's Home:*

> When the family is instituted by marriage, it is man who is head and chief magistrate by the force of his physical power and requirement of the chief responsibility; not less is he so according to the Christian law, by which, when differences arise, the husband has the deciding control, and the wife is to obey.[43]

Indeed, the "Victorian patriarch" is a figure that remains in the public consciousness today. "Of all the images associated with the nineteenth century American family," note historians Steven Mintz and Susan Kellogg, "none has proved stronger or longer-lasting than the picture of the bewhiskered Victorian father presiding over his dutiful wife and submissive children."[44]

Our contemporary image of the Victorian father, however, partially conflicts with the reality. Even in Victorian times cultural expectation did not always match behavioral reality. As the modern nuclear family evolved, women gradually replaced men as the reigning domestic power, and male authority in the home was eventually to become largely symbolic. Already in the 1840s, in her tour of America, the Swedish feminist Fredericka Bremer admired the high place accorded women, "the center and lawgiver in the home."[45] At about the same time, Tocqueville described the diminished powers of the American father:

> Everyone has noticed that . . . a new relationship has evolved between the different members of a family, that the distance formerly separating father and son has diminished, and that paternal authority, if not abolished, has at least changed form. . . . The master and the magistrate have vanished; the father remains.[46]

Fatherhood in the Victorian family became a part-time activity. From once having had a wife as the assistant in the running of the home, a man increasingly was considered the part-time assistant to his wife. In a highly significant shift, kinship relationships, which in the preindustrial family centered around the husband, fell under the aegis of the wife. It was her relatives that came to be most important to the family.

The causes for this dramatic shift away from patriarchy are numerous. With men's new dependency on large work organizations and growing absence from the home during the day, the position of family patriarch became more and more difficult to maintain. Undercutting the father's authority still further was the declining importance to families of real property, one of the most important bases of traditional paternal control.[47] And the rise of mandatory schooling in the primary grades, for children aged six to about twelve, served to minimize a traditional paternal role, that of moral tutor and practical teacher.

Victorian culture, at the same time, was intent on enthroning women as the preeminent figures in the household and having them essentially replace men as the primary parents of children. Both female and male writers glorified women's domestic roles, urging women to rise to new heights of morality and spiritual perfection and use their domestic powers to the utmost in shaping civilization.[48] Childrearing advice literature, which formerly had been directed at fathers, refocused almost entirely on women and grew relatively silent about what men should do. Replacing the traditional distrust of maternal indulgence was an elevated appreciation of maternal tenderness and of female qualities in general. Such qualities as patience, kindness, and affection were now thought to be necessary not only for good childrearing but for human progress and the very salvation of the social order. "The foundation of our national character," expounded the popular nineteenth-century writer Josiah Gilbert Holland, "is laid by the mothers of the nation."[49]

The rejection of the Calvinist notion of innate child depravity, which had mostly occurred prior to the departure of men from the home, made eminently reasonable the turning over of children's care to the maternal, more affective, less instrumental side of the family. In the 1830s, following the industrialization of printing, there was a surge of childrearing guides directed toward women which reflected the new view of children. Indeed, the belief arose that women were morally superior to men— pure, upright, sensitive, and the true civilizing force in life. It was now women who were supposed to raise their children to be morally straight (and also to keep their men on the proper moral path in an increasingly complex society.) The very idea of "home" came to be defined by most nineteenth-century Americans as, in the words of historian Barry Levy, "a sheltered location where American women cultivated motherhood to nurture conscience in America's children."[50] In time, women became the teachers of religion, even taking over the long-time male activity of leading the family in its daily prayers. And inevitably it was now women on whom all the blame was placed should their children go astray!

The enthronement of women in the home and family and the displacement of men are nowhere better exemplified than in the legal changes that occurred. The English common-law doctrine held that children, like everything else in a marriage, were the "property" of their fathers. Children were not literally the father's property, as in slavery, but rather fathers had the right to the association and services, especially labor services, of their legitimate children (and also the responsibility to take care of these children).[51] At the time of divorce or other family disputes when children's custody had to be resolved, therefore, children were almost invariably awarded to their father's care by the courts.

Beginning in the antebellum years, however, the courts came to rule that the father's rights were only presumptive and could be put aside if the mother was better able to serve the child's interests. Gradually, the courts shifted still further, arguing that both parents had equal rights and that custody decisions should be made "in the best interests of the child." Eventually, in what came to be known as the "tender years doctrine," the custody of young children was routinely awarded to mothers as the more nurturing parents.[52]

With all of the attention focused on mothers, surprisingly little was actually written about the role of fathers in the early nineteenth century. "In important ways," writes historian Stephen Frank, "fathers and fatherhood were a lost chord in the antebellum fanfare for mothers and the power of mothers' love."[53] Then as now, what writing there was about fathers often came from the conservative side. Conservative writers of the time bemoaned the loss of male authority in the home brought about by the new division of labor between breadwinning husband and homemaking wife, and there was growing talk of "paternal

neglect." Men were urged not to spend so much time in the marketplace and to remember that they were the rightful leaders of the home
and that their families needed them. It was not at all clear in the minds
of these writers, to put it mildly, that maternal governance in the home
would be up to the task. As the Reverend John S. C. Abbott wrote in
Parent's Magazine in 1842:

> There is a *sentiment,* perhaps unexpressed in words, yet constantly acted
> upon, that it is the duty of the father to provide needful support for the
> family, while it is the duty of the mother to guide and govern the children.
> This sentiment has been the ruin of many families, and has brought down
> the gray hairs of many a father with sorrow to the grave. It is very rare that
> a family can be well regulated, unless there be cooperation of both parents
> in watching over and governing the children.[54]

The father role of family disciplinarian was regarded by conservatives
as second in importance only to the provider role. Yet increasingly
mothers were regarded as perfectly capable of being disciplinarians,
and fathers were relinquishing this task to them. Partly it was that the
preferred form of discipline was shifting away from the harsh, corporal
variety toward reasoning and moral suasion, an approach which was
more amenable to female sensitivities. European commentators of the
time frequently noted that the fathering in America was characterized
by an informality and permissiveness not found in their nations.[55]

By the mid-nineteenth century thoughts of the "new father," the
nurturant father, were creeping into the culture for the first time. Advice literature began to admonish fathers for harsh discipline and to encourage them to become more tender and loving with their children,
especially their older children; to try to be close to them, to play with
them, to befriend them. It was believed that male capacities for nurturing both could and should be greatly strengthened.

Today we hear a great deal about women's two roles, one at work and
one in the home. We have come full circle. In the nineteenth century
the talk was about men's two roles. Even as they left the home and their
household authority declined, fathers were expected to remain dedicated to their children and actively involved in their children's upbringing. Paternity was considered to be a major component of the male sex
role; the masculine ideal included the strong desire for marriage and a
family and the willingness to sacrifice for them. The good father was expected not only to be a good provider but, just as importantly, his wife's
auxiliary in creating and maintaining a home environment that manifested the highest domestic virtues. Although they were losing authority
within the home, many fathers continued in their roles of occupational

guide and model for their sons. It was common in both the middle and working classes, for example, for fathers to take their sons to work with them to "show them the ropes." And fathers largely held forth as intellectual leaders and as final arbiters in family discipline.

Like working women today, fathers sometimes anguished over how to allocate their time between work and family, yet it is hard to detect among the mass of fathers any special sense of crisis or concern about the changing nature of fatherhood. Most fathers seem to have been able to combine work and family in what was to them an entirely satisfactory way.

ASSESSING THE VICTORIAN FAMILY

The lambasting of the Victorian family by scholars has been relentless.[56] It has been charged with patriarchy and gross female oppression and seen as a "domestic tyranny"[57]—a place which men abandoned for the greater glory of the workplace; a family system where people were so repressed sexually that they became emotionally damaged for life; a hierarchy that suppressed children's natural instincts and stifled emotional expression, leading to lifelong psychological difficulties. In short, it has been seen as a historical family form whose departure should be a cause for little short of celebration.

Judged by today's standards, there is undoubtedly some truth to each of the charges leveled against the Victorian family, but the more appropriate perspective is that of the era preceding the Victorian from which it evolved and from which its historical imperatives were derived. At the same time, the seemingly intractable social problems of the late twentieth century throw into bold relief the strengths of the Victorian family—not only in contributing to personal security and well-being but also in creating a viable and remarkably successful institution for raising future citizens and for promoting principles that buttressed the social fabric and the national good.

Examinations of our past in an attempt to draw reasonable lessons for today are often dismissed as mere "exercises in nostalgia." The underlying assumption of this invocation seems to be that every aspect of our life has improved, and life in the past is something either negative or better left forgotten. In positing the general unsuitability of the nostalgia charge, I could not agree more with my Rutgers history colleague Jackson Lears:

> The assault on nostalgia could come only from an intelligentsia drunk on disowning the past. Where else are the visions of the good society to come from, if not from our own memories that life was different, and maybe bet-

ter, than it is here and now? From schematic agendas set by managerial theorists? In imagining more humane ways of life, why are recollections of the past held inferior to fantasies of the future? Perhaps because the myths of progress continue to mesmerize intellectuals at all points of the political spectrum . . . [58]

The most remarkable thing about the nineteenth-century Victorian family was its great stability—the rate of voluntary family breakup was extraordinarily low. The stability was especially remarkable because the Victorian family was based heavily on love and affection. Lawrence Stone has suggested that this was "the first family type in history which was both long-lasting and intimate."[59] As we now know, marriages based solely on personal affection tend not to be very durable; personal affections change, and seemingly preferable alternative love partners are in constant supply. The family stability was also surprising in view of the greater longevity of both men and women. One of the arguments for the high divorce rate of our time is that people now live so long—or as one wag put it, "Every marriage ends in divorce—it is just that some people die before they have that opportunity."

How was the durability of the Victorian family achieved? The best answer, especially from the women's side of the equation, is that the tie of economic dependency, a tie that marriage has always represented, was still largely in place. Generally prohibited from being in the workforce, married women were completely dependent upon their husbands for economic support. They realized that even if they wanted to leave a marriage, the economic and social consequences would be disastrous. Needless to say, the very restrictive laws about divorce also played a role.

But it is also the case that male commitment to family life in the Victorian era remained enormous even though the work of men had left the home and their family authority had dwindled. Men took their breadwinner role with utmost seriousness and strongly identified their success in the workplace with the happiness and security of their wives and families. To be a man was to be an economically successful family provider. "In fact," as Karen Lystra has pointed out, "nineteenth century men claimed they worked for women and children in a way analogous to an earlier generation of Americans who claimed they worked for God."[60] Within the home many men sought to live up to their vows to "love, honor, and *cherish*," just as women sought to respect their vows to "love, honor, and obey." And just as wives had an economic dependency on their husbands, so did husbands develop a strong emotional dependency on their wives.

Although Victorian marriages were initiated on the bases of love and personal choice, older religiously based value systems of commitment and obligation were still largely in place. Marriages were held together less by the thin reeds of intimacy and affection, as is the case today, than by a deep sense of social responsibility and spousal obligation. In the words of historian Elaine Tyler May, "Husbands were to provide the necessities of life, treat their wives with courtesy and protection, and exercise sexual restraint. . . . A wife's duty was to maintain a comfortable home, take care of household chores, bear and tend to the children, and set the moral tone for domestic life."[61] With children parents had a built-in attitude of self-sacrifice, renouncing many of their own personal satisfactions for the good of the family unit. As writer Henry Seidel Canby recollected about his Victorian upbringing in the 1890s, "We knew . . . from our own impulsive desires that the father and mother denied themselves every day, if not every hour, something for the sake of the family."[62]

When a marriage ended, it was due more to a serious breakdown of spousal role obligations than to the loss of love.[63] Either wife or husband was simply unable to fulfill her or his marital duties. The Victorians deeply valued marital love, but its loss alone was not deemed sufficient to end a binding relationship.

The Victorian era was one dominated by a culture of "character," a belief that it was each person's supreme duty to live a life governed by a high moral code and to suppress any natural inclinations to the contrary. "By the middle of the nineteenth century," notes historian William L. O'Neill, "Anglo-American society had formulated a moral code based on three related principles—the permanency of marriage, the sacredness of the home, and the dependence of civilized life upon the family."[64] This moral code and the belief in the importance of character provided the interpersonal glue in marriage that love alone is incapable of providing. Once this moral code evaporated—in the twentieth century—the fragility of love as the sole basis for marriage became all too apparent.

The Victorian Father

A strong case can be made that fathering in Victorian times, even though it had become a more part-time activity, was an improvement over what it was in prior eras. Victorian fathers still regarded family life as very important, typically the most important dimension of their lives; they made a substantial commitment to their families in both resources and emotions. Yet compared with their predecessors, they were much less authoritarian and punitive with their children and more sensitive to their children's emotional needs. The running of the family had become more a cooperative partnership than a hierarchy. And even though father-child contact was probably diminishing overall, by the late nineteenth century many fathers became more domestic, devoting a larger portion of their nonwork time to family activities and to emotional engagement with their wives and children.

This domesticity was particularly true for the new "organization man," who "enjoyed the security of a regular salary, a predictable rise through the company hierarchy, and greater leisure time."[65] The company men tended to gravitate to the new streetcar-oriented suburbs that were emerging around many cities, where family life was accentuated. The distancing effects on fathers of industrialization and the movement of work outside the home, in other words, were partially compensated for by increased leisure time and job security and a "family togetherness" that was promoted by the new suburban lifestyle.

It is difficult to say what being a Victorian father meant to men; how much they bemoaned their loss of domestic power and status, for example, or how much they regretted the sexual strictures that held them in check. Certainly there is little utility in viewing the attitudes and feelings of Victorian men—or women—through a lens that incorporates the cultural baggage of our own time. Although the home had been turned into an all-female world, men still enjoyed some leadership and male dominance as well as a warm, well-run place to come home to each night. They had faithful, obedient wives and children. The exciting new public life was theirs and theirs alone and brought many satisfactions. They had the pleasure of seeing their children raised well without a heavy parenting input on their part. Men who were reasonably successful may have had the best of all worlds: both roots and wings. Indeed, male contentment in the middle class of the last century must have been great.

Because marriage and a strong family are civilizing forces of no mean proportions for men, male civility during the Victorian era should also have been great. And by all accounts it was. As virtually the only way that a man could have some assurance of emotional security, companionship, and sex, marriage was something to which virtually all men aspired and which almost all men achieved. Being married and having a family were regarded as a fundamental mark of manhood.

The Victorian Mother

The situation of women in the Victorian family has been meticulously evaluated by reams of scholars. By today's standards, to be sure, the situation appears rather grim. The man was still the inegalitarian head

of the household in most cases. His wife had no representation and little impact in political affairs, not even the opportunity to vote. The
doctrine of separate spheres required that married women spend most
of their lives within the home, devoting their time to the creation of a
warm domestic arena and to the well-being of their children and husbands. As time went on, this domestic isolation conflicted head-on
with women's rising expectations for self-fulfillment and participation
in public life.

A "cult of true womanhood" is said to have dictated the measure of
the good woman: piety, submissiveness, purity, and domesticity.[66] Having been put on a pedestal, women compromised these virtues at their
peril. Yet intrinsic to such virtues is the fact that they imply a lack of acceptance of real human beings and their individuality, needs, and special talents.

Sexually, this was an era of considerable restrictiveness for women as
well as for men, although the lack of "healthy sexuality" among Victorian women has probably been overstated.[67] Certainly, the sexually ad-
venturous woman was an outcast, and even the sexually curious
woman was suspect. Although contraceptives were not yet available,
birth control, which was limited to either abstinence or *coitus interrup-
tus,* had become the desire and practice of most middle-class families.
This situation alone was probably responsible in large part for the enormous anxiety and frustration with which Victorian sexuality was
fraught, to say nothing of its repression and denial, especially in the
case of female sexuality. Without contraception women's roles necessarily remained highly circumscribed.

Despite its patriarchal and repressive qualities, however, what we
now call the traditional nuclear family represented for women a significant advance in many ways over their situation in the premodern family. Throughout the nineteenth century and into the twentieth, an increasing proportion of women were experiencing a typical or preferred
family life cycle. More women married, bore children who survived,
and had husbands who lived jointly with them until at least the age of
fifty years.[68] Partly this was due to lower infant mortality and greater
longevity. But it was also due to the remarkable stability of the Victorian family, in which voluntary family breakup was minimal. While this
may well have been a psychological nightmare for some women—those
stuck in an abusive or emotionally empty marriage—it was a social
boon to many others.

Culturally, women now had a realm of their own, fully appreciated
both by men and by society at large, in which their own values and interests could be pursued. As historian Glenna Matthews says in her

book *"Just a Housewife": The Rise and Fall of Domesticity in America,* "For the first time in American history, both home and women's special nature were seen as uniquely valuable."[69] The nineteenth-century housewife, she says, had great satisfaction and self-respect. There is little evidence that most women of the time felt anything but pride in their domestic position. The values of the modern nuclear family were endlessly praised, for example, by the female writers of the time, such as Louisa May Alcott.[70] By some accounts the sex-role expectations of men and women were endorsed and upheld by men and women from all classes and occupational groups.[71]

In addition, women's relationship with their husbands had become more egalitarian than probably ever before in recorded history. As Carl N. Degler has noted: "The marriage which initiated the modern family was based upon affection and mutual respect between the partners, both at the time of family formation and in the course of its life. The woman in the marriage enjoyed an increasing degree of influence or autonomy within the family."[72] In general, women were no longer considered to be inferior to men. In the words of historian Nancy Cott, "By 1830 'different' had overwhelmed 'inferior' in usage to depict woman's place."[73]

Indeed, women, again for probably the first time in history, were accorded in major respects a moral supremacy over men. The new role prescription for the middle-class family man called for him "to temper his authority, respect his mate's moral superiority, and make every effort to be a true companion to his wife and children."[74] Even the sexual double standard between men and women was minimized although by no means absent. To a large degree, men subscribed to sexual fidelity and espoused marital commitment.[75]

Some scholars have suggested that a "status decline" took place for women with the rise of industrialization, owing to their removal from the productive workforce. In becoming housewives, they argue, women lost some control over their working conditions.[76] It is hard to believe that most women of the time thought in those terms, however. The dedicated and ceaseless scramble of nineteenth-century women in menial and unpleasant jobs to marry, leave the workforce, and become "just a housewife" suggests that something else was in their minds.[77]

The full-time mother-homemaker, freed from some of the menial drudgery of times past, ruled over a home that had supplanted the community as the center of sociability and social life. The middle-class homes of the day had grown more spacious and were embellished with whole new lines of domestic goods as well as the presence of domestic servants.[78] With family sizes still relatively large, there was a constant round of daily activity. As historian Susan Strasser argues in her book *Never Done: A History of American Housework,* "Men had bosses; married women bossed themselves, deciding what needed to be done according to the task and not the clock, controlling their own work process."[79] The middle-class home, in nineteenth-century America, was where most women wanted to be.

Victorian Children

The group that benefited most from the emergence of the modern nuclear family, however, was certainly children. "As motherhood gained in status, so did childhood," notes historian Anne M. Boylan.[80] Children became a central focus of the family as they never were in prior centuries in the West, going back thousands of years. By the end of the nineteenth century, in a profound cultural change, children had become highly sentimentalized and even sacralized, with many people coming to believe that it was almost better to be a naive and innocent child than an adult. In children's literature the American child was portrayed as "naturally good and capable of realizing all our national dreams, from the sublime to the trivial."[81] The care and nurturing of children came to be regarded as almost the measure of life and certainly society's best hope for a rewarding future.

Parental investments in the well-being of children became enormous. With declining birthrates, parents could afford to invest more time and energy and money in each child. Indeed, to be able to invest more heavily in each child was one of the major reasons for limiting pregnancies and having fewer children. As Carl Degler observes:

> The attention, energy and resources of parents in the emerging modern family were increasingly centered upon the rearing of their offspring. Children were now perceived as being different from adults and deserving not only of material care but of solicitude and love as well. Childhood was deemed a valuable period in the life of every person and to be sharply distinguished in character and purpose from adulthood. Parenthood thus became a major personal responsibility, perhaps even a burden.[82]

In preindustrial Europe, by way of comparison, parental care of children does not seem to have been particularly competent, and such practices as infanticide, wet nursing, child fosterage, and the widespread use of lower-class surrogate caregivers were common.[83] According to evidence assembled by demographer Sheila Ryan Johanson, "Malparenting in the form of extreme parental neglect (or even abuse) must have been widespread."[84] Child care undoubtedly improved in the preindustrial families in America. But even there the childrearing regime was harsh, coercive, and based on a perception of children as "naturally depraved."

The Victorian family may even have recaptured elements of childrearing that are deeply rooted in human biology. Evolutionary scientists Patricia Draper and Henry Harpending suggest that one of the greatest achievements of the modern nuclear family was a return to the high-investment nurturing of children by their biological parents, the kind of parenting characteristic of our hunter-gatherer ancestors.[85]

Fathers were leaving domestic activities for work outside the home, to be sure, and children did not see as much of them. But even so, any loss of function in childrearing on the fathers' part was probably more than made up by the increased attentions of mothers. A notable feature of the Victorian family was the intense bond, the emotional closeness, between mothers and their children, the kind of bond that is commonly found today in tribal societies. Using modern terms, there was very strong mother-child attachment. Some feminist scholars have attacked the importance of this strong bond, suggesting that perhaps it stifled individual development, led to the "overdependence" of children, and produced various personal pathologies.[86] Yet the evidence now indicates overwhelmingly that a strong mother-child attachment in infancy and childhood is critical to a person's optimal development.[87]

The family stability of the Victorian era helped children enormously. Cultural sanctions against divorce and out-of-wedlock births were powerfully enforced, and thanks to ever-lowering death rates, both parents typically were able to care for their children to adulthood. With the struggle for existence greatly diminished and a stable family structure firmly in place, children became ends in themselves more than ever before, individuals whose happiness and sound upbringing were of the utmost importance to parents and to society.

This new childrearing regime—a combination of stability and love— seems to have paid large dividends in the health of children. According to physician and epidemiologist Leonard A. Sagan, the rise of the modern nuclear family may be a more important explanation for improved standards of health than even the new medical technologies of the time. "Parenting patterns associated with the modern nuclear family," he writes, "produce healthier children who are not only physically bigger and brighter, but are more resilient, more resourceful, and better survivors."[88]

Social Well-Being

We don't often think of the Victorian period as a time of great psychological well-being. Among others, Sigmund Freud punched a gaping hole in that perception. It may well have been "psychologically superior" to previous eras, but of that we cannot really know. What we do know is that it was a time of great *social* well-being.

As the nineteenth century plunged on, an extraordinarily high measure of peace and social order, civility, optimism, and a sense of social progress and achievement came to prevail in much of the United States. By the end of the nineteenth century, for example, rates of crime and deviance reached lows that have never before or since been seen.[89] As social analyst James Lincoln Collier has summarized, "Pre-marital pregnancy rates dropped sharply; alcoholic intake was down two-thirds from the dizzying heights of the previous era; church attendance rose dramatically; homes, farms, and streets became cleaner, casual violence was curbed."[90] And all of this occurred amidst waves of extraordinary new technological and organizational inventions and the rapid movement of people off the farm. Let us not forget, however, that this was not yet a time of great economic well-being; a third or more of the population still lived in poverty.

The social well-being of the time stemmed in large part from the high levels of self-discipline and sense of obligation, as well as personal achievement, that the late Victorians espoused. Using today's terminology, this era was highly communitarian in character, marked by a strong sense of shared values and reciprocal responsibilities. "The main thing that Victorians can teach us," writes historian Gertrude Himmelfarb, "is the importance of values—or, as they would have said, "virtues"—in our public as well as private lives."[91] Indeed, the values that today we desperately clamor to regain—honesty, trustworthiness, respect, responsibility, and citizenship—are the very values which characterized the Victorian period.[92]

The personal and civic virtues of Victorians almost certainly were developed in and nourished by their families. The aim of Victorian child-rearing was to develop adults who could be autonomous individuals of strong character imbued with an ethic of responsibility. "One of the foremost human achievements of the bourgeois family," sociologists Brigitte and Peter L. Berger point out, "has been the balance it provided between freedom and restraint, between individual self-realization and social responsibility."[93] The philosophers of the Enlightenment seem to have been right—that a stable nuclear family system could become a seedbed of civic virtue, a place where strong, independent, and democratic citizens could be generated who would in turn be able to achieve both social order and progress.

More pointedly, the rise of mothers as the primary parent, with their intensive devotion to childrearing, is one of the most salutary things to happen to children in modern times. The new maternal role was largely

made possible by an expanding economy and the breadwinning ex-
ploits of fathers, who, through enabling their families (both women
and children) to remain out of the workforce, provided their wives time
for childrearing and their children time for childhood. In the Victorian
family we have a classic example of a rather indirect yet stable fatherhood that paid enormous social dividends. Fathers were losing their
hands-on role with children, but the roles they played—provider, protector, stabilizer, and guide—were of paramount importance.

In summary, the achievements of the Victorian family should not be
taken lightly. Certainly there was a dark side to Victorian family life, as
is the case for family life in all times and places. But the harsh, patriarchal regime of the preindustrial family had been dropped in favor of
more democratic family relations; family life became far more affectionate and emotionally rewarding between both husband and wife and
parents and children; parents remained highly obligated and dedicated
to their children's physical and social well-being; and the massive father absence of modern times had not yet taken place. Although there
is no way that we could return to this family form—the external conditions of society, along with the desires of men and women, have
changed too much for that—let us not disregard the majestic significance of the Victorian family when viewed from the broad perspective
of human history and civilization.

4. The Shrinking Father and the Fall of the Nuclear Family

In the social and cultural life of modern times, nothing stays the same for very long. So it was with fatherhood and the modern nuclear family of the Victorian era, discussed in the last chapter. With the loss of paternal authority and the movement of men's work outside of the home, the seeds of later father absence, unfortunately, were sown. The path down the slope of fatherhood's decline had steepened. Fathers were beginning to move away—first from the home, later from their children, and ultimately from marriage.

The economic, social, and cultural trends that eventually led to the decline of the modern nuclear family and massive father absence are typically thought of as twentieth-century phenomena, and that is the century in which they flourished, but their roots can unmistakably be found in the late nineteenth century. The Victorian family continued on into the early twentieth century but was heavily buffeted by the winds of change.

THE LATE-NINETEENTH-CENTURY ROOTS OF FATHERHOOD'S DECLINE

As virtually every student of American women's history knows by now, women in the late nineteenth century were beginning to feel resentful of—or at least restive at—their separate-sphere existence, desiring a more active role in public life. Modern feminism was taking shape. In the 1890s there was much talk of the New Woman, a more bold, physically active, and socially aware woman. Yet the feminism of the time, which extended through the Progressive era, was not designed to get women out of the home and into the workplace, as was the case with feminism later in the twentieth century. Rather, it was organized around the attempt to civilize the public world in terms of the values of the middle-class home, to socialize men to female values, and thus to achieve equality with men on female terms. New women's organizations were spreading like wildfire, many of which were designed to bring more "private virtue" into civic life. A "purity crusade," for example, sought to banish prostitution and the "white slave" traffic, along with men's double standard of sexuality, to bring about the triumph of love over lust.[1] Other crusades focused on male alcoholism and the reform of public schools.

Less well known is the fact that men, too, on a wide cultural scale, were beginning to feel the need to break away from the established social order. And that was just as consequential, if not more so, for the Victorian family. The Victorian era was not an easy time to be a man, especially a man of the working classes. Society depended on men who could be successful, and the standards of both character and achievement were high, higher than many men could attain. This was on top of the normal stress and danger that had long accompanied the male obligation to be an economic provider. The expected level of male sexual self-control was experienced as extreme by many men who desired more chance for sexual expression and experimentation. Thus, some sense of failure among men was almost assured. Preferring male bonding, adventure, or just the chance to get away from looming failure, a growing number of men in the second half of the nineteenth century fled from their families. Many headed West.

Even economically and socially successful men found reasons to be away from home more often. The intimate, domestic, highly feminized home was more than some men could confidently relate to. Fraternal orders and men's clubs proliferated like locusts in the nineteenth century, providing men an "alternative domesticity" on male terms and enabling them temporarily to escape the home ties.[2] And of course, some men escaped to their places of work and became consumed by their business and professional ties. With the sharp separation of the realms of work and home, two cultures emerged that were often in conflict with one another, the one favoring competitiveness, ambition, and aggression and the other emphasizing patience, kindness, and cooperation. Maneuvering between these two disparate cultural realms became an increasingly difficult task, something that today's working mother realizes all too clearly.

As the nineteenth century wore on, according to historian Stephen Frank, a shift of great symbolic importance in the cultural expectations for family men occurred. The principal male family role became defined, especially by female writers of the time, more in terms of being a husband than of being a father.[3] The "good father" became not a person who fathers per se, but one who devotes himself to helping his

wife fulfill her natural maternal and domestic obligations. It was a subtle but telling indicator of father slippage. With this new cultural norm
fathers retreated further from the direct care of their children; now
their relationship with their children was seen to be primarily through
their wives. The strong cultural message was that fathers were both less
qualified and less necessary in parenting and that mothers were the
"natural parents."

Fatherhood and the New Masculinity

Another cultural current of major importance, arising in the 1890s, was
a change in the very definition of masculinity. A male minirebellion
took place against the standards of masculinity that had guided middle-class men of the prior generation. For a growing number of younger
men, masculinity came to be defined less in terms of self-control and
family obligation, including responsible fatherhood, and more in terms
of competition, ambition, assertiveness, and virility.[4]

The new masculinity, centering on male "toughness," became a
major theme of popular culture for males in the late nineteenth and
early twentieth centuries. There was a new glorification of competitive
athletics and other forms of strenuous recreation, physical prowess,
and virility, together with a growing scorn for effeminacy and frailty.
These themes were fed by an enormous new body of cowboy, adventure, and escape literature and the rapid emergence of spectator sports.
Intercollegiate athletics flourished, and in 1896 William Randolph
Hearst's *New York Journal* created the modern sports page. As men
turned in droves to the Great Outdoors, a new cult of the wilderness
developed. Even militarism became popular again, the Civil War having
become a distant memory.

The conditions were ripe for this redefinition. The 1890s, which
Henry Steele Commager called a watershed of American history, was
an era in which there "was everywhere a hunger to break out of the
frustrations, the routine, and the sheer dullness of an urban-industrial
culture."[5] Men were caught up in large, complex work organizations
which threatened their former independence and sense of manly accomplishment. From being self-made small businessmen and farmers,
they were becoming cogs in bureaucratic machines. The felt need for a
rebellion against an emasculating new organizational bureaucracy and
the growing routinization of life was in the air.

The redefinition also reflected male cultural rebellion against the
excessive refinements of the Victorian home and a concession to the
new values of the ever more complex and compelling public or market sphere in which men increasingly were encapsulated. This sphere

was becoming more commercial—and therefore highly competitive—and more removed from the leavening effect of small-town values. As men were pulled into the public sphere, the female-defined virtues of the home looked more deficient and confining to them. Why should the female values of the home govern them, why should control of their passions be their foremost virtue, and why are the competition and aggression of the marketplace such morally questionable traits? Some men saw themselves as revitalizing their primitive instincts, much like today's "Iron John" devotees. The new masculinity may also have been one means by which men were compensating for their loss of social power within the home brought about by the decline of patriarchy.[6]

The new masculinity may even have stemmed, in part, from something deeper within the Victorian family. There is a sense in which the Victorian family contained the seeds of its own destruction, a phenomenon we shall encounter again with the 1950s family and its aftermath. The goal of Victorian male childrearing was to generate individualistic male adults who could be independent, who could stand on their own two feet. It was perhaps inevitable, therefore, that the young males of the Victorian family would carry that individualism a step further in a radical direction, toward an expressive individualism relatively unfettered by social structure and social bonds and oriented more to the satisfaction and development of the self. Modest though the trend still was at the time, male individualism as self-discipline was giving way to individualism as self-expression.

This shift in the definition of masculinity—away from family protector-provider toward an expressive individualism—was damaging to fatherhood. A locker-room mentality among young males was growing. Male excitement and adventure were emphasized, and masculine humor grew disparaging of marriage and family responsibilities. Children were increasingly left out of the male equation. More men were leaving their families. In the late nineteenth century, as historian Peter N. Stearns attests, "there is little doubt that the number of 'irresponsible' fathers and husbands increased."[7]

In fact, a new hint of desperation about fatherhood entered the social debate. Unlike motherhood, which was believed to be the fulfillment of woman's nature, fatherhood came to be regarded as more cultural in content. Male biology was viewed as inherently suspect and constantly posing the threat of tempting fathers away from home and family. From being considered a central, natural, and unproblematic aspect of being a man, as it had been with the Puritans, fatherhood became something which needed to be promoted by the culture.

In keeping with an ever more secular and individualistic age, the main themes of the new cultural promotion of fatherhood came not from the religious realm but from the realm of self-improvement. Fatherhood was characterized by moral leaders and writers of the time as something that was "good for men's health and happiness." It was even said to be a means by which men could actually assert their "true virility" and thus perfect their own masculine natures. One by-product of this was that the central theme of the fatherhood message became, not what men can do for their children, but what fatherhood can do for men.[8]

Fatherhood and New Concerns About Youth

Around the turn of the twentieth century, with the continuing shrinkage of the father role, one dimension of this role took on particular social significance. Much was written about how important it was for fathers to at least be good "role models," especially to their sons. Because being a role model is something at which fathers can excel with relatively little concrete effort or family involvement, it may not be far off the mark to suggest that the importance given to role models was in part a rationalization for the more limited scope of fatherhood that had developed. But the new concern about role models emerged mainly from alarm over the changing social conditions of youth. Apprehensions were growing about overly aggressive or hypermasculine, as well as hedonistic, behavior in boys, traits that even then were known to be associated with father neglect and father absence.

The development of a boys' peer culture, with values that run counter to those of the adult world, can be traced well back into the nineteenth century, as historian E. Anthony Rotundo has pointed out. Such peer cultures were closely associated with the movement of fathers out of the home and mothers' becoming the primary parents; boys felt a growing need to break loose from the female-dominated setting. The prevailing spirit of these boyhood groups "emphasized exuberant spontaneity . . . allowed free rein to aggressive impulses and reveled in physical prowess and assertion"; they were not only independent of adult men but often quite hostile toward them.[9]

Early in the twentieth century a new stage of life called adolescence was identified, and it was among adolescents that the youthful, countercultural peer groups reached their apogee.[10] Enhanced by the new culture of masculinity, some of these adolescent peer groups—called youth cults at the time—became not only socially deviant but socially destructive, especially in cities. Their deviance and divisiveness was nothing, of course, compared to what was to come. Male adolescent peer groups, now called gangs, have become the scourge of urban areas in the late twentieth century.

Declining Paternal Authority and Family Function

Over the course of the nineteenth century, the erosion of paternal authority was reflected in, and also to some extent promoted by, legal changes and the expansion of government. In addition to the gradual shift in child-custody awards from fathers to mothers, virtually completed by the end of the century, government increasingly encroached upon what had once been the father's prerogative by taking over various family functions, especially when the family was failing.

In order to protect the safety and individual rights of children and women in an increasingly complex society, courts and governments took over numerous rights and obligations that had traditionally been held by the family patriarch.[11] Earlier in the nineteenth century, for example, in response to the desperate condition of impoverished and abused children, state-run asylums, designed for out-of-control children and runaways as well as orphans and the poor, began to appear.[12] The courts ruled that such children could be taken away against their parents' wishes when the parents (typically the father) proved unworthy. It is important to note in this case, however, that the state had merely incorporated a power formerly held—and intermittently utilized—by many traditional small communities.

A far more extensive and compelling intrusion into what was formerly the realm of paternal authority was the rise of compulsory schooling, which came to require the attendance of all children aged six and older. The most cherished principles of democracy—in particular, universal suffrage—required a literate and educated citizenry, but removing parental consent for education eroded further a paternal prerogative. The extension of compulsory public schooling to all regions of the nation was virtually complete by the end of the nineteenth century. This was followed, in the Progressive era of the early twentieth century, by much-needed child-labor laws and an entire new juvenile-justice system.

By 1900 many of the traditional family functions had been shorn away. Gone were economic production, formal education, and in some instances health and welfare activities in the care of the elderly, the poor, and the mentally ill. Having lost much of their household authority, few fathers any longer anchored their identities in the role of domestic patriarch. Their new role was to be a reliable economic provider and also to take care of "practical matters" around the home, such as house maintenance and yard work. Respect for the kind of authority that fathers once held was also in steep decline, as egalitarianism swept the country and a world once dominated by unquestioned acceptance of traditional hierarchy and social obligation became one measured by democratic principles of equality and fairness, individual liberty and achievement.

The Replacement of Fathers by Mothers

The connection between work life and domestic life had been largely severed by the end of the nineteenth century. The home had clearly become the sphere of women, and within this sphere there was growing resistance by males to participation in day-to-day domestic activities.[13] This was the family pattern, for example, that Robert S. and Helen Merrell Lynd found in "Middletown" (Muncie, Indiana) in the 1920s.[14] The wives of Middletown were wholly responsible for the organization of household affairs, for child care and the disciplining of children, and for arranging the family's social life. "Without a commanding, patriarchal role to play in the family," notes E. Anthony Rotundo, ". . . men let their wives take full responsibility for the children, rather than fall into a secondary role and suffer a blow to their masculine pride."[15]

Thus, the home replacement of fathers by mothers was complete, and many men became ever more remote from the daily exigencies of family life. In time, fathers even came to be depicted in American popular culture as "incompetent" around the home compared to mothers.[16] Left with breadwinning as their only clear-cut family role, it should come as no surprise that fathers would flounder and not know what they should be doing when, late in the twentieth century, even that role on an exclusive basis was lost to them.

THE FIRST AMERICAN FAMILY CRISIS

"The family of our father's time has almost entirely gone," wrote Chauncey J. Hawkins in 1907 in his book *Will the Home Survive: A Study of Tendencies in Modern Literature.*[17] He was referring to the demise of the older, self-contained patriarchal family. But the title of Hawkins's book suggests new anxieties about the modern nuclear family. By the turn of the twentieth century, real danger signs in the new family form were beginning to appear, and the country became alarmed, not so much about father absence as about "family decline." The alarm was not misplaced. The modern nuclear family, while highly successful in its day, was not to last out the new century.

Several widely publicized statistical trends became a source of special concern. There was a rapidly falling birthrate, from 7 children per native-born white family in 1800 to only 3.56 children per family in 1900. The drop in the birthrate was especially strong among newly college-educated women. When it was discovered that the rate of child-bearing among immigrant women was nearly twice that of native-born white women, President Theodore Roosevelt promptly warned the nation about "race suicide."

The rapid movement of women into the labor force was also a source of worry for some. By 1900 nearly one fifth of the total labor force consisted of female wage earners, and between 1880 and 1910 the proportion of females (aged fourteen and over) in the labor force nearly doubled. These were mostly low-level jobs, and only a small percentage of workers were married women (only 5 percent of married white women worked outside the home in 1900). Still, the handwriting was on the wall, and concerns about women's key role in the family were simmering. Also, married women, while not yet in the labor force, were becoming more interested in politics and social reform movements, which had the effect of taking them away from home activities.

But the main trigger for America's first named national "family crisis" was divorce. America awakened at the turn of the century to find that it had the highest divorce rate in the world. Following a climb in the divorce rate in the 1880s and 1890s that was three times that of the population increase as a whole, the rate jumped another 100 percent between 1900 and 1920. With the exception of a period in the 1930s and the 1950s and a slowdown in the 1980s and 1990s, it has been increasing ever since.

By the early decades of the twentieth century, the so-called companionate marriage had come into full flower. Wives and husbands were each other's "best friends." Many marriages were warmer and more egalitarian than ever before. Unfortunately, however, affection alone often proved an inadequate basis for a lasting marriage. As marriage lost its religious nature and its traditional economic tie and became based mainly on emotional considerations, more marriages began to dissolve.

Divorce was almost unknown in colonial America, and the rate remained exceedingly low up until the Civil War. While legal under certain highly restrictive circumstances (the first Massachusetts law permitting divorce dates from about 1639), it was regarded as grossly immoral, something akin to prostitution. Prior to the Civil War efforts were undertaken in many states to make the divorce laws more permissive, but typically these efforts failed. In the decades following the Civil War, however, climbing divorce rates were accompanied by legislative changes that eased restrictions on divorce and by the growing use of "divorce colonies"—the migration of those desiring a divorce to certain areas of the nation, mainly in the mid- and far West, where the laws were less restrictive.[18] After reviewing the trends, the eminent early twentieth-century psychologist John B. Watson predicted, "In fifty years there will be no such thing as marriage."[19]

Many new professionals and professional groups, notably the emerging profession of sociology, reacted to the new family trends with alarm. Introducing the section on the family in his *Outline of Practical Sociology* (1898), Carroll D. Wright, president of Clark College, referred to "the menace to which the family is exposed through the complications of modern society."[20] As U.S. commissioner of labor in the late 1880s, he had written a special government report on marriage and divorce that was generated by pressure on Congress to address the new concern about divorce. In 1908 the third annual meeting of the newly formed American Sociological Society was devoted to problems of the family. The titles of many of the papers presented at the meeting raised questions we still grapple with today: "Are Modern Industry and City Life Unfavorable to the Family?" (answer: yes); "How Does the Access of Women to Industrial Occupations React on the Family?" (answer: poorly); "Is the Freer Granting of Divorce an Evil?" (answer: no, but increasing divorce is a serious problem); "How Far Should Members of the Family Be Individualized?" (answer: not too far).[21]

There was also great concern in the Progressive era that living conditions were getting worse for children and that government "child savers" were needed to step in. During what historian Joseph M. Hawes has called "the age of the child," 1890–1920, reformers sought to devote great national attention to the problems of children. Their concern was for working-class, especially immigrant, children in the burgeoning cities of the nation. In the thirty-year period from 1885 to 1915, the American population almost doubled, and much of the population growth consisted of relatively unassimilated urban-dwelling immigrants. The exemplary environment of children in the middle-class home provided a powerful new standard of how things should be in the rest of society. With the new view that childhood should be a special time of life with its own norms and removed as much as possible from adult responsibilities, a groundswell of opinion led eventually to laws that prohibited the paid employment of children below a certain age.[22]

Despite all the talk of crisis, the Progressive era was a highly optimistic one. The rapidly emerging class of social-service professionals believed that they had both the knowledge and the capability to move the nation forward. Social reform was in the air as never before. The time seemed right to coalesce the nation around the middle-class values that had been generated so successfully by the Victorian family. It was thought that society could develop in such a way that all children would be provided a happy, stable home with devoted parents. This optimism was reflected in the first major history of the American family, published in 1917–1919, by Arthur W. Calhoun. "On the whole it cannot be doubted that America has entered upon 'the century of the child.' . . . As befits a civilization with a broadening future, the child is becoming the center of life."[23] How wrong he turned out to be!

HEADED TOWARD THE 1960s

What the Progressives failed to realize was just how fast an ideology of radical individualism would devour marriage and family life and leave a chaotic culture in its wake. Not everyone was blind to this possibility, however. In a remarkable discussion on the future of the family, published in the *North America Review* in 1901 in an article entitled "Anticipations: An Experiment in Prophecy," H. G. Wells clearly foresaw that "the institution of permanent monogamous marriage" was due for "a considerable relaxation:"

> It is foolish . . . not to anticipate and prepare for a state of things when, not only will moral standards be shifting and uncertain, admitting of physiologically sound *ménages* of every variable status, but also when vice and depravity, in every form that is not absolutely penal, will be practised in every grade of magnificence and condoned. . . . Outside the system of *ménages* that are now recognized . . . there will be a vast drifting and unstable population grouped in almost every conceivable form of relation.[24]

When romantic love became so important in the nineteenth century, the die was probably cast on the future of marriage. Romantic love was a potent generator of what later became radical expressive individualism through its emphasis on emotional bonds, which focus on the unique and separate features of another individual, and on sexuality as "an emotional expression of the romantic self" rather than merely a reproductive function.[25] In essence, romantic love is a cultural commitment to individual differentiation, and it heavily involves the exploration of the "true self,' the identification of feelings, and appropriate self-expression and self-disclosure.

In many respects, as Karen Lystra has observed, romantic love was influential far beyond the realm of interpersonal relationships. It was a major player in the secularization shift, from a God-centered to a person-centered universe of meanings. When romantic love first arose in the nineteenth century, "few abandoned God or religion, but they began to find ultimate fulfillment and the central symbol of their life's meaning in the new theology of the romantic self."[26] Eventually, of course, this process extended much further, undercutting traditional religion and replacing God with "me" as the main focus of values and meaning. With the loss of religiously based transcendent meaning, the days of socially oriented Victorian values were numbered.

Marriage and Families in the Culture of the Twenties

By the 1920s, the Victorian era was virtually over and the age of modernism had begun. The 1920s saw the early stages of many social and cultural trends which were to become so prominent in the 1960s, when they finally burst forth to challenge the basic validity of the modern nuclear family. Especially for the more than 50 percent of Americans who had become city dwellers, a more affluent economy of mass production focused on personal and household consumption, together with a rapidly expanding organized entertainment industry generating movies, dance halls, and urban amusements, were radically changing the values by which Americans' lives were governed. A culture based on the wisdom of age and experience was giving way to one based on youthful innovation and constant technological and social change. Victorian values such as self-reliance, self-sacrifice, frugality, and sexual self-control were being replaced by a "new morality" of self-expression and self-gratification.

A new youth- and leisure-oriented lifestyle geared to self-development and pleasure emerged in the cities in the 1920s. As historian Paula S. Fass has written, "Youth appeared suddenly, dramatically, and even menacingly on the social scene."[27] Accompanying the arrival of a youth subculture was what has been referred to as "the first sexual revolution," wherein both men and women became more sexualized and sexual mores became more peer-determined and thus more permissive.[28] Much talk of nonmarital "free love" was in the air.

Helped by the rise of the automobile and commercial entertainment, the process of "courtship" shifted from its carefully supervised and formal Victorian version (including chaperonage) to the individualistic, privatized, and peer-controlled "dating and petting" system which was to last for the next fifty years.[29] For men, the entire Victorian sex code, anchored around premarital chastity, marital fidelity, and "respect" toward women, was beginning to crumble. A 1938 study of northern California middle-class married couples by Lewis Terman found that only 32.6 percent of men born between 1900 and 1909 were virgins when they married, compared to 50.6 percent of men born before 1890.[30]

Feminism took a new direction. Whereas feminism in the Victorian and Progressive eras had concentrated on trying to civilize the public world with the values of the Victorian home, the new feminism sought to liberate women from the home and achieve female equality in male terms and on male turf. The New Woman again made an appearance in various guises from flapper to career woman. Women wanted to have the same education, access to jobs, and careers as men. They wanted to be full participants in public life. And if not seeking a sexual life identical to that of males, they at least wanted to move far away from the Victorian sexual double standard.

This new version of feminism was made possible by an unprecedented drop in the birthrate to just one or two children per woman, which, together with increased longevity, enabled women for the first time in history to spend a large portion of their lives outside of motherhood. The birthrate drop can be attributed in large measure to the widespread use of contraceptives, especially in the middle class. Also, the changing nature of work was a major factor. Almost all productive activities had left the home, and the economic system saw the rapid rise of people-oriented and symbol-manipulating "service" jobs which were as well, if not better, suited for women as for men.

For urban males, the new complexity and uncertainty in personal relationships, including fear and anxiety about the New Woman, together with the growing availability of sex outside of marriage, led to a waning interest in marriage. More males were eschewing stable family commitments in favor of hedonism and the pursuit of self-improvement. The marriage rate dropped throughout the 1920s. A *Collier's* writer of the 1920s, observing the life of young men in New York City, stated: "The general opinion seems to be that the young men of today do not wish to marry."[31] And for men who found themselves married to the new working women, there was growing anxiety and feelings of discontent.

The cultural saga of redefining masculinity continued apace. The turn-of-the-century emphasis on strident virility and toughness was weakening, in part because of the devastating damage done by the experiences of World War I to the male military ideal. Gender roles were gradually becoming indistinct: Men were less interested in differentiating themselves from women, and all-male associations gradually gave way to increased intermingling between the sexes. The separate sphere, that pillar of Victorianism, was crumbling.

In summary, the family in the 1920s became a less integrated unit than ever before and more a constellation of individual personalities, each of whom was trying to make his or her own way in the new and complex world. As Christopher Lasch put it in his classic work *Haven in a Heartless World,* citing sociological analyses of the time, "Relations within the family took on the same character as relations elsewhere; individualism and the pursuit of self-interest reigned even in the most intimate of institutions."[32]

The Ever-Shrinking Father

The role of father was left hanging and unresolved in the culture of the 1920s. Or perhaps in the minds of many men it was settled and needed no further elaboration. Male roles were focused on the workplace, and female roles on the home. The man as provider was the dominant motif of the family-oriented male. There were virtually no other male family roles around which a man could organize his life. Other than a provider, it was no longer clear what a father should be or what he should do. Almost all the other dimensions of the Victorian father role had been taken over by women. Women had become, or at least were well on the way to becoming, the chief family educator, disciplinarian, accountant, and overall family head.

The father role was made still more precarious due to the fact that mothering, under the tutelage of a growing body of social science experts, was becoming more "scientific." The domestic sciences had arrived. Child-development and parenting studies were underway across the land, the results of which were widely distributed to middle-class mothers. In a "relocation of authority," women turned more and more to outside experts instead of to their husbands for advice. The advice they received was probably an improvement over traditional sources but at the cost of ever-more-superfluous fathers who were left out of the process, for the most part, as both donors and recipients.

As long as the mother was doing a good job of childrearing, there was not much concern on the part of family experts about father neglect. One of the major contributions to social science in the early 1930s was the monumental collaborative study conducted by the President's Research Committee on Social Trends. In the long chapter on the family, fathers are barely even mentioned, much less regarded as in any way problematic. They are absent from the "Problems and Trends" section, as well as from the section on "Parents and Children," which states: "The influence of the mother, who has repeated and frequent contacts with her offspring, is probably greater than that of any other member of the family, with the child's brothers and sisters, if there are any, coming next."[33]

A few experts of the time did begin to worry about diminished paternal influence. A *Parents' Magazine* article in 1932 pronounced that the new American family was becoming "fatherless."[34] Experts advised fathers to continue to be good role models but, even more, to become, as befits the new companionate family, companions to their children, especially their sons. Patriarchy and authority, they suggested, should continue to give way to love and affection and closer psychological involvement. This, of course, was a continuation of the "new father" idea that had been gaining ground over the decades. From a feminist perspective, the historian Robert L. Griswold maintains that the problem with this idea was that it merely served to prolong the existence of the modern nuclear family and "redefine patriarchy at a critical historical moment."[35] The real problem, however, was that it said little about what was unique and irreplaceable about fatherhood, a problem that remains with the "new father" role to this day.

With the father role ever shrinking, men were increasingly consumed by the nonfamily world. E. Anthony Rotundo has suggested a useful typology for the new ideals of manhood that emerged.[36] These types unfolded as the century wore on, and all are demonstrably still with us.

The most common ideal, the *team player*, is linked to the bureaucratized workplace and community and not so much to the family. Using competitive athletics as a model, the team player extends the idea of aggressive teamwork into his work life, sublimating his own immediate interests for the long-run benefit of the corporation. In the 1950s this type came to be popularized as the "organization man." Two other male ideals that emerged are fundamentally antifamily and antifather; they grew in popularity in the decades starting with the 1960s. One is the *existential hero,* the man who distrusts much of modern civilization and lives on the margins of society, eschewing much of middle-class social structure. This type was popularized by the movies and by many of the novels of the day. And then there is the out-and-out *pleasure seeker,* made especially popular in the pages of *Playboy* magazine, which had its debut in 1953.

Fatherhood and Family Life in the Great Depression

The trend toward radical individualism and cultural "modernity" was set back by the Great Depression and World War II, as national values became more communitarian in response to national threats, both economic and military. People hunkered down into family and community and fell back, to the extent they were able, on traditional values and roles.[37] But in both periods, for different reasons, the authority position of fathers in the home, already badly shaken, took yet another hit. Having made breadwinning their main family contribution, men's lives were shattered as unemployment reached over 25 percent in the depression and the burden of family responsibility fell more to women. Although efforts were made to keep married women out of the labor force so as to provide work for men, the percentage of married women in the labor force actually increased in the 1930s.

The depression sharply pointed up the fragility of the disempowered male position in the companionate family. Few features of the depression are so firmly stamped on our minds as that of the unemployed dad, a kind of dismissive third thumb around the home. In his important longitudinal study of depression-era adolescents in Oakland, California, sociologist Glen Elder found that economic hardship "emphasized the centrality of mother in family matters and children's sentiments."[38] It became strikingly clear that men now had to earn their position as family head; headship was not automatically assured to them by cultural tradition.[39] The unemployed male could maintain his family standing but only through the voluntary acceptance of family members. In this respect the new father was considerably better off than the old father. The normative expectations about marital gender roles had still not changed very much, however, and those families where the father's role had weakened were regarded as abnormal or deviant and certainly not a desirable pattern for the future. Traditional work roles were still widely accepted: A 1936 Gallup poll found that 82 percent of the population (and three fourths of all women) believed that wives of employed husbands should not work outside the home.[40]

The Great Depression was also the period, of course, when government came to the aid of families in a major way, as national assumptions and expectations about the role of the national government underwent a significant shift. In addition to aggressive policies designed to generate employment, the New Deal began seriously to address the traditional family tasks of helping the widowed, the disabled, the young, the sick, and the elderly when the families themselves were unable to do so. While many social benefits ensued, political conservatives regarded this as a further intrusion of government into family life and a further weakening of male authority, issues which are still very much alive today.

Social trends during the depression ignited new concerns about family decline. There was a growing anxiety about the negative influence of Hollywood, which in the 1930s actually upheld much of traditional morality but which was beginning to confront the modern nuclear family through glorifying the lives of single women and condoning divorce.[41] Statistically, marriages were being delayed for economic considerations, as were births. The birthrate during the mid-thirties reached a new historical low for America of 2.1 children per woman, slightly below the level of fertility necessary to replace the population. The divorce rate, after leveling off in the early 1930s, began to climb toward the end of the decade, and even more than divorce, marital separations increased. The 1938 report of President Roosevelt's National Resources Committee predicted that fewer Americans would marry, more adults would live outside of marriage for longer periods of their lives, and the birthrate would steadily decline. Virtually no expert fore-saw the dramatic family turnabout that was to come after the war.

Fatherhood and World War II

World War II put a severe strain on many families, entailing as it did mass migrations, much consumer privation, and the longtime separa-tion of family members from one another. Yet it also helped to rejuve-nate the modern nuclear family system in certain ways. Thanks to a massive revival of the nation's economy, poverty declined dramatically. Full employment was achieved by 1943, enabling more family forma-tion, and both marriage rates and birthrates returned to their prede-pression levels.[42] Many military men married, partly in order to have a home tie while they were away at war; marriage was strongly encour-aged by government policy. On the home front the shared sense of na-tional emergency forced people to pull together and find strength among their own small circles of family and community. Moreover, there was widespread sentiment that a primary purpose of the war was "to preserve the American family." The family was seen to be the very symbol of democracy, freedom, and the good life—the basis of all na-tional strength. Its possible loss was reason enough to fight a war on distant soil.

The impact of World War II on fatherhood was ambiguous. The au-thority of fathers was certainly undercut. For the first time in American history, fatherlessness—albeit involuntary and temporary—occurred on a mass scale. Fathers were pulled away for military duty, and de facto single-parent, mother-headed families became common across America. Under the circumstances, these families functioned with a reasonable measure of success, proving that mothers could run the household by themselves and that the physical absence of a father was not a fatal flaw. Also, the percentage of married women in the labor force rose sharply, from 17 percent at the end of the 1930s to 25 per-cent by the end of the war.[43] Thus, foretelling a major trend to come, a growing portion of wives made an incursion into the breadwinning role and had a taste of work life.

But in other respects World War II proved to be a boon for father-hood. Not only was the breadwinning role of many men restored by the war, due to full employment, but one of the most ancient father roles of all, that of protector, became highlighted. Men were again back in their element, being vigorously masculine in the cause of protecting their families, albeit a long way from home. The away-from-home father was a hero glorified by public opinion, quite unlike the absent father who had abandoned his family through divorce or desertion.

At the same time, great national attention came to be focused on the social importance of fatherhood and on what a tragedy it was not to have fathers in the home. When the war began, fathers were considered so important to their families that they were exempt from the draft by special deferment (although many fathers rushed to enlist, part of a virtual stampede to defend the country and be part of the war effort). When it became apparent in 1943 that more men would be needed for the war effort and that fathers would have to be drafted, a battle in Congress ensued. A majority of Americans and many experts at the time favored keeping fathers out of the war, and there was a national outpouring of support for the idea of fatherhood that has perhaps never before or since been witnessed.[44] Charlotte Towle, a leading social welfare authority, wrote:

> That the pregnant woman and the mother of children needs support, psychological as well as economic, of her husband during wartime is also well recognized. The absence of the father has a different import for children at different ages, but at all times he is needed.[45]

The fight to keep fathers from being drafted was eventually lost, giving way to military necessity ("fathers can help their families even more by defeating the fascist dictators"), but not before alerting the nation to the importance of fatherhood.

The war revealed one of the inherent dangers of fatherlessness, although it was not clearly recognized at the time. Wartime economic conditions provided teenagers new opportunities for financial and social independence, and teenagers became recognized as a major new consumer group through the publication of the teen magazine *Seventeen,* launched in 1944. Teenage peer cultures boomed, but with them came an increase in serious juvenile delinquency and crime. The percentage of juvenile court cases jumped alarmingly in the later years of the war, and delinquency became one of the most disturbing social problems of the era.[46]

Yet the etiology of delinquency was believed to be due more to the changing role of women and to wartime dislocation and "family stress" than to fatherlessness. While the wartime work of mothers was mostly part-time and short-lived and typically made necessary by father absence (most married women worked for economic reasons or because they wanted to support the war effort more actively), the "dark specter" of working mothers was raised to a new level. There was much talk about "latch-key" or "eight-hour orphan" children, maternal neglect, and too-permissive childrearing. In fact, the nation may have caught its first glimpse of the negative social consequences of simultaneous paternal and maternal neglect.

Mothers who weren't neglecting their children faced another charge that had lingered from the 1930s—maternal overprotection. It was said that children, especially those in the middle class, had become subject to excessive maternal influence and domination, a phenomenon labeled "momism" in a best-selling 1942 book by social critic Philip Wylie.[47] The problem was envisioned as not simply war-generated but part of a long-term social trend. There was particular apprehension about the rapid increase in "sissy" boys, a throwback to concerns about masculinity earlier in the century, reemerging in tandem with the hypermasculine climate of wartime. In order to assure that their children would grow up to be mature adults with appropriate gender roles, women whose husbands were away were urged to find father substitutes, especially for their sons.

Balancing all of the positive and negative considerations, World War II seems to have strengthened the importance of fatherhood in America. After the war, in numerous postmortems of wartime social conditions, social scientists found that, on many counts, father absence during the war had left scars on the young, on the men themselves, and on the social fabric. The facts indubitably showed that fathers were needed at home. And that is precisely where the returning GIs headed, generating the greatest outpouring of familism and family values of the century.

FIFTIES FAMILISM

Before its collapse in the 1960s, the modern nuclear family had a final moment of flowering in the so-called fifties, the era that roughly spans the years from 1946 to the end of the baby boom in 1964. And what a flowering it was. This was an era of remarkable familism, with high birthrates that had not been seen since the prior century. Women bore their first child at a younger age, they had more children on average, and fewer couples were childless. The domestic, child-centered family flourished. Both men and women of this era showed an extraordinary desire to marry. Age of first marriage dropped to one of its lowest levels ever, and 96.45 percent of the women and 94.1 percent of the men eventually married, making it the most marrying generation on record. The stability of these marriages was high; after a steep jump in the immediate postwar period, the divorce rate leveled off and even dropped. Sociologist Andrew Cherlin has noted that "those who married in the decade or so following the war were the only cohorts in the last hundred years to show a substantial, sustained shortfall in their lifetime levels of divorce."[48]

High employment and high incomes brought back the strong male breadwinner and, to some extent, the head-of-household male leadership role as well. The new affluence enabled many families to move to the suburbs and purchase their own single-family houses; home ownership doubled between 1940 and 1960. Especially in the new suburbs, "old fashioned family values" and traditional husband-wife roles were reaffirmed in America in a big way.

To a remarkable degree, women who had worked during the war returned home and expressed strong contentment with their new role of full-time housewife and mother. Surveys showed that they appreciated being their own boss again and having more control over their own lives. Even well-educated middle-class women had little to say on behalf of paid work and careers. An influential best-seller at the time, *Modern Woman: The Lost Sex,* was a strident attack on women who put careers ahead of motherhood. When asked in a survey what they thought they had sacrificed by marrying and raising a family, an overwhelming majority of postwar married women replied, "Nothing."[49]

That no one predicted the enormous family turnaround of the 1950s indicates how great a departure it was from family trends of the 1920s and 1930s. Still today, considerable scholarly disagreement about the causes of 1950s familism remains. Probably the most popular theory is that it was the result of a "pent-up demand" for families and children generated during the depression and World War II, when both marriage and fertility had been postponed. This theory is true as far as it goes, but it does not account for why the birthrate after the war kept going up and up and up. The peak baby-boom birthrate of 3.7 children per woman didn't occur until 1957, some twelve years after the war had ended. The happy parents at that time were still children when the war ended. Nor does the "pent-up demand" theory provide a reason for the return to an almost Victorian family form, with Rosie the Riveter readily leaving the job market and becoming "just a housewife."

The best explanation for fifties familism is a combination of economic prosperity and sociocultural demand. This was a time of unparalleled affluence in America, the most sustained period of prosperity in the nation's history. The gross national product increased a remarkable 250 percent between 1945 and 1960, and there was an enormous growth of discretionary spending power. By 1960 some 65 percent of American families had achieved a middle-class standard of living, compared to only 30 percent in 1929.[50] Contrary to the disaffection toward the Victorian family that some segments of the educated middle class had started to express in the 1920s and 1930s, the working class had been waiting quietly in the wings to achieve their dream of having a middle-class lifestyle—a husband who could be the sole breadwinner, a wife who no longer had to work, and a single-family house of their own filled with children. Postwar prosperity finally made this dream come true for a huge segment of the American working-class population.

Fatherhood in the Fifties

In some respects family gender roles in the 1950s did indeed remain quite traditional; the trends of modernism that had been reshaping women's and men's roles, especially in the 1920s, were set back. Partly this was a legacy of the war, with its radical escalation of masculinity and the male protector role. Partly it was the result of a feeling of confidence on the part of stay-at-home housewives that their breadwinning husbands would remain with them.

Husbands of the time, in reaction to depression and wartime deprivations, looked to home and family as a great source of security and satisfaction. Marriage, children, family togetherness, and domestic consumption in the suburbs were what the good life was supposed to be all about. As in Victorian times, there was a widespread feeling on the part of men that the reason they were working was to provide a good home for their family; that is also what they had fought for, as the GIs in World War II had been repeatedly told. Male authority in the home also may have been enhanced temporarily by the changing nature of work. It was thought that the hardworking new "organization man," who had lost much of his independence and power in the emerging megabureaucracies, ought to be able to retain or regain some of his authority within the confines of the domestic sphere.

For a short moment in history, fatherhood again became a defining identity for many men, a fact that was highlighted by such popular television characters as Ward Cleaver and Ozzie Nelson, whose lives beyond the confines of their father role always remained vague and amorphous. At the same time, as these fictional "good fathers" pointed out, the father role was changing in a new and modern direction. Gender roles were still relatively traditional in terms of the overall division of labor, but compared to their Victorian counterparts, the 1950s middle-class fathers were both more nurturing and more egalitarian in outlook. Ward Cleaver and Ozzie Nelson were heads of household, but they were a far cry from Victorian patriarchs.

In 1954 *Life* magazine pronounced the domestication of the American male.[51] Especially in the middle-class suburbs, the "new father" had come into style. Psychological principles were widely purveyed in books and in the media, suggesting that fathers should be more friendly and open with their children, more democratic and nurturing, and less what psychologist Kyle Pruett has referred to as the "distant, remotely involved patriarch, perpetually absent from the nursery."[52] Men were urged to become sophisticated assistants to their wives, with the goal of developing the full intellectual and psychological capabilities of their children. Indeed, a trend toward greater flexibility and egal-

itarianism in marital gender roles was said by a leading family sociologist of the day to be one of the most striking characteristics of suburban life.[53] Yet due to their breadwinning responsibilities, the actual
contribution of most fathers to the day-to-day care of children remained minimal.

According to psychologist Joe Pleck, this new father-role image was
"the first positive image of involved fatherhood to have a significant impact on the culture since the moral overseer model of the colonial period."[54] But as we have seen, what we today call the "new father" role
had been brewing for a very long time. Its practice had been enhanced
by the shorter workweek and the growth of leisure time, together with
the suburban "captivity" of fathers on weekends, which partially offset
the ever longer commutes to work. Suburban men of the time reported
in surveys that after they moved to the suburbs, they spent more time
at home.[55]

Child-Centeredness

The increase in fathers who nurtured was not the only way that childrearing in America was changing in the 1950s. This was an enormously child-centered era, an era in which parental preoccupation with
the needs and interests of children was paramount.

Childrearing became more "permissive," due in part to the highly influential *Baby and Child Care* of Dr. Spock, which first made its appearance in 1946. But it was not permissive in the modern sense of "neglect,"
"spoil," and "let kids do what they want." It was permissive in that parents became more thoughtful, responsive, comforting, and geared to the
needs of the child rather than being rigid, strict, and demanding, the pro-
tocol for childrearing in earlier times. Indeed, it was a highly time-intensive form of childrearing, and mothers and perhaps also fathers spent
more time directly engaged in this task than perhaps ever before in American history. This, too, was partly enabled by postwar prosperity.

Another important element of 1950s childrearing, one that was to
have a major impact in the following decades, was the gradual decline
of traditional gender distinctions. Girls were being raised and treated
more like boys, and vice versa, although strong differences remained
among the social classes, with working-class families hewing more to
tradition. Gender equality in childrearing was influenced by the fact
that each sex was receiving substantially the same education, especially
at the primary and secondary levels but also including college—the
percentage of girls going onto college increased substantially during
this period.

FIFTIES FAMILISM: A POSTMORTEM

For many American citizens, the fifties were an enormously peaceful and satisfying period. A strong sense of optimism, the Cold War notwithstanding, pervaded the land. People's incomes were increasing on a regular basis, and a world of consumer products had arrived that would have been almost unimaginable to earlier generations. The huge pockets of poverty and the racial inequality that still existed were mostly overlooked by the popular culture. The future looked bright indeed.

Yet the era suddenly ended, the birthrate plummeted, and the dramatic "social revolutions" of the three decades following the fifties— the sexual revolution, the divorce revolution, and the women's liberation movement—were launched. As women went into the labor force, young men in large numbers rejected domesticity and even the masculine ideal. The laid-back and thoroughly family-rejecting hippie became a model for many men, and all "rigid gender roles" became something to be eschewed at all costs. Marriage fell out of fashion, replaced by the rapidly growing phenomenon of living together outside of marriage. After an historical moment of glory, the modern nuclear family came apart at the seams. And in the vanguard of the family revolt were children who came from intact families—the centerpiece of 1950s life— that were supposedly so warm, friendly, and nurturing.

What happened? Just as no one had predicted fifties familism and the baby boom, no one predicted sixties antifamilism and the baby bust. It came as a great surprise to expert and lay person alike. Hindsight, however, shows the pieces were in place for a radical change of social direction.

The Situation of Women

Perhaps most importantly, the 1950s proved to be a far-from-ideal time to be a woman. Especially for women in the suburbs, social conditions were substantially different from those of Victorian times when the modern nuclear family thrived. A man could center his life on his suburban family because he also was engaged in the world of work and public life. But for his wife, suburban life was not to prove so sustaining.

A comparison of Victorian social conditions with those of the 1950s is highly revealing. The Victorian home was set typically in a small town. The organized entertainment industry had not yet emerged, transportation was limited, neighbors were friendly, and fathers worked nearby. Home was the true center of social life, and family togetherness was more than an expression, it was a daily reality. The home was a bustling place filled with children, visiting relatives, neighbors, servants, and the many daily, time-consuming domestic activities, such as laundry, baking, cooking, cleaning, and bottling, that preceded the invention of labor-saving home technologies. There was really no place else for a middle-class woman to be and no place else she would want to be.

Fifties suburban life for women was in many ways the polar opposite of this, despite the fact that couples typically sought out the suburbs to gain "a sense of community." The home was still the one and only center of life, but it was a relatively lonely home, isolated from relatives and now without servants. The daily chores, which no longer had the same urgency as in Victorian times thanks to modern technology, were accomplished by women working alone without the presence of other adults. Fathers were physically absent much of the time during the week due to the increasingly long commute. Town centers were often far distant and not easy to get to; surrounding the home was merely a sea of other homes containing women similarly situated. Except for the commanding presence of children, the suburban community was relatively lifeless.

For all of these reasons, many mothers of the time had strong, if often unexpressed, feelings of boredom, loneliness, and social isolation—that "real life" was taking place somewhere else. And taking place elsewhere it was, mostly in the distant and male world of the city. The social isolation was made worse by the fact that a growing number of suburban women had a higher education almost equivalent to that of their husbands, the proportion of bachelors' and masters' degrees received by women having increased from 24 percent in 1950 to over 35 percent in 1960. Women stashed away at home were unable to utilize most of this education.

On top of this, a higher percentage of women got married than was the case in Victorian times, including, perhaps, many women who did not have a serious interest in marriage and family life. And they married when they were very young, especially those who married toward the end of the baby boom. The median age of first marriage for women momentarily dipped as low as 19.9 in the late 1950s, compared to 22 in 1890. Marriage at an early age has proven to be one of the surest tickets to divorce.

This was the set of conditions that led Betty Friedan in 1963 to write *The Feminine Mystique*, helping to launch the modern women's movement and the remarkable and dramatic shift of mothers out of the home and into the workplace.[56] The proportion of married women in the labor force, already a quarter in 1950, climbed to about a third by 1960. Long before Betty Friedan raised the consciousness level of women concerning their situation, a minority of married women had grown restless and unhappy at having the sole role of motherhood; or they went to work, especially as their children grew older, because the suburban lifestyle was expensive and more money was needed to pay off the new-house debts; or they wanted full-time careers. Whatever the reasons, as more married women entered the labor force, the fundamental axis of the modern nuclear family fell by the wayside.

The Situation of Men

Men, too, were becoming restless in the modern nuclear family. Barbara Ehrenreich has suggested in her classic book *The Hearts of Men* that a "male revolt" took place during the 1950s, away from the breadwinner role and into the playboy role.[57] The growing "unreliability" of men as fathers and husbands was a major reason, she maintains, for female flight from the modern nuclear family. Although the conditions for male revolt did not suddenly arise in the 1950s with the publication of *Playboy*, it is undeniable that, fueled by the media, the expressive life of self-development and self-gratification became more and more attractive to men. The sexual revolution was gradually taking hold.

The early median age of first marriage in the late baby-boom years was even more significant for men than for women. That age was just 22.6 in 1955 versus 26.1 in 1890 at the height of the Victorian era. Arguably, these young married men had not yet had time to sow their wild oats before marrying, and when new sexual opportunities opened up, they found them harder to resist. Spurred by the longer periods of time during the day in which men were away from home in work and public places, together with the increased presence of women in those locales, rates of male marital infidelity increased.

Teenage Subculture

Also making life in the 1950s unstable—and certainly containing the seeds of social change—was the continued growth of a teenage subculture. The teenage phenomenon that had emerged during the war became a tidal wave, and the peer-oriented subculture of teenagers boomed under the careful prompting of advertisers and the mass media that were feeding on the new, prosperity-driven purchasing power of youth. Movies, radio, popular magazines, comic books, and records became in aggregate probably a more important influence on the young than education or even their parents. To these was added television, the most ubiquitous, influential, and consequential medium of them all. In 1946 only a fraction of 1 percent of American households had television sets; by 1960, 90 percent did.[58]

Through increasingly distinctive dress, music, and mannerisms, many teenagers and young adults of the era demonstrated that they desired an existence separate from and beyond the control of their parents. Their values became more liberal, sometimes radical or deviant. Coming from economically secure and intact families, they could afford to take stable family life and bourgeois virtues for granted; what many sought instead was a youthful excitement, adventure, and stimulation. In the process, they gradually picked up the threads of modernism that had been left dangling by the onset of the depression and World War II.

The mass media and entertainment industries helped in this endeavor both by exposing the imperfections, pretensions, and dishonesties of the bourgeois lifestyle and by serving as an accessible source of countercultural values. Thanks in part to the mass media, such as the enormously popular *Mad* magazine, the intellectual life of the young was becoming heavy with cynicism and nihilism. Thanks to the movies and to popular music, a more open sensuality was palpable.

It was said at the time that many youth were becoming "alienated." A clear source of alienation was the crass materialism of the era, a theme that resonated in J. D. Salinger's runaway best-seller *Catcher in the Rye,* first published in 1951. One path for the alienated was to "drop out." Another was to become highly idealistic. Coming from relatively secure and prosperous families, many idealistic young people were shocked to learn that poverty, deprivation, and racism were still very prevalent in America, and they embarked on a campaign to eradicate them.

Still another path was delinquency. Juvenile delinquency in both city and suburb increased substantially during the 1950s, and that issue overshadowed all others at the White House Conference on Children and Youth in 1960. Youth in the deteriorating inner cities became isolated and often lived in poverty. And the suburbs, which had many attributes desirable for raising infants and children, proved to be relatively unsuitable for teenagers. Teenagers found them dull and boring, with few facilities and services catering to their needs, and the suburbs' virtually complete automobile orientation left teenagers heavily disenfranchised in terms of geographic mobility.[59] From an adult perspective, the informal mechanisms of social control, such as neighborhood vigilance, which had been so effective in small-town America, were breaking down.

The Psychological Interior of Fifties Families

Very little of a negative nature was written at the time about the psychological life of 1950s families. The social critics leveled their most pointed attacks at the rise of complex organizations, the new conformity in the world of work, and the fall of "inner-directed" man, which essentially meant the decline of Victorian "character." Yet the youth rebellion from this family form in the 1960s was so severe that something must have been wrong. If these families were so warm and democratic and child-centered, why did so many youth forsake them?

The psychological interior of many structurally intact and seemingly together families in the 1950s was not quite how it appeared to outsiders. The family, like other social institutions, had quietly become an arena not just for the expression of social obligation but even more for adult self-fulfillment. And a supercharged arena it was. Expectations for love, happiness, and the good life within the family had reached new heights, and social alternatives were few. With such high expectations many adults were bound to end up disenchanted, disappointed, and discontented. And this is what happened to both husbands and wives.

As psychologist Herbert Hendin long ago pointed out:

> More than any generation before them, the mothers [of the fifties] had great hopes for personal fulfillment and growth that were likely to conflict with the needs and demands of small children. . . . Women who had given up or postponed career aspirations sometimes felt engulfed in resentment of their children and self-hatred for letting themselves down as well.[60]

In the socially isolated world of the modern suburb, many of these unhappy mothers in their "companionate" marriages had only their husbands to rely on for emotional support. Yet many men, when faced with unhappy wives and the seemingly endless emotional turmoil of a large family, a psychological realm for which they felt constitutionally ill suited, simply withdrew into their work or the company of friends. Their commute to work, as it were, became longer and longer; their psychological distance from the family greater and greater. The result: not only unhappy mothers but increasingly distant and unavailable fathers and, of course, children who were caught in the middle.

And so, with discontented, stir-crazy mothers and disgruntled, psychologically distant fathers and youth who abandoned it, the cultural reign of the modern nuclear family, after only a one-hundred-fifty-year existence, was coming to an end. The attempt to resurrect the Victorian family had failed.

CONCLUDING REMARKS

Many of the underlying social trends that eventually struck down the modern nuclear family, as we have seen, had their origins as far back as the last century. The overreliance on romantic love to the exclusion of social obligation; the increasing focus of marriage on the self-fulfillment of adults; the decline of a religious bond; the growing role specialization of fathers and their removal from day-to-day family activities; the movement of married women into the labor force. These are all trends of "modernity"—of rationalism, secularism, individualism, materialism. And up to now, at least, these trends have been on a linear course. No modern, Western society has become continuously less rational, secular, individualistic, or materialistic, although that could happen sometime in the future. From this perspective, the fifties are best seen as an aberration or temporary cyclical variation in some aspects of the long-term trend, an era when Victorian values showed a final burst of energy before becoming exhausted.

It would be nice if we had a precise date of death for the modern nuclear family, but we don't. Indeed, in sizable segments of the population, this family form lingers on to this day. Let us just say that as a widespread cultural ideal it died during the 1960s and 1970s. Most women today are relieved that it is gone, but the attitude of men is not so clear. In any event, there is no going back. Families are not only shapers but products of society, and the historical conditions that generated the modern nuclear family are no longer with us.

Yet the modern nuclear family was a signal human achievement in the organization of intimate lives, and it still has much to teach us. This is especially so since, to date, no fully satisfactory alternative has been discovered. This family represented a bargain between men and women. Men would sacrifice for their wives by working hard to provide economic support and constraining their sexual appetites if women would sacrifice for their husbands by staying at home and providing them with sex, children, and a warm domestic environment. Both husband and wife would sacrifice for their children.

For much of its history, there was not a strong sense of self-sacrifice in this bargain on the part of either husband or wife. Family behavior was seen simply as a necessary part of the struggle for existence and the optimum survival of children. Today not only is there a growing sense of real, personal sacrifice, but the bargain has largely been broken. Women no longer want to stay at home, and men have lost their exclusive breadwinning role. Both husband and wife can get all the sex they want outside of marriage. And where the bargain still remains, trust that both husband and wife will hold to it in the long term has badly deteriorated.

The greatest legacy of the demise of the modern nuclear family is the decline of fatherhood, the dimensions of which were described in chapter 1. For the simple reason that motherhood is more natural and fatherhood more cultural, the cultural bonds of the modern nuclear family were always more important for men than for women. Women are still having children but without men to help care for them. Men are still having children but feeling little obligation to help raise them.

To bring women and men back together and to hold them together for the sake of the children requires some kind of new bargain between them. In this, while we cannot go back, we can certainly learn from the past. What will it take to hold men to their children? And what should their new role in the family be, now that exclusive breadwinning is lost? That discussion is to come in the final chapter.

Part Three

Why Fathers Matter

5. What Do Fathers Do?

What is it that fathers actually do for children and families, such that their absence could generate the profound negative consequences discussed in earlier chapters? Drawing on an array of evidence from the social sciences, this chapter attempts to provide answers to this crucial question. As we shall see, the involved father not only greatly benefits his children but the children's mother as well—in a surprising way.

Much of what fathers contribute to child development, of course, is simply the result of being a second adult in the home. Other things being equal, two adults are far better than one in raising children. As the distinguished developmental psychologist Urie Bronfenbrenner has noted, the quality of interaction between principal caregiver and child depends heavily "on the availability and involvement of another adult, a *third party* who assists, encourages, spells off, gives status to, and expresses admiration and affection for the person caring for and engaging in joint activity with the child."[1]

In fact, as detailed earlier, children with two adults to take care of them have an enormous advantage over children with only one parent. Childrearing is a demanding, stressful, and often exhausting activity that continues nonstop for at least eighteen years. Two adults can not only support and spell one another; they can help counteract each other's deficiencies and contribute to each other's strengths. Two adults will invariably bring different skills and perspectives to a child, and they will bring access to two different social networks of relatives, friends, acquaintances, and work associates. They will likely be able to provide more economic resources as well.

But beyond being merely a second adult or third party, fathers—men—bring an array of positive inputs to a child, unique and irreplaceable qualities that women do not ordinarily bring. Despite their many similarities, males and females are different to the core. They think differently and act differently. Differences have universally been found in aggression and general activity level, cognitive skills, sensory sensitivity, and sexual and reproductive behavior. By every indication the expression of these differences is important for child development.

Moreover, the biological father—not just any man—is the most likely person to bring these inputs. The biological father is by far the most plausible candidate for enduring third-party status. He not only has the genetic tie to his child but also, usually, the sexual and emotional tie to the child's mother. His biologically based interest in the well-being of the child is generally far greater than that of any other male. Especially in modern societies, a child who does not have a close and sustaining relationship with her or his biological father is far less likely to have such a relationship with any adult male.

It is a father's task to help raise his children so that they can be constructive members of society, to transmit to his children those cultural values they must have to succeed in life. Many tomes have been written on the topic of what men bring to this task that women cannot, or ordinarily do not, bring; the list of possible factors is great. Much of the writing is speculative and based mostly on intuition or personal experience. Here I shall stick to those fatherly traits that have a body of social science evidence in their support.

PROTECTING AND PROVIDING

The first father roles that men presumably played in human evolution were protector and provider for women and children. Males tend to be physically stronger than women; they are also more aggressive and take more risks. In times past, families without male protectors were highly vulnerable. Even today, when families are not so vulnerable, it is almost always the man—if available—who is expected to go downstairs at night when a strange noise is heard or break up the fight between neighborhood children or lead the way in the dark.

Despite the rise of police forces, armies, and criminal justice systems, the male as protector has by no means outlived his usefulness. Fathers act as protectors of their daughters from child abuse by strangers, protectors of their sons from violence, protectors of their wives from rape and assault, and protectors of their homes and neighborhoods from intrusion and disorder. As James Q. Wilson has observed: "Neighborhood standards may be set by mothers but they are enforced by fathers, or at least by adult males. Neighborhoods without fathers are neighborhoods without men able and willing to confront errant youth, chase threatening gangs, and reproach delinquent fathers."[2]

Even when men are not actually engaged in protecting, of course, their physical strength is often well put to other uses. Their gender advantage of at least 25 percent more "upper body strength," as every woman knows, can prove indispensable for changing tires, lifting heavy boxes, and repairing the plumbing.

Throughout human history men have also been the main providers for their families; they were expected to garner resources and share those resources with their wives and children. Yet men have typically shared the task with women, just as they do today in advanced societies. Originally it was man the hunter, woman the gatherer; in agricultural societies both women and men typically "worked the farm." The male as *exclusive* breadwinner, the pattern in the modern nuclear family of industrial societies, has not been widespread historically.

To the degree that providing is thought of as the only father role, then, it is no wonder that some people today think of fathers as superfluous. Mothers can now be breadwinners on an almost equal footing with men. Moreover, there is a realization that the government can step in and be the provider if need be.

Still, the provider role of men should by no means be discounted. It is a universal male role, and one that most family men in America feel morally compelled to play. Indeed, many men feel that breadwinning is almost an innate quality of being an adult male and father. The loss of a job, for example, is often catastrophic for a man's sense of worth and self-esteem.

Most women, no matter how much they themselves may contribute to the family's resources, still expect the male to be a resource provider. Few males are more scorned by women than ne'er-do-well bums. Indeed, the world over, breadwinning potential ranks as a primary reason males are selected as mates. As evolutionary psychologist David M. Buss has recently noted, "The evolution of the female preference for males who offer resources may be the most ancient and pervasive basis for female choice in the animal kingdom." He finds that, even today, women "value good financial prospects in a mate roughly twice as much as men do."[3]

It is often said that just as females most want to be "cherished" by their mates, males most want to be "needed" by theirs. More than anything else, "being needed," for a man, involves his ability to provide resources.

THE UNIQUE CONTRIBUTIONS OF FATHERS

Protection and provision only scratch the surface of what fathers do in modern societies. With most other male and female adults gone from the childrearing scene, fathers have come to play an indispensable direct role in childrearing. They are expected to give their children guidance, instruction, encouragement, care, and love. In giving these things, men bring to their children something quite different from what mothers bring. The unique contributions of fathers, in turn, are strongly related to successful child outcomes.

Role Models

One of the most significant qualities of being a father, and certainly the most frequently cited, is serving as a role model. Imitation, or modeling, is one of the most potent learning processes. As someone once said, "Children want to see a sermon, not hear it."[4]

Fathers are role models for both their sons and their daughters. For the lack of male role models, father-deprived children of each sex are at a marked disadvantage in human relationships. As a recent research review concluded: "Fathers who are available provide important experiences and models for children that can help them gain greater competence and maturity . . . the responsive participation of fathers in their children's lives, both when they are young and when they are adolescent, has a significant impact on those children's later lives and will be evident years later during their children's early adult years."[5]

Through identification and imitation, sons learn from their fathers, as they cannot from their mothers, how to be a man. Making the shift from boyhood to constructive manhood is one of life's most difficult transitions, especially since boys as they grow up must break away from the comforting female arena of their mothers. They typically do this through identifying and bonding with their fathers.[6]

Involved fathers, assuming that their sons love and respect them, can have an enormous impact on the development of appropriately masculine character traits in their sons. Sons learn from their fathers about male responsibility and achievement, about how to be suitably assertive and independent, and how to relate acceptably to the opposite sex. Sons who experience a rejecting, incompetent, or absent father often grow up with a highly conflicted sense of masculinity, what psychiatrist Samuel Osherson, based on a longitudinal study of 370 men plus his own extensive clinical practice, calls "a wounded father within."[7]

Adult male role models are especially important for controlling the behavior of teenage boys. The discipline and authority that men bring to raising boys are very difficult for a woman alone to achieve. Without adult males around, teenage boys will necessarily turn excessively to their peers and to the antisocial behavior that male teenage peer groups often engender. We shall look below in detail at the process through which boys who lack adult males in their lives become so much more prone to teenage delinquency and violence.

The pathway to adulthood for daughters is somewhat easier than it is for sons in the sense that daughters need not break away so fully from their mothers' domain. But they still must learn from their fathers, as they cannot from their mothers, how to relate to men. They learn from their fathers about heterosexual trust, intimacy, and difference. They learn to appreciate their own femininity from the one male who is most special in their lives, again assuming that they love and respect their fathers. Most importantly, through loving and being loved by their fathers, they learn that they are love-worthy.

In addition, daughters learn from their fathers much that will be of value in their work and professional lives, especially the skills they need for coping in a still male-dominated world. They learn about assertiveness, independence, and achievement. Girls with supportive fathers are, in general, more successful in their careers.

Fatherless girls are generally disadvantaged at a later stage in life than fatherless boys, but the effects are no less striking. We shall see below how the input of fathers is critical for the prevention of teenage female promiscuity and unwed childbearing.

Different Parenting Styles

In almost all of their interactions with children, fathers do things a little differently from mothers. What fathers do—their special parenting style—is not only highly complementary to what mothers do, but by all indications important in its own right for optimum childrearing.

Play. An often overlooked dimension of fathering is play. From their children's birth through adolescence, fathers tend to emphasize play more than caretaking. This may be troubling to egalitarian feminists, and it would be wise for most fathers to spend more time in caretaking. Yet fathers' play should not be taken lightly. Although its full importance remains to be determined, play in various forms among the young appears to be critical for later development. This is an important recent finding of animal studies. Offspring who do not engage in sufficient play activities suffer a variety of negative developmental consequences.[8]

For human beings, the fathers' style of play seems to have unusual significance. Fathers' play is likely to be both physically stimulating and exciting, typically consisting of what has been called a rough-and-tumble approach.[9] Among infants it involves more bouncing and lifting. Among older children it involves more physical games and teamwork that require the competitive testing of physical and mental skills, and it frequently resembles an apprenticeship or teaching relationship: "Come on, let me show you how."

Mothers, of course, also play with their children. In fact, because they spend so much more time with their children, mothers actually play more with children than fathers do. But mothers' play is different. Mothers' play tends to take place more "at the child's level." Mothers provide the child with the opportunity to direct the play, to be in charge, to proceed at the child's own pace. In the short run, at least, children seem to prefer their fathers' more physically arousing style of play. In one study of 2½-year-olds who were given a choice of play partners, more than two thirds chose to play with their fathers.[10]

The benefits of fathers' play have shown up in child development areas ranging from the management of emotions to intelligence and academic achievement. Fathers' play appears to be particularly important for the development of socially acceptable forms of behavior that do not include violence and aggression—in other words, for the development of the character trait known as *self-control*. According to one expert, "children who roughhouse with their fathers . . . usually quickly learn that biting, kicking, and other forms of physical violence are not acceptable."[11] They learn when "enough is enough" and when to "shut it down."

A committee assembled by the Board on Children and Families of the National Research Council (a group sponsored by the National Academy of Sciences and the Institute of Medicine) concluded, "Children learn critical lessons about how to recognize and deal with highly charged emotions in the context of playing with their fathers. Fathers, in effect, give children practice in regulating their own emotions and recognizing others' emotional clues."[12]

Experimental studies with animals have found that certain forms of play in childhood are crucial to controlling later aggression. And studies among humans have found that self-control is a trait notably lacking among adult criminals. The findings of a study of convicted murderers in Texas are probably not based on coincidence—90 percent of the murderers either did not play as children or played abnormally.[13]

Competition, Risk Taking, Independence. Through their play, as well as in their other childrearing activities, fathers tend to stress competition, challenge, initiative, risk taking, and independence. Mothers in their caretaking roles, in contrast, stress emotional security and personal safety. On the playground, for example, fathers will try to get the child to swing ever higher, higher than the person on the next swing, while mothers will be cautious, worrying about the possible dangers. On an outing in the woods, fathers will want to hike the extra mile, while mothers will be more concerned about fatigue and the coming storm. (My own daughters remember fondly various family outings which included activities that my wife considered, at the time, to be "life threatening.")

These fundamental differences in parenting styles show up in the way fathers and mothers communicate with their children.[14] Fathers' conversations tend to be briefer and to be more directive and focused on specifics; they less often occur face-to-face. In content, fathers' conversations more often relate to issues of independence and autonomy. Mothers are much more likely to share their feelings and to engage in extended conversations; they are less directive and more verbally encouraging. The content of mothers' conversations emphasize interpersonal relationships.

Male-female differences even show up in the way infants are held. Psychologist Jerrold Lee Shapiro, who has interviewed thousands of dads and observed hundreds of families, finds that while mothers use touch in order to give a child comfort, fathers more often use touch in order to excite:

> When a mother picks up her infant, she tends to wrap the baby up toward her breasts, providing comfort, warmth, and security. By contrast, a father may well hold the child at arm's length and make eye contact, toss her in the air, turn her around so that her back is against his chest, or prop her up to look back over his shoulder. Each of these "daddy holds" underscores a sense of freedom.[15]

The complementarity of male and female parenting styles is striking and of enormous importance to a child's overall development. It is sometimes said that fathers express more concern for the child's longer-term development, while mothers focus on the child's immediate well-being (which, of course, in its own way has everything to do with a child's long-term well-being). What is clear is that children have dual needs that must be met: one for independence and the other for relatedness, one for challenge and the other for support.

Discipline. Differing parenting styles also show up strongly in the area of discipline. Because of their greater size and strength, fathers virtually everywhere are seen by children to be more powerful, threatening, and "authoritative." But in addition to this, the disciplinary approach of fathers tends to be "firm" while that of mothers tends to be "responsive." Mothers' discipline varies more from time to time, involves more bargaining, and is adjusted to the child's mood and context. It is seemingly based on a more intuitive understanding of the child's needs and emotions of the moment. Fathers, without the "special understanding" of mothers, necessarily rely on rules and principles. Based on this distinction, of course, mothers are often accused of being too soft, while fathers are accused of being too arbitrary and rigid.

That fathers almost everywhere have been the "disciplinarians of last resort" is no accident. When the emotional and context-tailored approach of mothers falls short, as sometimes happens, the fatherly rules and natural authority come into play. Fathers set the limits; they must be obeyed. Several studies have found that fathers are more effective than mothers at getting quick action ("clean up the toys").

If educational psychologist Carol Gilligan and her followers are correct, the two disciplinary approaches are rooted in a fundamental difference between men and women in their moral senses. Men stress justice, fairness, and duty (based on rules), while women stress sympathy, care, and helping (based on relationships).[16] This difference is apparent even in early childhood. Infant girls show more interest in people and faces than do infant boys. And in his classic study of the play of young children, the famed psychologist Jean Piaget found that girls are more concerned with relationships and boys with rules.[17]

In the area of discipline we again clearly see a complementarity of opposites in the parenting styles of men and women. While mothers provide an important flexibility and sympathy in their discipline, fathers provide ultimate predictability and consistency. Both dimensions are critical for an efficient, balanced, and humane childrearing regime.

Gender-Differentiated Parenting

The burden of social science evidence supports the idea that gender-differentiated parenting is important for human development and that the contribution of fathers to childrearing is unique and irreplaceable. A broad review of psychological research in the journal *Child Development,* for example, concluded that children of parents who are sex-typed are more "competent."[18] And a major study of the outcome of childrearing styles on adolescent development found that the most effective parenting was that which was both highly demanding and highly responsive.[19]

The significance of gender-differentiated parenting undoubtedly is related to something fundamental in the human condition. Psychosocial maturity and competence among humans consists of the integration of two factors: *communion,* or the need to be included, connected, and related; and *agency,* or the drive for independence, individuality, and self-fulfillment.[20] These terms (and many others could be substituted, such as expressive and instrumental, bonds and choice, or roots and wings) refer to the balance of psychic and social forces of which human life consists. One without the other is a denuded and impaired humanity, an incomplete realization of the human potential.

For many couples, to be sure, these factors are not rigidly divided along standard female-male lines. Significant overlap can exist among females and males in the range of gender-differentiated traits they express (and the degree of overlap is no doubt affected by culture and by environmental circumstance.) For some couples, there may even be a "role reversal," with men largely assuming the female style and women the male style. But these are exceptions that prove the rule. Throughout the world, gender-differentiated parenting occurs naturally in most father-mother families. And certainly, let us not forget, the factors of communion and agency are extremely difficult for either a man or a woman *alone* to combine effectively.

Gender-differentiated parenting is of such importance that in childrearing by homosexual couples, either gay or lesbian, one partner commonly fills the male-instrumental role while the other fills the female-expressive role. Unfortunately, we do not yet have good data about the child outcomes of these same-sex arrangements. Not enough such couples have been studied, and there has not been enough follow-up time to see results.

In focusing on the independent contributions of males and females, of course, the profound significance for children of the relationship that a father and a mother have *with each other* should not be overlooked. Children learn about male-female relationships by seeing how their parents relate to each other. Children learn about trust, intimacy, and caring between the sexes. Most importantly, their parents' relationship provides children with a model of the most meaningful heterosexual relationship that the great majority of individuals will have during their lifetimes—marriage.

FATHER INVOLVEMENT AND CHILD OUTCOMES

The behavioral research conducted over the past few decades indicates that children benefit greatly from a high level of father involvement. The more that fathers are involved in the day-to-day activities of their children—assuming the fathers are warm and sensitive to their children's needs—the better off in life those children will be.[21] After reviewing the accumulated evidence in his recent book *Fathers and Families: Paternal Factors in Child Development,* the noted psychologist and longtime student of fatherhood Henry B. Biller sums up: "The father is extremely important for the child's intellectual, emotional and social development."[22]

Fathers the world over become especially influential in the lives of their older children, with whom they have more direct contact. But as the research just discussed suggests, they can have a significant impact on their younger children as well. Of special importance is the fact that early bonding between father and child is strongly associated with a father's later desire to want to maintain contact with that child. In other words, father care, more than mother care, is learned behavior; to be a good father to their older children, it is critical for men to develop strong attachments to those children when they are young.

Intellectual Competence and Academic Achievement

Father involvement is related to improved quantitative and verbal skills, improved problem solving ability, and enhanced academic achievement in their children. For daughters, several studies have found that the presence of the father is one of the determinants of proficiency in mathematics.[23] And one pioneering study found that the amount of time fathers spent reading was a strong predictor of their daughters' verbal ability.[24]

For sons, who can more directly model their father's behavior, the results have been even more striking. A number of studies have uncovered a strong relationship between father involvement and the quantitative and mathematical abilities of their sons. Other studies have found a relationship between paternal nurturing and boys' verbal intelligence.[25]

The processes through which fathers bring these intellectual benefits are not yet clear. No doubt it is partly a matter of having a second adult devoted to the child and of having a higher income that enables greater access to educational resources. But it is probably also related to the unique mental and behavioral qualities that men bring to children, the male sense of play, reasoning, challenge, and problem solving, and the traditional male association with achievement and occupational advancement. Unfortunately, the current research does not enable us to distinguish among these different factors.

Empathy

Especially in individualistic and competitive societies such as the United States where, compared to traditional societies, everyday life is not so marked by cooperation and helping among kin and neighbors, the social order is heavily dependent upon children learning what is called "prosocial behavior"—behavior directed toward helping others. And nothing is more important for the development of prosocial children and teenagers than the teaching of *empathy*—the ability to experience the thoughts, feelings, and attitudes of another person. In other words, in order to have law-abiding, cooperative, and compassionate adults, we must first teach them as children to cultivate feelings of empathy.

We don't often think of fathers in connection with the teaching of empathy; it would seem to be more the province of mothers. But involved fathers, it turns out, may be of special importance for the development of this character trait. A twenty-six-year longitudinal study examined the relationship between parental behavior in early childhood and "empathic concern" in adults—"the tendency to experience feelings of sympathy and compassion for others." The researchers' main finding was "quite astonishing": the most important childhood factor of all is "paternal involvement in child care." Fathers who spent time alone with their children more than twice a week, giving meals, baths, and other basic care, reared the most compassionate adults. This single factor accounted for a greater percentage of the adult outcome than the three strongest maternal predictors combined, which included "maternal inhibition of child's aggression" and "maternal tolerance of dependent behavior."[26]

Again, it is not yet clear why fathers are so important. Perhaps merely being with their children provides a model for compassion. Perhaps it has to do with their style of play or mode of reasoning. Perhaps it is somehow related to the fact that fathers typically are the family's main arbiter with the outside world. Or perhaps it is because when mothers receive help from fathers and are thus freed from some of the instrumental demands of childrearing, they are more able themselves to promote empathic concerns. Whatever the reason, it is hard to think of a more important contribution that fathers can make to their children.

Psychological Well-Being

Involved and caring fathers are important, finally, for the psychological well-being of their children, including happiness, life satisfaction, and the absence of psychological distress. Many interview studies of happy and successful adults have discovered that a central fact of their lives was having had such fathers as children.[27] One study that looked at the life course of several hundred children, first interviewed in 1951, found that the offspring of warm and affectionate fathers were much more likely in 1986—when they were in their forties—to be happily married and mentally healthy and to report good relationships with friends.[28]

For young adults, having a continuing, close relationship with their fathers has been found to be a significant contributor to their sense of well-being. After taking note of the likelihood that most families in which fathers are highly involved are also those in which mothers are especially caring and competent, and that many studies of two-parent families have failed to separate the father's independent effect on well-being from that of the mother's, sociologist Paul Amato recently completed a study in which he carefully distinguished "closeness to father" from "closeness to mother" among older children and young adults.

He found that closeness to fathers, as measured by such indicators as understanding, trust, respect, affection, and fairness, makes a unique contribution to the psychological well-being of both daughters and sons. Young adults who feel emotionally close to their fathers tend to be happier and more satisfied in life, regardless of their feelings toward their mothers.[29]

Feeling emotionally close to one's father also has been shown to be of great psychological value for children who go through a divorce. The quality of the relationship between children and their divorced fathers, for example, is a strong indicator of how well adolescents are able to adjust to divorce.[30] It is important to note that the quality of the relationship between child and father seems to be more important than frequency of contact. The evidence is not entirely clear on this, but large national surveys consistently show only limited statistical association between nonresident fathers' visits and children's well-being.[31]

WHY BIOLOGICAL FATHERS?

We have discussed why fathers are needed in childrearing, but does it make a difference whether or not the father is biologically related to the child? According to the available evidence, the answer is a resounding yes.

One of the surprising findings of family-related research in recent years is that the presence of stepfathers may actually aggravate childrearing problems and thereby increase the level of negative child outcomes.[32] We saw in chapter 2 how the increase of surrogate fathers in the lives of children is strongly related to rising rates of child abuse, especially the most serious forms of child abuse. Similarly, stepfathers are implicated in juvenile delinquency.

In one 1985 study, a nationally representative sample of over one thousand families with children aged six to eighteen were interviewed, and about three quarters of the families were reinterviewed five to six years later. At both the initial and reinterview times it was found that children living with biological fathers exhibited the least delinquency, and children with stepfathers had the *most* disordered behavior. Single-parent children fell in between. These findings persisted even when ethnicity and social class were controlled.[33] Another major study of stepfamilies, which found similarly negative child outcomes, concluded that "stepfather-child relations became more negative over time . . . particularly for stepfathers and boys."[34]

In their recent review of the major studies, McLanahan and Sandefur found that living in a stepfamily was no better than living in a single-parent family in terms of child outcomes; the rates of high school dropouts and teen births in the two family situations, for example, were essentially the same. Of course, the income level of stepfamilies is well above that of single-parent families, and that is a distinct advantage. But the economic advantage is typically not enough to offset the many social disadvantages. They conclude that "stepfathers are less likely to be committed to the child's welfare than biological fathers, and they are less likely to serve as a check on the mother's behavior. Rather than assisting with the responsibilities of parenting, stepfathers sometimes compete with the child for the mother's time, adding to the mother's and the child's level of stress."[35]

Stepparents have been found in large numbers to become "disengaged" in the rearing of unrelated children, exhibiting relatively little warmth, control, or supervision.[36] This is a condition which likely has an evolutionary basis, as we shall fully discuss in the following chapter. Parenting is fundamentally rooted in human biology, and it is at least partly activated by the "genetically selfish" activity of favoring one's own relatives. From this perspective, childrearing by nonrelatives is inherently problematic.[37]

The parental relationship—fathering included—is unique in human affairs, evolutionary psychologists Martin Daly and Margo Wilson have pointed out. In most social relationships the reciprocity of benefits is carefully monitored, and an imbalance is regarded as exploitative. But in the parental relationship "the flow of benefits is prolongedly, cumulatively, and ungrudgingly unbalanced." Only biological parents are fully attuned to accepting such an unbalanced flow of benefits because "organisms have evolved to expend their very lives enhancing the fitness prospects of their descendants." "Parental investment is a precious resource," Daly and Wilson stress, "and selection must favor those parental psyches that do not squander it on nonrelatives."[38]

This is not to deny, of course, that strong feelings of parental love can be activated in substitute and adoptive parents nor to take anything away from the many devoted and involved stepfathers. The only point is that paternal feelings and paternal love—due to their very special nature—are inherently more difficult for men to develop toward children who are unrelated to them.

LOSING A FATHER THROUGH DEATH

The death of a father is no longer a major cause of father loss for children. Only about 6 percent of single mothers today are widows. Yet the consequences of losing a father through death are so different from losing a father through divorce or out-of-wedlock birth that a discussion of the phenomenon is important for presenting a complete picture of what fathers do.

Many studies have indicated that the negative effects on children of a father's death are far fewer than those of a father's divorce or absence through nonmarital birth. Sara McLanahan and Gary Sandefur determined the chances of dropping out of high school before completion to be 37 percent for children born out of wedlock and 31 percent for children of divorce but only 15 percent for children whose father died, a figure that had no "statistically significant difference" from the 13 percent for nondisrupted families. For becoming a teenage mother, the chances are 37 percent for girls born out of wedlock and 33 percent for girls of divorce but only 21 percent for girls whose fathers died; in this case, there was a statistically significant difference from the 11 percent chance for girls from nondisrupted families.[39]

Some common findings of social research are that both the daughters and sons whose fathers die are more likely than children from intact families to be submissive, dependent, and introverted—in other words, less traditionally masculine—and the daughters are more likely to be anxious and shy around men.[40] These traits are plausible effects of losing a male role model. At the same time, such children suffer much less than the children of divorce and nonmarital birth from a sense of rejection, with its associated loss of self-esteem and behavioral problems. This is because the nature of the father loss, based on uncontrollable external rather than interrelational factors, is entirely different. The marital hostility and discord, faultfinding, and family trauma that commonly precede divorce are absent. And the death of a parent typically involves fewer life changes for the child than does divorce; widowed mothers tend to be financially better off than divorced mothers, and relatives and friends are more likely to provide assistance.

After a period of bereavement, the child of a widowed mother normally comes to accept the "natural" reality of the loss. The lingering feelings of conflict, resentment, and guilt associated with divorce are absent, as are feelings of betrayal and abandonment by the absent father. Often, in fact, the child carries an idealized image of the dead father that can be consoling and even uplifting.

Ironically, a dead father is typically a more effective father than one who is missing.[41] When a father dies, his favorable reputation is still maintained; his picture still hangs on the wall; he is still a positive presence, a force, even an arbiter ("what would your father think of that behavior?") in the lives of his children. Thus, in a symbolic sense he continues to hold a position of authority, influence, and moral leadership in the home.

FATHERS AND TEEN DELINQUENCY AND VIOLENCE

The unique contributions of fathers can be examined in more detail by looking at several problem areas in which the presence of fathers is important. In chapter 2 we set forth the data linking fatherlessness to delinquency and suggested that fathers are needed to control the overly aggressive behavior of their children, especially their sons, if teenage delinquency and violence are to be curtailed. We are now in a position to describe what fathers do to help prevent delinquency and violence and the process through which they do it.

At the outset it is important to note that distinguishing the etiology of violent behavior from other forms of deviant or antisocial behavior is very difficult. We do not really understand why some antisocial people are more violent while others are less so. So the discussion is best framed in terms of what generates antisocial behavior in general.

One highly significant empirical finding can serve as starting point. There is strong evidence that tendencies toward antisocial behavior first emerge in childhood and are relatively stable across the stages of life into adulthood.[42] This is especially true of male aggressiveness.[43] Most adult criminals, in other words, manifested antisocial tendencies already in childhood (that is not to say that all antisocial children become adult criminals). As one researcher succinctly put the matter: "Early antisocial behavior is the best predictor of later antisocial behavior";[44] in the words of another, "Adult antisocial behavior virtually requires childhood antisocial behavior."[45] The strong relationship between childhood antisocial behavior and later criminality prevails even when childhood economic status and IQ are held constant.[46]

Antisocial behavior in children is thought, by most current experts in the study of human behavior, to result partly from childhood experience and partly from genetic inheritance. Indeed, the overwhelming evidence of most credible recent research indicates that genetically based factors are of much greater importance than most social scientists commonly grant.[47] Yet there are no indications that the genetic makeup of American children has markedly changed over the past thirty years, when rates of fatherlessness, juvenile delinquency, and violence have skyrocketed.

Which childhood experiences are most important? Family, neighborhood, peer group, and popular culture all play some role. General agreement exists within the social science community, however, that antisocial behavior in children is heavily a product of the socialization and social control processes employed by parents. James Q. Wilson, one of America's leading criminological experts, attests: "A large body of data has demonstrated beyond much doubt the powerful effect on aggressiveness and delinquency of being raised in a family that is discordant, lacking in affection, or given to inappropriate disciplinary practices."[48]

In their recent reanalysis of the pioneering data set first collected in the late 1930s and early 1940s by Sheldon and Eleanor Glueck of the Harvard Law School, researchers Robert J. Sampson and John H. Laub found strong corroborating evidence for the importance of early childhood experiences. The Gluecks' data set, designed to uncover the causes of delinquency and adult crime, compared the life course from childhood to adulthood of five hundred delinquents with five hundred nondelinquents, all of whom were white males who grew up in the Boston slums. The Gluecks collected data from a wide variety of sources, including teacher reports, psychiatric interviews, health and welfare records, employer assessments, and extensive interviews with the subjects and their families. Sampson and Laub reached this conclusion: "Low levels of parental supervision, erratic, threatening, and harsh discipline, and weak parental attachment were strongly and directly related to delinquency."[49]

A recent authoritative report entitled *Violence,* prepared by the Panel on the Understanding and Control of Violent Behavior of the National Research Council, summarizes what we now know: "Researchers have identified many correlates and antecedents of aggressive childhood behavior that are presumed to reflect psychosocial influences [including] early family experiences: harsh and erratic discipline, lack of parental nurturance, physical abuse and neglect, poor supervision, and early separation of children from parents."[50] The report continues: "Numerous studies show that violent offenders tend to come from certain types of family backgrounds. In particular, they tend to have been subjected to physical punishment, they tend to have alcoholic or criminal parents, and they tend to have disharmonious parents who are likely to separate or divorce."[51]

Where do fathers fit into this picture? A major contribution of involved fathers, according to researchers, is to teach their children two key character traits: self-control and empathy. People with antisocial and criminal tendencies lack both of these traits; that is, they "tend to be impulsive, insensitive, physical (as opposed to mental), risk-taking, short-sighted, and nonverbal, and they will tend therefore to engage in criminal and analogous acts."[52]

The lack of self-control in adulthood is closely associated with the absence of powerful and necessary "inhibiting forces" in early childhood, forces which can now be identified with some clarity following several decades of intense study by social scientists.[53] These inhibiting forces consist of parental childrearing practices which are able "to set clear rules, to monitor behavior, and to make rewards contingent on good behavior and punishment contingent on bad behavior."[54] The development of empathy in children, in turn, is strongly associated with childrearing approaches that involve reasoning with children (rather than disciplining without reasoning), teaching about the consequences of their actions on others, and eschewing authoritarian and/or harsh disciplinary methods.[55]

It is entirely possible, of course, for a single mother to follow these childrearing practices and bring up children who possess a high degree of social control and empathy, but it is certainly more difficult for one parent than for two. The well-known criminologists Michael Gottfredson and Travis Hirschi have aptly described the situation:

> The single parent (usually a woman) must devote a good deal to support and maintenance activities that are at least to some extent shared in the two-parent family. Further, she must often do so in the absence of psychological or social support. As a result, she is less able to devote time to monitoring and punishment and is more likely to be involved in negative, abusive contacts with her children.[56]

The single mother's predicament is borne out by extensive social science findings. Much antisocial behavior among teenagers is peer-group related, for example, and it has been found that children from single-parent families are especially susceptible to antisocial peer pressures.[57] The National Health Examination Survey of 1966–1970, a representative sample of 6,710 noninstitutionalized youth of ages twelve to seventeen which compared mother-only families with families containing both biological parents, concluded that:

> Mother-only households are . . . associated with particular patterns of family decision making and adolescent deviance, even when family income and parental education are controlled. In contrast to adolescents in households with two natural parents, youth in mother-only households are perceived as more likely to make decisions without direct parental input and more likely to exhibit deviant behavior. The presence of an additional adult in a mother-only household, especially for males, is associated with increased parental control and a reduction in various forms of adolescent deviance. . . . We believe that a major reason for the increased deviance of youths in mother-only households is the absence of the second adult."[58]

The Second Adult

Unfortunately, not just any "second adult" will suffice. What about a second mother? In addition to the obvious desirability of providing a male role model, something two women cannot do, a father brings to childrearing, as we have noted, qualities that are especially applicable to the development of self-control and empathy. Especially for boys, the role of fathers in setting rules and limits, enforcing discipline, and maintaining parental authority should not be underestimated. For children of both sexes, the father's style of play and his ability to protect are extremely important factors.

What about grandmothers? As biologically related adults their strong "evolutionary" tie to their grandchildren might suggest that they, in some respects, could make satisfactory father substitutes, improving the outcome in what otherwise would be single-mother families. But in McLanahan and Sandefur's major analysis of the data, children living with a single mother and a grandmother fared *worse* as adolescents than did those living with just a single parent.[59] For example, they were twice as likely to drop out of high school. Similarly, a study of multigenerational African-American families found that the quality of parenting was lower than in single-mother families.[60] The main problem with multigenerational mother-grandmother families seems to be that a diffusion of parenting responsibility between the two parties is often dysfunctional and filled with conflict.[61]

What about stepfathers? We saw above that they cannot ordinarily take the place of biological fathers. The evidence relating fathering to violence suggests that, to reduce delinquency and violence, the child must be reared by a biological father. The National Health Examination Survey, for example, found that stepfamilies are no better than single-parent families in supervising their children.[62]

Protest Masculinity

One of the most prominent findings about the importance of fathering in preventing juvenile delinquency and violence was first disclosed by cross-cultural evidence gathered by anthropologists and comparative psychologists. Psychologist Henry Biller explains this finding as follows: "Males who are father deprived early in life are likely to engage later in rigidly overcompensatory masculine behaviors. The incidence of crimes against property and people, including child abuse and family violence, is relatively high in societies where the rearing of young children is considered to be an exclusively female endeavor."[63]

The association of hypermasculine behavior—or "protest masculinity"—with the absence of fathering was an early focus of social scientists who called themselves "culture and personality theorists." Drawing on the work of Sigmund Freud, they believed that boys who grew up without father involvement had to disengage themselves from the dominance of their mothers and gain a male identity in a socially problematic way. Such boys may find it necessary as a "defense mechanism" to devalue and reject their mothers; in the process, they become angry and fearful, and hostile toward women in general.

Two of the most prominent social scientists working within this tradition were the Harvard University husband-wife team of Beatrice and John Whiting. They believed that protest masculinity, or attempts to prove manliness through threatening or violent behavior and daring acts of physical strength and athletic prowess, was based largely on "an unconscious fear of being feminine" that arose in the absence of male role models.[64] In their classic cross-cultural study of childrearing, published in the 1970s, they found strong support for their views. Most cases of assault and homicide were found to occur in the two most "father-distant" cultures that they examined.[65]

Evolutionary theorists have recently devoted much attention to the phenomenon of protest masculinity, reexamining the cross-cultural evidence and placing it in a new theoretical perspective.[66] Pennsylvania State University's Patricia Draper and Henry Harpending summarize the nature of the behavior:

> . . . rejection of authority, particularly when it is imposed by adult females; exaggerated masculinity; . . . rejection and denigration of femininity; greater interpersonal aggressiveness; increased risk of incarceration; and a relatively exploitative attitude toward females, with sexual contact appearing important as conquest and as a means of validating masculinity.[67]

In line with a central assumption of evolutionary thought that people are predisposed, mostly on an unconscious level, to want to maximize their reproductive potential, Draper and Harpending have argued that such hypermasculine behavior among adolescent males is associated with a particular "reproductive strategy" that is largely learned in their growing-up years.[68] Males from fatherless homes learn that they are not expected to contribute to child care and that therefore no reproductive advantage is to be gained by carefully choosing a compatible mate and postponing reproduction. Instead, such males engage in competitive struggles with other males for short-run sexual conquests, struggles which typically involve aggressive and exploitative behavior.

While a complete explanation for protest masculinity remains to be developed, only a person who neither reads nor watches television and lives in total isolation could fail to realize the applicability of this phenomenon to modern social settings. Protest masculinity, of course, is most associated with our nation's inner cities, especially the 180 urban neighborhoods recently identified where at least 90 percent of all families are without fathers![69] Like other dimensions of urban living, it is spreading.

FATHERS AND UNWED TEEN CHILDBEARING

Just as fathers are important for preventing male delinquency and violence, so are they important for preventing another of the major social problems of our time—unwed teen childbearing. And as in the case of male delinquency, we now have a good understanding of what fathers do that is so consequential.

The classic work on the relationship between father involvement and the sexual and personality development of adolescent girls was done in the early 1970s by the prominent University of Virginia psychologist E. Mavis Hetherington.[70] Although methodologically unsophisticated by today's standards, the study, which followed the lives of adolescent girls into adulthood, sharply points up some central themes that have been verified by later, more rigorous, analyses.

Hetherington classified her female adolescent subjects into three groups: those from intact, father-present families; those who had lost their fathers through divorce; and those who had lost their fathers through death. Even before analyzing her first interview results, she came up with a striking finding. The interviewing was done by a male interviewer seated in a room with a desk and three other chairs. One chair was located very near the interviewer, a second was on the other side of the desk, and the third was about three feet away. Remarkable differences between the girls in the three groups were revealed by which chair they selected and by their behavior toward the male interviewer.

Girls from the father-present families took the chair that was medium-distant from the interviewer, and they related to the interviewer naturally and with ease. Girls from the divorced families tended to take the chair closest to the interviewer and assumed a rather seductive, sprawling, open posture. They leaned forward toward the interviewer and smiled more than the girls from the other groups. The girls from widowed families took the chair furthest from the interviewer and tended to sit upright, often looking away from the interviewer and not speaking very much.

The interactions which these girls had with the interviewer proved to be highly indicative of the relationships they had with males in general. The girls from intact families related to boys easily and on their own terms. They showed a quiet confidence in heterosexual relationships. The girls whose fathers had died tended to avoid boys and to be shy and inhibited when boys were around. Similarly, it was learned that during recreation center dances at school, they stayed at the girls' end, often in the back of a group of girls.

The girls from divorced homes, in contrast, sought out boys more and were more seductive toward them. At the recreation center dances, they spent much of their time at the boys' end of the stag line. They tended to be relatively promiscuous, engaging in more and earlier sexual relationships. Later investigation showed that they were more likely to marry at an earlier age than females in the other groups, often to inappropriate men; to become pregnant before marriage; and eventually to divorce.

As might be guessed, the interview responses found that the girls from intact homes had generally positive perceptions of their fathers, while the girls of divorce had very negative perceptions. The girls whose fathers had died tended to remember their fathers with idealized images.

Fathers are the first and most important men in the lives of girls. They provide male role models, accustoming their daughters to male-female relationships. Engaged and responsive fathers play with their daughters and guide them into challenging activities. They protect them, providing them with a sense of physical and emotional security. Girls with adequate fathering are more able, as they grow older, to develop constructive heterosexual relationships based on trust and intimacy.[71]

A number of studies have found that girls with involved fathers have a stronger "internal locus of control." That is, they are more independent and self-possessed, more likely to assume responsibility for the consequences of their actions, and more likely to perceive themselves as masters of their own fate.[72] Stronger internal control has been found to be associated not only with lower levels of problem behaviors but also with higher academic achievement and overall self-esteem.

For girls whose fathers are not involved, many positive character and personality traits fail to be developed. Girls deprived of strong relationships with their fathers tend to grow up with the perception that men are irresponsible and untrustworthy. As adolescents they commonly become obsessed with heterosexual relationships. In a desperate search for substitute forms of male affection, some have inappropriate sexual contacts, become overly dependent on men, and allow men to take advantage of them. Studies in many different cultures have found the same pattern: Father-deprived girls "show precocious sexual interest, derogation of masculinity and males, and poor ability to maintain sexual and emotional adjustment with one male."[73]

Teen Promiscuity

There may be an evolutionary basis for the problematic sexual behavior of adolescent girls from father-deprived households, just as for the hypermasculine behavior of father-deprived adolescent males discussed above. In line with the central assumption that people are predisposed to want to maximize their reproductive potential, evolutionists argue that this pattern of adolescent sexual behavior, as in the case of boys, is linked to a particular "reproductive strategy," one learned by girls during their growing-up years.

The argument is this: A girl from a father-absent home learns that males are unreliable and that enduring adult heterosexual relationships involving a high male contribution to childrearing cannot reasonably be anticipated. Rather than postpone reproduction and seek the best man she can get, therefore, she takes advantage of every short-run sexual opportunity. "Seeking early investment from a succession of males," evolutionary thinkers suggest, "may be the only way in which she can regularly obtain any male parental investment at all."[74]

One recent paper written from an evolutionary perspective goes a step further to suggest that the experience of growing up in a stressful family, such as that generated by father absence, can affect not only behavior but physical changes in the body, specifically the timing of puberty. Taking note of the fact that the average age of menarche has been dropping and that daughters from divorced households were found to reach puberty a full six months earlier than age-mates from maritally intact families, the authors suggest that puberty will occur earlier among children who have stressful childhoods "dominated by rejecting or aversive parents."[75]

Lowered age of menarche is strongly associated with having sex and children earlier in life. Again, the explanation is that earlier menarche represents an opportunistic adaptation to a particular environment in which there is a low expectation for enduring adult relationships with men and male participation in childrearing. Whether the evolutionary thinkers are right or not, the kind of environment they describe sounds distressingly familiar to most Americans. Similarly, the motivations they reveal are those commonly expressed by the unmarried teenage mothers of our inner cities.

FATHER INVOLVEMENT AND THE STATUS OF WOMEN

The direct involvement of fathers in childrearing obviously eases the workload and reduces the stress on mothers, especially mothers who work outside the home. Yet it also appears to benefit women in a less obvious way—it may raise their public status. Some observers have suggested that the nuclear family is an obstacle to women's advancement and that getting men out of families might actually enhance women's status.[76] New evidence indicates that the opposite is closer to the truth—without male involvement in childrearing, the public status of women probably will remain low.

As the following chapter will detail, there is enormous cross-cultural variation in father-child relationships. When this variation is carefully examined, as sociologist Scott Coltrane has recently done by drawing on ethnographic description and quantitative data from ninety nonindustrial societies, it is found that "paternal proximity, affection, and responsibility for routine child care are positively associated with female participation in community decision making [and] female access to positions of authority."[77] In other words, the more that fathers help out with children, the more mothers are able to be full participants in their communities.

One does not need to look to nonindustrial societies to reach this conclusion. Among advanced societies, those which have the highest level of father involvement also have the most women in positions of authority. The nation in which fathers are most involved in childrearing, by all accounts, is Sweden. Some 25 to 30 percent of all Swedish fathers take some parental leave from their places of employment to care for their children. And Sweden is the nation which gained a new world's record in 1994 by electing a parliament (*Riksdag*) consisting of 41 percent women. Other Scandinavian nations are not far behind, both in father involvement and in the percentage of women in public life.

What is the connection between the direct involvement of fathers in childrearing and the public status of women? Women's primary responsibility for child care necessarily constrains their ability to exercise public power. Thus, male involvement in childrearing gives women more time to participate in nonfamily activities. Yet time alone does not translate easily into public power.

The study of women's participation in public life has focused less on father involvement as the underlying enabler than it has on the contribution of women to the economy. It is believed that women's public power is necessarily related to their economic power, their "control over the means of production." To the degree that women have control over money, it is argued, they will also have power.

But money and other economic resources apparently advance women only so far. Coltrane's study of nonindustrial societies found no consistent or statistically significant relationship between women's contribution to economic subsistence and their public status. And among industrial societies, while Swedish women have great power in public life, they do not have so much power in economic life. Virtually all Swedish women are in the labor force, for example, but they are significantly underrepresented in managerial positions in the Swedish economy.[78]

If it is not only their economic power that generates high public status for women, what other forces are at work? There is good reason to believe that women's climb to public power stems as much from the voluntary relinquishment of power by males as from a takeover of that power through economic means. The authority structures of virtually every society in the world have been, and mostly still are, dominated by males, yet in some societies men have been willing to share some of their power with women. What causes men to do this? The answer may lie in the way in which they were socialized in childhood. Here is what Scott Coltrane found: "Societies with father-present patterns of child socialization produce men who are less inclined to exclude women from public activities than their counterparts in father-absent societies."[79]

The linkage between male attitudes toward women in adulthood and the socialization of males in childhood was an early insight of Margaret Mead. In *Male and Female* (1949) she wrote of male exclusionary attitudes toward women in societies where men are relatively uninvolved in childrearing:

> In a great number of societies men's sureness of their sex role is tied up with their right, or ability, to practice some activity that women are not allowed to practice. Their maleness, in fact, has to be underwritten by preventing women from entering some field or performing some feat. Here may be found the relationship between maleness and pride; that is, a need for prestige that will outstrip the prestige which is accorded to any woman.[80]

Boys who grow up in societies where they have involved fathers and strong male role models, in contrast, do not have the same need to reject and dominate women and create exclusionary, all-male activities.[81] Moreover, just as a strong sexual division of labor in childrearing generates a strong sexual division of labor in society as a whole, as Nancy Chodorow has pointed out in her book *The Reproduction of Mothering,* so does male-female cooperation in childrearing lead to an expectation that there will be male-female cooperation in other areas of life.[82] Task sharing in the home seems to translate into task sharing in public life. It may also be the case that involved fathers sex-type their children less and thus promote in their daughters the kind of self-confidence and sense of autonomy that enables them to be stronger participants in the public sector. There is some evidence to that effect.[83]

The association between the contribution of fathers to childrearing and the public status of women needs more study and analysis, but the evidence available leads to the conclusion that as fatherlessness grows, women's status will drop. The underlying social process involved, again, is that the relationship boys (and girls) have with their fathers when they are growing up has a significant impact on their adult behavior and consequently on larger societal issues and problems.

CONCLUDING REMARKS

Fathers are far more than just "second adults" in the home. Involved fathers—especially biological fathers—bring positive benefits to their children that no other person is as likely to bring. They provide protection and economic support and male role models. They have a parenting style that is significantly different from that of mothers, and the difference is important in healthy child development. According to the evidence, fathers make important contributions to their children's intellectual competence, prosocial and compassionate behavior, and psychological well-being.

Father involvement in childrearing also brings an important benefit to women: It raises their public status. Children raised by involved fathers grow up to become adults who are more respectful of women and more willing to share with women broad social power and authority.

Clearly, expectations for fathers have been changing. From their ancient roles of protector and provider, men are being asked today to raise children pretty much as women have always done. Just how malleable are men in the fathering process? Are men really cut out to be "new fathers"? What did fathers actually do in the thousands of societies that existed prior to modern times? How are other societies organized to maximize paternal investments? To answer such questions we must go to the roots—to the biology of males and the male-female bond and to the evolution and anthropology of fatherhood. These are the subjects of the following chapter.

6. The Essential Father

A message found in a Chinese fortune cookie reads: "Every woman is at heart a mother; every man is at heart a bachelor." How much truth is there to this statement? What are fathers—men—"at heart?" Why have fathers been, universally, the protectors and providers? Are fatherhood and marriage really such a difficult leap for men? The search for the essence of fatherhood, for answers to the ultimate why, takes us deep into the evolutionary and anthropological record. We shall see that fatherhood is a unique combination of biological predisposition and cultural sanction.

A generation of social scientists has argued that fatherhood is merely a "socially constructed" phenomenon, a "gender role," something devised and taught by each society. The implication is that, because it is devised by society, it can be changed or even dropped altogether. This argument is often extended to most male and female differences. Such differences are thought to be culturally determined, even arbitrarily so. But it would be surprising indeed, given our current understanding of human biology and evolution, if this were so. In fact, the strict social constructionists are way off base.

The uniqueness of fathers is linked to male biology. Fathering, like all social behavior, represents a combination of nature and nurture, the innate qualities with which men are born and the way they are taught. Precisely where biology ends and culture begins is, to be sure, impossible to determine. But from the new and rapidly advancing fields of evolutionary anthropology and evolutionary psychology, we have strong clues about the nature of male biology and the biological basis of fathering.

The biological nature of human beings is a product of millions of years of evolution. We have evolved with certain species-typical traits, biological and psychological predispositions and drives that continually give shape to our lives and to the human condition, whether it is the need to eat and sleep, feelings of jealousy or aggression, or the desire to love and be loved.[1] Certain behavioral patterns make us feel comfortable and able to thrive, while others make us uncomfortable and compromise our ability to survive. And according to a growing body of evidence, human males and females differ in many of their inborn predispositions regarding thought, behavior, and emotion.

The evolutionary and anthropological record suggests that the human male is endowed genetically with the capacity to be a social father in some form—at minimum to provide resources and protection to his childbearing mate. Universally in human societies, the record shows, biological fathers are identified where possible and play some role in their children's upbringing. Fatherhood thus appears to be an inherent part of the human repertoire, and fathering, or paternal behavior, is a fundamental part of men's nature.[2] Indeed, as we shall see, the fathering capacity in human males was a critical component in the evolutionary success of our species.

At the same time, nature is perverse. Men are not ideally suited biologically to being the kind of fathers societies want them to be; so all successful societies have imposed social sanctions on men to encourage their fathering behavior. By far the most important of these sanctions is the institution of marriage, the most universally found social institution of all, and the very social institution that in modern societies is in such sharp decline.

HUMAN EVOLUTION AND FATHERHOOD

The great Russian American biologist Theodosius Dobzhansky, who helped to establish evolutionary genetics as an independent discipline, once said, "Nothing in biology makes sense except in the light of evolution."[3] The fundamental proposition of evolution is that all organisms, including humans, are shaped or designed by what is termed "natural selection"—those best adapted to an environment are more likely to survive, reproduce, and produce successful offspring. The term itself can be misleading because no active selection in the sense of "choice" is involved; the selection is called "natural" to distinguish it from what human breeders of domestic animals accomplish through conscious design when they systematically mate individual animals to achieve certain genetic traits.

Natural selection operates mainly through differential reproduction—some organisms reproduce more than others, and it is the genetic traits of those organisms that tend disproportionately to survive into the next generation. The issue is not just which organisms produce the most offspring but which produce the most offspring that themselves survive and reproduce. In higher animals this involves the careful rearing of offspring after they are born so that they may have more success as reproductive adults.

Most educated people today have little difficulty in accepting the proposition that human anatomy and physiology are products of evolution by natural selection. But they often have enormous difficulty when it comes to human behavior, taking the view that almost all human behavior is learned and can be explained entirely by culture. With respect to behavior, in their view, humans are entirely different from animals. This is despite the fact that we share more than 98 percent of our DNA with chimpanzees, our closest living relatives in the animal kingdom; genetically we are as close to the chimpanzee as the dog is to the wolf or the horse to the zebra.[4]

"There is no reason to think," the biologist Katharine M. Noonan has stated, "that behavior is different from other kinds of traits in relation to genetic influence."[5] Although human behavior is thought of, and experienced, as conscious and willful, and complex behavior is not determined in any rigid or obvious way by genes, no scientific basis exists for leaving such behavior out of the evolutionary equation.

Because successfully raising children to adulthood is so much a part of the survival of the human species, not only mating and reproduction but also parenting—both fathering and mothering—are the key phenomena of human evolution. One important concomitant of this is that human beings have evolved to be parental as well as sexual. Predispositions toward raising children are very likely as much a part of human makeup as are predispositions toward sexuality. If this were not the case, we probably would not be here.

Mating, reproduction, and parenting, however, are not the only ways that individuals pass on their genes into the next generation, thus insuring their genetic futures. A second means is known as "kin selection" and is based on the fact that people share their genetic makeup with blood relatives. A child receives half its genes from its mother, half from its father, and shares half its genes with full siblings, one eighth with first cousins, and so forth. One's genetic posterity can also be achieved to some extent, therefore, through nurturing these genetic kin. Not a single animal species has been found in which organisms, if they are social at all, do not behave preferentially toward their close kin. This must surely be a reason why people the world over tend to favor close relatives and why modern societies have had to develop rules against "nepotism."

"Inclusive fitness" is the term used by evolutionary theorists to refer to the sum of an individual's own reproductive fitness together with his or her influence on the fitness of relatives. The concepts of "kin selection" and "inclusive fitness" are so straightforward and plausible you would not guess that in the early 1960s, when they were first proposed by a young British biologist named William Hamilton, they created a stir in the academic community.[6] They proved to be one of the master keys to unlocking the secrets of evolutionary psychology. The inherited anatomy, physiology, and behavioral dispositions within each of us have been designed to maximize inclusive fitness.

The Human Line

In order to understand the evolutionary importance of fathers and the innate capacity for fathering that men have, it is necessary to consider first the ancestral beginnings of human beings. The human line in the animal kingdom branched off from a common ancestor with the chimpanzees in Africa some seven and a half million years ago (which is barely 1 percent of the history of complex life on earth.) Due to a cooling climate, the first hominids, or immediate human ancestors, were pushed out of shrinking forests into the surrounding savannah environment, consisting of mixed woodlands and grasslands. The early hominids probably lived in small, family-based bands of twelve to twenty-five individuals, gathering food in the vicinity and scavenging for meat, cleaning up the carcasses of animals that had been killed by other animals.[7] They were essentially still "bipedal apes," and their social behavior probably was not much different from their forest-living relatives.[8]

After some five or six million years of hominid existence, and possibly as the result of a further cooling of the earth's climate, our genus, *Homo,* emerged a million and a half to two million years ago. Concurrent with the development of an enlarged brain, a more complex language, and the ability to make tools, the size of these early human bands grew to some fifty to one hundred individuals. Increasingly, these bands came to rely on hunting big game, in addition to gathering plant materials and scavenging—thus the term "hunter-gatherers."[9] These early human bands were made up of close relatives and were probably relatively cooperative and egalitarian; they had a strong sexual division of labor in which males did most of the hunting and females most of the gathering.[10] Meat, presumably a richer nutritive source essential for the enlarged brain, became an important food source. Meat and other food materials were typically shared among the group members, a practice not commonly found among lower animals, and such cooperative sharing was a major source of group ritual and, eventually, other complex social behaviors.

Markedly different from the situation of our closest animal relative, the chimpanzee (a forest-dwelling, individual-foraging, less cooperative, and mostly plant-eating animal), these were the living conditions of most human beings until about ten thousand years ago. Hunting, food sharing, and the division of labor between the sexes gave early humans a remarkable adaptive advantage over their animal relatives, and proportionately more human young were able to survive to adulthood. Because biological change through evolution takes so long—occurring only over many, many generations—this hunting-gathering lifestyle in the savannah is probably the social and ecological environment for which humans today are biologically best adapted. It is often called by evolutionary experts the "environment of evolutionary adaptedness." This is an important point to stress: The inherent and inherited predispositions toward such behaviors as sexuality and parenting that we have today are likely based on natural selection, not in our current, modern environments, *but in the particular environment of evolutionary adaptedness in which most of human evolution took place.*

Human culture is entirely dependent on our biologically evolved capacity for language, the most remarkable trait that separates us from the higher animals. Language enables what is learned by each generation to be passed on to future generations, thus enormously enlarging our ability to adapt. Language-based cultures also "evolve," but unlike biological evolution, many cultural changes, even major changes, can take place in a single generation or less.[11] Consider the recent sexual and civil rights revolutions in America, which in the space of thirty years have radically transformed the way we behave toward one another. That biological and cultural evolution occur at such vastly different rates of speed is a source of continuing difficulty in human affairs.

The Evolutionary Basis of Sex Differences

There is every reason to believe that the marked division of labor between males and females that occurred over the several million years of human evolution in the savannah has left its mark on the biological endowment of each sex. The division of labor was one in which males were protectors and females were nurturers, males were hunters and females were gatherers, and both focused on the feeding of juveniles. Sex differences related to parenting behaviors have not escaped the forces of evolution; indeed, they lie at the very heart of the evolutionary process.

The most obvious biological differences between human males and females are the larger body size of males and the presence of larger fat deposits in females, especially in the breasts and buttocks. These characteristics are directly related to the different mating and reproductive processes of each sex.[12] Going deeper, the neural and endocrine systems of males and females differ significantly as well. And a growing body of recent evidence has led to the conclusion that male and female brains are "wired" differently.[13]

In the environment within which humankind evolved, men's hunter role required them to be aggressive, to travel long distances, and to navigate in foreign terrain. Men today, on average, show a higher aggression and general activity level than women. Men also have better developed spatial, long-range route-finding, and targeting skills, which show up in better vision, spatial visualization, and mathematical reasoning. Males are better at object manipulation in space, rotating objects in their minds, reading maps, and performing in mazes; they also have a better sense of direction.[14] These cognitive and behavioral patterns are affected by hormonal differences. Male skills are better developed when androgen ("male hormone") levels are high, for instance. Women are more skilled in these areas to the degree that their estrogen ("female hormone") levels are low, which occurs both after menopause and at certain times during the monthly cycle.

Women's childbearing, home-tending, and local food-gathering roles have similarly left a biological mark. This shows up most strongly in the areas of nurturing and social relationships. Women have greater sensitivity to touch, sound, and odor; they have better developed fine-motor capability and finger dexterity, and they are more sensitive to social context and to facial expressions. Their perceptual discrimination is more sensitive to small changes in an infant's appearance and behavior. Women pick up nuances of voice and music more readily than men, and they are six times more likely to sing in tune!

Such female skills are also related to differential hormonal levels. A high level of androgens in females has been shown to be associated with a low level of nurturance. In one animal study, testosterone (one of the male hormones) administered experimentally to various mammalian females acted to reduce their nurturant behavior. In another study, preadolescent male rhesus monkeys raised in total social isolation were more aggressive and less nurturant towards infants presented to them for the first time than were preadolescent females raised under the same deprived conditions.[15]

Many of these male-female differences appear at a very early age and are therefore unlikely to be culturally based. This does not mean that cultures don't strengthen or diminish them in various ways, emphasizing some rather than others. It also does not mean that men and women can't be *taught* to excel in traits that are more pronounced in the opposite sex. While women are biologically more attuned to infant care, for example, some studies have suggested that men—with suitable training—can do the job nearly as well.[16] Yet no matter how they are trained, men and women will probably continue to bring to parenting the underlying "styles" of their sex, styles that are based in the very different reproductive roles of our evolutionary past.

The Fathering Capacity

Men have a biological capacity for fathering. Although their actual fathering roles have varied, fathers have a biological predisposition to assist with child-rearing. Fathering behavior—and to a certain extent monogamous pair-bonding—is built into the nature of men.

Within the animal kingdom the human species stands out as one in which males and females cooperate in raising a relatively few "high quality" young. Parenthood among humans has expanded to include a very long period of child care. Particularly important and unusual is the special role of males. Unlike many other species, in which vast numbers of offspring are produced and males and females abandon each other after insemination, human males appear to have an inborn tendency to "pair-bond" with females for the purpose of helping to raise their offspring. Thus, monogamy—the exclusive mating of one female with one male—may be built into human nature.[17] This does not necessarily mean lifetime, "till death us do part" monogamy, however. In the environment of evolutionary adaptedness, the practice of monogamy may have meant only that a man stayed with a woman until their child was out of infancy, possibly for a period of about four years.[18]

Put in the terms of evolutionary psychology, human parenting distinctively involves on the part of men a relatively large paternal investment, a wide range of activities and resources that a father contributes to the survival and fitness of his offspring. In the words of anthropologists Jane and Chet Lancaster, "The evolution of the human husband-father role can be summarized as the channeling of male parental energy into the rearing of young."[19]

In this sense, the rise of fatherhood should be considered the key dimension in the evolution of the human family and, ultimately, of human civilization. The Lancasters elaborate this notion:

> In the course of evolution, the keystone in the foundation of the human family was the capturing of male energy into the nurturance of young, most specifically for the collaborative feeding of weaned juveniles. The human family is a complex organizational structure for the garnering of energy to be transformed into the production of the next generation, and its most essential feature is the collaboration of the male and female parent in the division of labor.[20]

Fathering is a part of the human biological makeup as it is not for most animals. Both monogamous pair-bonding and significant male care of the young are relatively rare in the animal kingdom; in only about 3 percent of all mammal species (which includes humans) do males form a long-term relationship with a single female.[21] In virtually all human societies men play some version of the father role with their biological children. The most universal, and therefore arguably most fundamental, elements of the father role are the physical protection of the family unit and the provision of resources—breadwinning—necessary for the family's survival.

Fatherhood and Evolutionary Advantage

The development of the fathering capacity has been a source of evolutionary advantage. High paternal investment in offspring has been decisive in the survival of the species.

Why did such relatively high paternal investment and monogamous fathering patterns develop in the human species? One answer is our unique bipedalism. As they left the forest for the savannah, our ancestors evolved to walk on two legs instead of four; this is the most distinctive anatomical difference between humans and apes. A leading explanation for bipedalism based on evolutionary adaptation is that it "was a response to the need to forage for food in open environments, where patches of food were widely spread apart."[22] The ability to stand upright presumably helped the early humans to see over the tall grasses, to travel longer distances, to fight enemies. Over time, having the hands free also enabled them to make and use tools.

Yet walking on two legs created a special problem for mothers. Among our forest-dwelling forebears, infants clung to their mothers' abdomens or rode on their backs. But the new upright mother had to carry her infant in her arms. This hampered her ability to protect herself from the dangers that lurked everywhere and limited her ability to collect food. She had to depend more on others for protection and provision, or she would not survive.

Bipedalism is only one answer to the puzzle of high paternal investment and monogamy among humans. A more common explanation is that human young have a longer period of dependency on adults than any other animal. In all mammals offspring grow internally within the female for a relatively long period of time, and after birth, due to the function of lactation, they require close attachment to the mother as their food source. But as many biologists have pointed out, humans are mammals whose infants are in a sense born "too soon," and they therefore have a longer period of dependency outside of the womb. For almost a year after birth, for example, the human baby still lives almost like a dependent embryo. Human newborns cannot grasp onto their mothers as the newborns of other primates can, and following weaning, human infants must have all of their food brought to them by their parents, whereas weaned apes gather their own food.

An important reason for this premature birth is that the human brain, and therefore head size, became so large that human babies had to be born early so they could pass through the mother's birth canal (whose size was restricted by anatomical constraints imposed by the demands of bipedal locomotion). To produce an infant destined to have a very large brain, therefore, requires that the infant be born at a relatively immature stage; the human brain then continues to grow at a rapid rate outside the womb for the first year after birth.

As humans evolved, the period of childhood dependency was further extended by the growth of an increasingly complex culture. Children had to be taught by adults how to make and use tools, how to hunt, sew, and cook, and how to understand and speak the language. Thus, the childbearing woman in the environment of evolutionary adaptedness needed an inordinate amount of help from others, and the most likely helper was the nonchildbearing father, the person who genetically had the most at stake. According to evolutionary theory, those children who were most likely to survive came from women who managed to secure mates who would stay with them after fertilization and help them during their dependent years. Stated as an evolutionary proposition, monogamy occurs when the need of the mother to obtain her nutrition interferes with the care of the young.[23]

For such reasons the human pair-bond, or nuclear family, the most primeval form of human social organization known, was generated. It is important to note that, from this evolutionary perspective, the human family is primarily an arrangement for raising children. In the words of biosociologist Pierre L. van den Berghe: "The human family is, very simply, the solution our hominid ancestor evolved over three to five million years to raise our brainy, slow-maturing . . . highly dependent, and, therefore, very costly (in terms of parental investment) babies."[24]

It is not difficult to see why pair-bonding benefits childbearing women. Women need help in raising their children. But why should men be adapted to pair-bonding, to staying with women and helping them raise their children? Like the males of many other species, why shouldn't they mate with as many women as possible and go for quantity not quality in their offspring? As is well known, some men do act this way; so this impulse has by no means been eradicated in the human species. But as evolutionists have suggested, two biological mechanisms evolved in human females to minimize such male behavior—to promote pair-bonds and hold men to them during their child-bearing years.[25]

The first mechanism is the human female's continuous sexual receptivity; they do not go into periodic "heat," or estrus, as other mammals do. Women are, so to speak, continuously available for sex far beyond the necessity for reproduction, and one reason for this may be to keep men around. Second—also unlike in all other mammals—ovulation in women is "concealed"; men do not know when the woman's fertile period occurs. This provides another biological reason for the man to stay close to one woman.[26] He never can be sure which of his sexual acts will result in reproduction, and to insure fertilization (as well as to guard against his woman having another man's child instead), he must seek to copulate regularly with her.

An even more important evolved mechanism that helps to hold couples together is our predisposition for love—the "affective attachment" between men and women. Although we tend to think of love attachments as being highly social in character, they also have a strong biological component.[27] They involve feelings of infatuation, the sense of well-being when in the company of a loved one, and feelings of jealousy and protectiveness when others try to intrude into our relationship—each of which, in turn, is related to biochemical processes and reactions in the brain.

THE FATHERHOOD PROBLEM

Nature is perverse. Men have a strong capacity to father, but male biology pulls men away from long-term paternal investment and pair-bonding.

If the human family is a biologically evolved mechanism for insuring our survival, and if men contain some impulse to pair-bond, why is fatherhood a problem? Why is fathering so often filled with tension? Why do so many fathers in modern times not get the biological message? Why am I writing this book? There are many cultural forces working against fathering today, but some fatherhood difficulties are rooted in the biological nature of males. In effect, fathers are pulled by their biological nature in several directions at once. In other words, just as some inherent biological mechanisms promote pair-bonds, others operate to pull them apart.

As anthropologist Donald Symons has summarized, "Human sexuality, especially male sexuality, is by its very nature ill-designed to promote marriage, and gender differences in sexuality do not seem to be complementary."[28] Men the world over are more sexually driven and "promiscuous," while women are more concerned with lasting relationships. The pioneering sex researcher Alfred Kinsey once said, "Among all peoples, everywhere in the world, it is understood that the male is more likely than the female to desire sexual relations with a variety of partners."[29] Also, men universally are expected to initiate sex, while women are expected to set limits on the extent of sexual intimacy. Such conflicting forces and tensions lie at the heart of what is said to be the longest running battle in human social life, the battle of the sexes.

Sexual Strategies

To understand the male sex drive and the fragility of human pair-bonds, we must carefully consider the radically dissimilar sexual and reproductive strategies of males and females from a biological point of view.[30] While it is necessary for the female to produce eggs, her main reproductive function is to carry the human fetus to term. The female reproductive rate is strictly limited—first by the availability of eggs for only a brief time during a monthly cycle and then by the physical and time requirements of childbearing. The primary reproductive function of males, on the other hand, is to inseminate. Males, with their far more numerous sperm, have the capacity to acquire many mates and reproduce at much higher rates than females. One man with a hundred mates could have hundreds of children, but one woman with a hundred mates could not have more children than she could have with just one mate.

It follows that a distinctive sexual strategy is most adaptive for each sex. For reproductive success females have the incentive to gain paternal investment—to keep a male around for the protection and support of herself and of the relatively few children she can have. Males, on the other hand, have the incentive to spread their abundant sperm more widely among many females. A male may decide that his best tactic is to care for the mother and baby, to ensure the latter's survival, but also to continue inseminating other females (if he can get away with it) to further solidify his chances of genetic posterity.

In all of these respects, humans show their strong relationship to other animals. The radically different sexual mating and reproductive strategies of males and females throughout most of the animal kingdom have been summarized by the evolutionary psychologists Martin Daly and Margo Wilson as follows:

> In most animal species, the female's greater investment in each offspring means that her maximal reproductive potential is lower than the male's. Males therefore compete among themselves for fertilization opportunities. Investing little in each offspring, males are selected to sow their seed wherever opportunity arises. Investing considerably in each offspring, females

are selected to exhibit greater selectivity in their choice of mates. One feature on which females may exercise selectivity is the male's willingness or ability to make an effective parental contribution.[31]

Human males, more than females, could be said to be at least mildly polygamous by nature. Many things point in that direction, such as the male's larger body size and degree of aggression, features not commonly found in fully monogamous species, and the fact that 84 percent of the 853 premodern cultures on record either permit or prefer polygamy (in modern societies polygamy is banned by law).[32] Of course, most men in these cultures are not able to live polygamously; only 10 percent to 15 percent of men in avowedly polygamous societies have more than one wife at a time. The relatively equal sex ratio (same number of women as men) in most societies makes unlikely more polygamy than that, to say nothing of the disgruntled men who are left out of the bargain.

Paternity Confidence

The Roman jurist Baius observed long ago, "Maternity is a fact, paternity is a matter of opinion."[33] From an evolutionary viewpoint, if a man is to stay with one woman rather than pursue many, he will desire a very high degree of "paternity confidence," the belief that offspring are really his. There is no genetic advantage to him for investing in another man's child. For this reason, some evolutionists believe that monogamy arose first and that high paternal investments evolved only after monogamy had produced increased paternity confidence.[34]

The paternity-confidence phenomenon has been clearly discerned in today's premodern societies. Anthropologists Steven Gaulin and Alice Schlegel carefully analyzed and compared the sexual norms and practices in 186 preindustrial societies for which adequate data are available, concluding that a male tends to invest in his mate's children only when his paternity confidence is high. "Cultural patterns leading to heavy male investment in a wife's children are common only where mating patterns make it likely that such investment benefits bearers of the male's genes."[35] Other studies have shown that mating systems in which paternity is relatively unacknowledged and downplayed and paternal investments are minimal are those in which confidence of paternity is low.[36]

Paternity confidence remains an important phenomenon—and a mostly unexamined one—in modern societies. If paternity confidence is on the wane, which certainly appears to be the case, it helps to explain today's downward spiral of fatherhood.

Male Sexual Strategies

While female sexual strategies have been pretty much the same the world over, male strategies have ranged from the faithful and monogamous Puritan fathers of American colonial history, who were devoted to their children, to fathers who spend their lives trying to sleep with as many women, and who pay as little attention to their children, as possible. Evolutionary scientists Patricia Draper and Henry Harpending have postulated that the male reproductive strategy ranges from the promiscuous and low paternal-investment "cad" approach, in which sperm is widely distributed with the hope that more offspring will survive, to the "dad" approach, in which a high paternal investment is made in a limited number of offspring.[37] It is because of the greater range and flexibility in the male than in the female reproductive strategy that the male strategy can be, and is, so heavily shaped by culture.

Why don't all men subscribe to the "cad" approach? Male promiscuity is kept in check by the strong moral proscriptions found in many cultures, as well as by the human pair-bonding predispositions already discussed. Another good deterrent is the presence of other men. Men don't want other men breaking into their relationships with the possibility of generating paternal uncertainty. All things considered, the "dad" approach with monogamous pair-bonding provides a trade-off that most men find acceptable. At the cost of having to make a relatively high paternal investment in their children and having a reduced access to other females, men gain greater paternity confidence and are able to maintain more stable bonds with other men, bonds that can prove useful to them.

In evolutionary terms, it may be a smart strategy for a man to cuckold other men and get them to raise his own children. Yet for the same man to be cuckolded by others is a disaster from his genetic perspective. This may be the principal reason why men tend to be far more upset with their mate's sexual infidelity than vice versa (women tend to be more upset by the loss of their mate's emotional fidelity, which threatens long-term commitment and support).[38] Throughout recorded history (until recently), legal codes on every continent have strongly prohibited adultery among married women while ignoring that of married men. And constraint of female sexuality by threat of male violence also appears to be a cultural universal.

"Scarce" eggs and the issue of paternity confidence clearly have the potential to set in motion an endless competition among men that can lead to violence, and such has often been the outcome. Male sexual jealousy is the leading motive in spousal homicides in North America, for example, and if one includes disputes among men over women, it may be the leading motive in all homicides.³⁹ Lethal male violence, however, is not necessarily "built into our genes." The virtually cease-less male rivalry, tension, violence, and wars that have been a hallmark of human history seem to have been generated mainly by the use of or-ganized power for despotic purposes that accompanied the rise of more complex human societies some five to ten thousand years ago. Such destructive violence was probably not so characteristic of the environ-ment in which we were biologically formed.⁴⁰

THE EVOLUTION OF FATHERHOOD

Fathering is different from and much more variable than mothering. But in many periods of our evolutionary history, when local and ecological conditions permitted or required it, father involvement with children has been very high.

The early evolution of fatherhood consisted of increasing investments of male parental energy into the rearing of the young. There are a variety of ways that fathers can make parental investments in their young. Just as with their sexual and reproductive strategy, the parental role of males is more variable than that of females. This does not mean, however, that fatherhood is an arbitrary social role that anyone can play.

Male parental investment occurs in two forms within the animal kingdom: *indirect care,* which involves the protector and provider roles, including defense of the home territory against intruders, food provi-sion, building shelters, and helping the pregnant and nursing female; and *direct care,* which includes feeding the young, carrying infants, baby-sitting, grooming and playing with the young, and sleeping in contact with the young.⁴¹ Two additional paternal roles are commonly found among humans: authority figure (head of household, disciplinar-ian, and leader of rituals) and culture transmitter or teacher.

Although the evidence is still scant, we can speculate that the evolu-tion of fatherhood took place along the following lines:⁴² Among the immediate ancestors of human beings—the more apelike hominids who lived on the forest edge in East Africa and relied on gathering and some scavenging for meat—the father role was probably minimal. A male would stay close to a female, providing some protection, probably in exchange for future sex, but both sexes were essentially independent in food gathering. The male's interest was in the female and not in her child. The child benefited only indirectly from the exchange, mainly in the form of extra protection against predators and other environmental dangers. Thus, protection was probably the first element of the human father role that came into existence.

Over time—surely with the arrival some 1.5 to 2 million years ago of our own genus, *Homo,* and the hunter-gatherer lifestyle—mothers became increasingly dependent. Provision—the second of the major elements of the father role—came into being as males (the hunters) became the main source of food. Later, with the rise of language, tools, and rudimentary social organization, the father role of culture transmitter emerged. The technology of big-game hunting, for example, which was very important to the survival of the group, had to be taught by fathers to their sons.

The appearance some 120,000 years ago of our own species, *Homo sapiens,* further accentuated the development of the father roles of protection, provision, and cultural transmission. As long as big-game hunting remained a major food source, the direct involvement of males in child care remained minimal (a conclusion based on the experience of the remaining big-game hunting societies that still exist today.) But as hunting technologies improved and hunting became less of a full-time activity, the time available for fathers to be involved in the direct care of their young children increased. The direct care of children by fathers also was promoted through the strengthening of monogamy and the consequent increase in paternity confidence. Although they probably were seldom involved in the direct care of unweaned infants, fathers gradually came to have more contact with weaned infants and children.

Parenting Among the !Kung San

How do we know so much about fathering and social life in general in our environment of evolutionary adaptedness? Most of our knowledge is highly conjectural. One key source of knowledge is the study of still-extant human societies (sometimes called "living fossils") that many scholars believe closely resemble the societies of our ancestors. A community regarded as quite similar to the human societies of our evolutionary past is the !Kung San (sometimes known as Bushmen), a relatively isolated, seminomadic hunter-gatherer group that lives in a semiarid region of northwestern Botswana on the edge of the Kalahari desert. They were featured in the popular movie *The Gods Must Be Crazy* of a few years back.

The !Kung San live in bands of some thirty people, which consist of a number of nuclear families together with the extended families of either or both spouses. Few restrictions are placed on premarital sex, but marriage occurs at early adolescence for girls and young adulthood for men. The San family is usually monogamous; only about 5 percent of unions are polygamous, and those involve no more than two wives.[43]

The women gather food in the nearby vicinity, and the men hunt on regular excursions away from the camp. But the land is relatively bountiful, and not much time has to be spent on provisioning. One anthropologist has referred to hunter-gatherers as the original leisure society.[44]

The !Kung San spend a great amount of their time with children. Both parents are very indulgent with infants and young children, as indulgent—according to anthropologists Mary Katz and Melvin Konner, who lived with the San—as has ever been described for a human population. Women carry infants more than half the waking hours, sleep with them, and nurse them several times an hour. Older children have much freedom and few responsibilities.

Fathers are closely involved with their children, and spend much of their free time with them. They are involved in subsistence activities no more than half the days of the week. Fathering practices among the !Kung San have been summarized by Katz and Konner:

> They often hold and fondle even the youngest infants, though they return them to the mother whenever they cry and for all forms of routine care. Young children frequently go to them, touch them, talk to them, and request food from them, and such approaches are almost never rebuffed. Boys are not expected to become involved in hunting activity until early adolescence at the soonest and then follow their fathers and uncles on hunts for years before being able to conduct hunts themselves.[45]

It is tempting to think that this is the "natural," inborn mode of human fathering, the kind of fathering to which males are biologically adapted. Indeed, many of its features are highly recommended today by most pediatricians! But it is doubtful that we will ever have enough evidence to be sure.

Hunter-gatherer societies like that of the !Kung San have numerous other features that many people today would regard as admirable.[46] The San are a completely stateless and classless society, without even so much as a headman with any real power. They are highly egalitarian, with prestige based mainly on individual merit and performance. Although clearly a male-dominated society, as virtually all human societies have been, the !Kung San men seldom mistreat women and children and are known to have relatively low levels of aggression and violence. Katz and Konner note that "homicidal violence occurs in this society, but wars were apparently very rare historically, and no wars had occurred for many decades at the time of the study. Preparation for fighting did not occupy the men in any way, and learning to fight was not considered an important skill for boys."[47] One reason for the low level of warfare may well have been the very low population densities, as well as the lack of threat from competing groups.

The !Kung San were first studied by anthropologists many decades ago, before they had significant contact with Western influence. Although recent research has shown that the San have always interacted with other African societies around them and may have descended to their present region from more fertile areas relatively recently, they have preserved an independent hunter-gatherer lifestyle over centuries, even millennia. Anthropologists today vigorously debate the degree to which one can draw inferences about our past from such a group, basically because the San also have evolved over a long period of time and may not have been then what they are today.[48] But the conditions of their lives are so remarkably close to those which are thought to have prevailed among our hunter-gatherer ancestors that the San may have much to tell us.

The Rise of Civilization

Gradually over the course of our evolutionary history, culture took command of human affairs. Such cultural features as rituals, mores, laws, organized religions, and state authority, with an interconnected dynamic of their own, became the main determinants of human behavior and social change. Fatherhood came to be influenced more by cultural preferences and exigencies than by biological predispositions.

The warming of the earth led to the end of the Ice Age some ten thousand years ago. Since then (an extremely short period of time in the course of our evolution), human social life has changed dramatically.[49] In the twilight of the Ice Age, plant food resources increased and big-game hunting declined in importance. This was also the time when rudimentary technologies of agriculture and the domestication of animals were discovered. New economic subsistence patterns and a more settled lifestyle came into being, bringing an end to most hunter-gatherers. Thanks to a richer resource base, human societies grew in size, and technological sophistication and population density increased.

These changes caused a fundamental shift in people's attitudes toward reproduction.[50] When the resources necessary to sustain life and reproductive success were perceived to be plentiful and generally available to all, as with the traditional !Kung San and presumably our evolutionary ancestors, the optimal reproductive strategy was simply to have as many children as possible. Reproduction, though, was still limited by the need of parents to sustain themselves. For this reason, women may have given birth to children only about once every four years (as do the !Kung San women). Made possible largely through the contraceptive effects of long-term breast feeding, this remains the reproductive strategy among people in remote parts of the world.

With increases in population density and the growth of wealth, however, resources once regarded as abundant came to be perceived as

finite. Over the course of the past ten thousand years, this new perception, together with the realization that the control of resources was all-
important for the survival of one's offspring, gradually caused a shift in
reproductive strategies. No longer could one think merely of procreat-
ing as many children as possible with the hope that some would survive to reproduce themselves. Rather, children needed to be given
whatever advantages the parents could bestow upon them—in the
form, for example, of education or inherited wealth—to provide them
the best chance of competing against others.

As social life became more complex, family structure changed substantially. The predominance of the nuclear family gave way to complex, extended family forms. Kinship linkages often became highly
elaborate, with suprafamilial clans controlling economic production
and distribution; this was characteristic of the early Middle Eastern
city-states, formed some five thousand years ago. The nuclear family
typically became submerged in these larger kinship groupings, almost
(but never entirely) to the point of extinction.

In keeping with the new importance of control over resources, the
roles of fathers shifted. The male role of authority figure grew greatly in
prominence. This was accompanied by increasing concern for the intergenerational transmission of property, with elaborated new rules of inheritance. Also, new controls over sexuality and the concept of "legitimacy" became widespread, a concept based on cultural disapproval of
casual sexual unions that create a child without married parents and,
especially, an identified father.

At the same time, the status of women deteriorated. Women were
increasingly considered just another form of property. Up until the industrial era, in fact, the status of women may have been linked to a society's complexity. At least that is what sociologist Martin King Whyte
found in a comparative analysis of ninety-three preindustrial societies
of modern times: "In the more complex cultures, women tend to have
less domestic authority, less independent solidarity with other women,
more unequal sex restrictions . . . and fewer property rights."[51]

In summary, the development of agriculture, food surpluses, and a
settled lifestyle led to massive social shifts. In the new "agrarian" societies people had to rely on strangers to meet many of their basic needs,
and their means of livelihood became subject to expropriation by others. New class hierarchies and states emerged to deal with the changed
social conditions. The traditional social order of hunter-gatherers,
which was based on cooperation and trust among kinfolk, was
eclipsed. Fathers were constantly pulled away to fight, and in some respects the situation of children must have deteriorated. It didn't take
long for the domination of the many by the few to generate the endless

violent conflicts over the control of resources that have characterized recorded human history.[52] Such is the mixed blessing of "civilization."

Fatherhood in Premodern Societies Today

The indirect-care protector and provider roles, found universally among human fathers around the world today, can be considered the primal father roles. A remarkable cross-cultural consistency exists among adult human males in that, when they produce or extract food provisions, these are redistributed to children either directly or through the mothers. With equal predictability, adult males serve as defenders of their own kith and kin when hostilities threaten. In virtually all of the world's societies the father, or at least an adult male, is also an authority figure (head of household, head of clan), and most fathers are active transmitters of culture to their children, particularly their older children.

On the other hand, direct care of the young by fathers is found only infrequently. No human society is known to exist where males provide more infant and child care than females, and in every society caregiving or nurturing is regarded as primarily a "feminine" activity. Human males around the world today do very little caregiving during infancy.[53] In one cross-cultural comparison of 186 societies, mothers were the "principal" or almost exclusive caretakers of infants (two and under) in 90 percent of the societies, and in the remaining 10 percent their role was at least "significant." In no society were the mothers of infants not involved, or were fathers the principal caretakers.[54]

Today, we expect fathers to at least have strong *contact* with their infants even if they don't directly care for them, just as with the !Kung San. And such contact is a much more common occurrence around the world than caretaking, as one might expect. In only 4 percent of the 186 societies did fathers have a "regular close relationship" with infants, but in 76 percent they had "frequent proximity" or "occasional proximity." In just 20 percent of the societies was there "rare proximity" or "no proximity."[55] In another cross-cultural study of 31 societies, fathers held their infants on a regular basis in only 3 of the societies, but on an occasional basis they held their infants in the great majority, 23 of the 31. In only 5 societies were infants never held by their fathers.[56]

The father's contact with, and also provision of direct care to, children increases as they grow older in most cultures. In all of the 186 societies, the father's direct caregiving role increased as the child reached early childhood (ages two to five), while that of the mother's decreased. Indeed, in 69 percent of the societies, fathers had regular or frequent proximity with children at this older age level.[57]

Implications

What can we reasonably conclude from this venture into the evolution of fatherhood? In every premodern society, fathers have played the roles of protector, provider, and culture transmitter. And fathers have virtually everywhere been authority figures, although more so following the rise of civilization. These, then, are the earliest evolutionary roles of fathers and the primary roles around which men have organized their lives over the course of history. They are also, presumably, the roles for which men are biologically best adapted. Beyond this, the roles that fathers have played depend heavily on local cultural and ecological factors; no one specific set of father roles is best suited to all circumstances. In some societies fathers are extremely involved at least with their older children and provide them with substantial direct care, while in other societies fathers remain largely uninvolved. In the great majority of premodern societies, fathers have at least some contact with their infants, although they do not directly care for them.

A problem for modern societies is that fathers often are no longer needed to fulfill the primary and traditional father roles. The roles toward which men are biologically most inclined are the very roles from which they have been, at least partly, removed. Men like to be the protector, provider, teacher, and authority figure. But modern societies want them to be something else—infant and child tender, the role that mothers have always had. Traditionally, mothers have received the help of close relatives, especially other women. Today, in the companionate form of marriage, where husbands and wives are closely associated with one another and living apart from most of their relatives, husbands are needed as never before in the direct care of children.

It is highly doubtful whether men should, or reasonably could, be expected to take over the traditional maternal role of child care, as will be discussed in the concluding chapter. But innumerable examples exist around the world where men are closely involved with their children, guiding them in their own unique way toward adulthood, and where they also provide extensive assistance to their wives. In fact, if the example of the !Kung San is any indication, this may be a father role for which men also are biologically well adapted, one from which they receive intrinsic psychic satisfaction.

Throughout history, however, even with a full set of fatherly roles from which men can gain satisfaction, fatherhood—unlike motherhood—is not something societies have been able to take for granted. To maximize the male parental investment, it has been necessary for women to provide men with a sense of paternity confidence—that the child in which the man is being asked to invest his time, energy, and resources is really his. And all societies, even those with relatively high paternity confidence, have sought to tie men to their children through the institution of marriage, realizing that this was necessary to prevent them from straying sexually.

What are modern societies really asking of men today? That men largely give up the main roles they have had throughout history and assume one that they have never had—the direct care of children. And do this not only with an increasingly lowered sense of paternity confidence but often with children they positively know are not theirs. It is possible that many men can be induced to accede to this request but probably, for most, only with their natural children and *only if the marriage bond is stronger than ever.* Let us turn, then, to the issue of fatherhood and marriage.

FATHERHOOD AND MARRIAGE AROUND THE WORLD

Because men are only weakly attached to the father role and because men's reproductive and parental strategies are variable, culture is central to enforcing high paternal investment. In every society the main cultural institution designed for this purpose is marriage. Father involvement with children is closely linked to the quality of the relationship between husband and wife.

It is reasonable to say that the social institution of marriage has some biological basis. Marriage is structured around the primitive, monogamous pair-bonds of our evolutionary ancestors. As one indication of its biological basis, marriage is a universal social institution—the preferred way of mating in every known society—and the vast majority of humans marry sometime during their lives. Almost all marriages the world over take place between just one man and one woman at a time, although in many societies men may subsequently marry additional women while still married to their original wives (simultaneous polygamy), and in most societies both men and women may marry subsequently if their first marriages are broken by divorce (serial monogamy or "successive polygamy"). The subsequent marriage of one already-married woman to additional men (polyandry) is quite rare in human societies, and group marriages—a man or woman marrying more than one spouse at a time—are virtually absent from the human scene.

We will probably never know for sure whether our prehistoric ancestors had marriage ceremonies, much less how much importance they placed on the institution of marriage. What we do know is that, among the premodern societies of the world today, marriage is one of the most important and certainly the most universal of social institutions. It has been defined simply as "a relationship within which a group socially approves and encourages sexual intercourse and the birth of children."[58] Group approval, rather than merely individual preference, has always been a major component of the institution. Throughout most of recorded history the majority of marriages have probably been arranged (with the principals having some say in the matter); they were less alliances of two individuals than of two kin networks, typically involving an exchange of money or goods between the networks.

There are many theories about the fundamental purposes of marriage, but surely one major purpose is to keep men attached to their mates so that offspring will have the best chance of survival. Through marriage, societies normally hold the biological parents responsible for each other and for their offspring. In addition, because marriage includes sexual obligations and rights, one of the most central being the male's right of exclusive sexual access to his wife, the institution helps to prevent men from openly pursuing other men's wives. This, in turn, increases paternity confidence.

Marriage is thus the institution through which societies have sought to engage the basic problem of fatherhood—while biology pulls men in one direction, culture has sought to pull them in another. Margaret Mead once suggested that there is no society where men will stay married for very long unless culturally required to do so.[59] The marriage ceremony, infused with ritual and public acknowledgment, symbolizes the cultural pull. It stresses a strong social bond which includes the long-run commitment of the male, the durability of the marital relationship, and the importance of the union for children.

Yet the power of culture has never been entirely successful, obviously, in holding men to the pair-bond. Divorce is also an omnipresent fact in human societies, and in many societies the right of divorce is granted exclusively to men. Lifetime fidelity to one spouse seems not to be built into the human psyche, certainly the male psyche, although it is clearly well within the realm of human possibility and has been achieved by many couples throughout the world. Anthropologist Helen Fisher has suggested that the modal divorce around the world, which occurs four years into a marriage, may reflect the birth spacing in the environment of evolutionary adaptedness.[60] In other words, males would stay with one female until their child was four years old (straying occasionally, she suggests) and then move on.

Societies differ greatly in the degree to which divorce actually takes place, but there are few societies from which it is totally absent.[61] Low-divorce societies tend to be those in which women have little relative autonomy, especially in the economic sphere. By the same token, the growing economic autonomy of women is a principal factor accounting for increased divorce in modern societies over the past one hundred fifty years.[62] The leading direct causes for divorce in premodern societies, however, are drawn directly from the realm of evolutionary biology—adultery and infertility, both mainly on the part of women.[63]

In over 80 percent of the world's premodern societies, marital polygamy for men is condoned, as noted above, and in many of these societies it is actually preferred and practiced to the extent possible. Why do some societies permit polygamy while others do not? There is no definitive answer to this question, but many researchers have investigated it.[64] Polygamy was probably quite limited in the environment of evolutionary adaptedness. In all likelihood it increased with the rise of agriculture, due to the generation of great wealth and attendant inequalities. Wealth is essential for securing mates in polygamous societies; in all polygamous societies well-to-do men are most likely to have plural marriages. The polygamous system may have reached its peak in the harems of some Middle Eastern potentates, which consisted of as many as one thousand wives.

For any given society, the amount of father involvement can be predicted with some accuracy through knowledge of that society's economy and marriage form.[65] Father involvement is highest in those premodern societies that are economically dependent upon gathering (not hunter-gathering) and primitive horticulture, in other words, societies in which women are major providers of subsistence resources and men are not so critically needed as hunters. Father involvement also tends to be high in societies without accumulated resources or capital investments that must be defended; such societies do not regularly engage in warfare and thereby free men from service as warriors. In marriage form, societies with high father involvement tend to be monogamous (rather than polygamous) and the degree of husband-wife intimacy is high.

Cross-cultural comparisons also lead to the following important conclusion: The more time that husbands and wives spend together, the greater the likelihood that fathers will be directly involved with their children.[66] As stated earlier, the evidence from modern societies provides additional support for this conclusion. For men, marriage and fatherhood are very closely linked, and the amount and quality of fathering that a man is willing to provide is highly dependent on the quality of his spousal relationship.

At the opposite extreme, father involvement with children is lowest in those premodern societies that practice herding and advanced agriculture—the agrarian societies. Both herding and advanced (that is, after the invention of the plow) agriculture are conducted mainly by men, and men thus provide most of the subsistence resources. These also tend to be warrior societies, intent on protecting or extending land holdings, the primary source of wealth. Father involvement is especially low in those agrarian societies that practice polygamy—where co-wives live in separate quarters and husband-wife intimacy is low and where nuclear families are deeply imbedded in extended family networks that tend to dilute the husband-wife relationship.

For the fate of fathering in modern societies, there is good news and bad news in all of this. The good news is that modern women are major providers of subsistence resources, and men are neither the sole source of support for their families nor required as hunters (and only sporadically as warriors). In addition, we have a monogamous marriage system with high husband-wife intimacy. These features are positive for father involvement. The bad news is that these same features are associated with a high divorce rate, a serious negative for father involvement.

SUMMARY AND CONCLUSIONS

Answers to the question, what are fathers—men—"at heart," can now be provided with some precision. The evolutionary and anthropological record of human beings indicates that men in all likelihood have a biological predisposition to be fathers. Fathering behavior, to put it another way, is built into the nature of men. In evolutionary terms, children whose fathers cooperated in nurturing them to maturity were more likely to survive, reproduce, and pass along their genes to posterity. Indeed, the conclusion of evolutionary scientists is that the development of the fathering capacity, with high paternal investments in offspring, was a source of enormous evolutionary advantage for human beings.

Moreover, the human family, a partly biological arrangement for raising children, has always involved fathers as well as mothers. The actual roles that fathers play vary considerably from society to society, but fathers universally play some role in their children's upbringing—at least that of protector, provider, and culture transmitter. In many societies, where local ecological and social conditions permit or require it, direct father involvement with the care of children is high. A man is likely to be directly involved in caring for his children if (1) he is sure they are his; (2) he is not needed as a warrior or hunter; (3) the mother contributes substantially to food resources; and (4) he is monogamously married and emotionally close to the mother, spends much time with her, and is encouraged by her to be involved.

Monogamous pair-bonding is also built into men's nature. The love attachments of marriage are more than just social constructs. Unlike most animals, human males and females have a predisposition to have some emotional affinity for each other beyond the sexual act and to establish pair-bonds. There exists an affective attachment between men and women that causes them to be infatuated with each other, to feel a sense of well-being when together with a loved one, and to feel jealous when others attempt to intrude into their relationship.

Yet men have other biological predispositions as well. The inherent, evolutionary-shaped sexual strategies of males dictate that fathers are pulled in other directions, away from monogamous pair-bonding and away from making large paternal investments in their children toward more detached behaviors. The "dad" strategy is in the genes of males, but so is the "cad" strategy. Men have the capacity to father but also the capacity to stray, and strong cultural sanctions are necessary if their paternal investments are to be maximized.

In those many premodern societies where men are heavily needed as warriors and hunters, fathers do not provide much direct child care. But their children nevertheless have a strong sense of being fathered. And the mostly absent fathers are compensated for in child care by the enormously large parental investments of mothers and close relatives.

In modern societies the primal protection and provision contributed by fathers have greatly declined in importance. Fathers are no longer as needed for these roles as they once were; the roles are shared with women and with the larger society. At the same time, the need for fathers in the direct care of children has become greater than ever before. Social complexity requires longer periods of socialization and dependency for children. To succeed economically in an increasingly technical society, children must be highly educated. To succeed socially and psychologically in an increasingly complex and heterogeneous culture, children must have strong and stable attachments to adults who love and care for them. With mothers increasingly in the workplace and close relatives living apart, large paternal investments have become essential for successful childrearing.

But at the very time in history when fathers are so badly needed, the cultural ties necessary to hold them to fathering have withered. Marriage is in decline and fathers are increasingly thought superfluous. To make matters worse, the sexual revolution has severely reduced paternity confidence. If fatherlessness is to be halted, if the unique attributes of fathers are to be made widely available to children, modern societies will have to change course. What they must do, how they must change, are the subjects of the concluding chapter.

Part Four

Conclusions

7. Reclaiming Fatherhood
and Marriage

Fathers play a crucial role in child development. Children develop best when they are provided the opportunity to have warm, intimate, continuous, and enduring relationships with both their fathers and their mothers. Yet if present trends continue, the percentage of American children living apart from their biological fathers will reach 50 percent early in the next century. Think about it. Half of all children without fathers to say good night to them. Many, when asked who their father is, will answer, "I don't have one."

Some of these absent fathers will try their best to take good care of their children. Many undoubtedly will wish they could be better fathers. But residential proximity is normally an essential for good fathering. Statistics show that, unlike mothers, fathers who don't live with their children tend to lose touch with them.

A growing number of children whose natural fathers do not live with them have surrogate fathers instead. As desirable as this may be in certain cases, the evidence suggests that surrogate fathers are generally poor substitutes for natural fathers, and there are sound biological reasons why this is so. Indeed, according to the data on child outcomes, a child is better off in terms of the chances for overall success in life with a dead father than with a surrogate father.

Just three and a half decades ago the percentage of American children living apart from their biological fathers was only 17 percent. That probably was an all-time low point because, throughout history, involuntary father absence from children has been very high due to a high paternal death rate. What a tragedy for children. Just at the time when modern medical technology enabled them to have a father who remained alive throughout their childhood, the fathers decided "voluntarily" to leave their families. The idea of social progress has been stood on its head.

We now know from a careful examination of the evidence that today's fatherlessness has led to social turmoil—damaged children, unhappy children, aimless children, children who strike back with pathological behavior and violence. Fatherless children have a risk factor two to three times that of fathered children for a wide range of negative outcomes, including dropping out of high school, giving birth as a teenager, and becoming a juvenile delinquent. The repercussions go far beyond children to include a steady deterioration in the lives of adult men and women. If present trends continue, our society could be on the verge of committing social suicide.

THE PATH TO FATHERLESSNESS

There are two immediate reasons for today's exponential growth of father absence. One is divorce, the rate of which has skyrocketed over the past thirty years. A first marriage entered into today has approximately a 50 percent chance of survival, and the presence of children has become an almost negligible factor in the decision to divorce. The second is nonmarital births, which have risen dramatically from 5 percent of all births in 1960 to more than 30 percent today.

Fatherlessness caused by nonmarital births now virtually equals that caused by divorce, and its effects on children have been shown to be even more deleterious than divorce on children's lives. In most divorce situations, children at least have had the advantage of a father's presence for part of their lives. For the majority of children born out of wedlock, the father is out of the picture from the very beginning.

The increase of fatherlessness has been mirrored by a dramatic "defining down" in our culture of the importance of fathers to children. One hundred, fifty, or even thirty years ago the premise that a child should live with a father in a nuclear family was universally held. Father absence was considered a tragedy, and a father who voluntary left his children was considered unmistakably deviant. Not so today. Divorce when children are implicated is well accepted by more than three quarters of the population. And there is a growing acceptance of childbirth without a father in the home, especially among the young.

Many factors are involved in this shift of cultural norms. To me the greatest single factor is the rapid and widespread growth of radical individualism in America, encompassing both men and women. We have always been an individualistic nation, but in times past we had a balanced or communitarian individualism. Self-development and achievement— self-reliance—were seen to be for the purpose of pursuing social goals: the betterment of family, community, and society. We were concerned as much with social responsibilities as with individual rights. In these cultural circumstances the family was unquestionably a *social* institution, intended expressly for the care and rearing of children. People had an active sense that strong families—consisting of both fathers and mothers—were the fundamental component of a good society.

Today self-development and achievement are thought of as purely individual pursuits. Self-reliance has turned into self-expression. Improve yourself so that you can be a happier person and get more out of life. The family, in turn, has largely become a *personal* institution, intended not for social purposes but for personal well-being; something to be shaped by our own immediate needs and desires. There is nothing intrinsically wrong with self-development. It is a quality we all crave. But when it is stripped away from social purpose, when self-development becomes sheer self-aggrandizement, we, collectively, become losers.

A contrary perspective on recent family-related cultural trends has made great inroads in American social thought, especially within the academic community. This perspective sees the father-mother nuclear family as inherently authoritarian, our cultural past as pervasively negative, and "alternative family forms" as representing social improvement. "There is a positive new diversity springing up in families and relationships today in Western society," writes Shere Hite in her recent book on the family. "This pluralism should be valued and encouraged."[1] Hite and others see the nuclear family model as "an essentially repressive one, teaching authoritarian psychological patterns, meekness in women, and a belief in the unchanging rightness of male power."[2] If men in families can't be reformed, the argument continues, let's throw them out.

This perspective typically envisions the nuclear family—sometimes referred to simply as "the family"—as a "patriarchal invention." It was presumably created by men so they could "imprison women in marriage" and have total control over their sexuality and their children. Yet a close examination of the evolution and history of the human family, as seen in the previous chapter, yields a quite different conclusion.

The Evolution of Families

Patriarchy is not a fundamental part of the human nuclear family system. To the contrary, it arose in conjunction with the rise of "civilization" and is most strongly associated not with nuclear families but with the complex, extended family systems in which most human beings have lived only for the past ten thousand years. In shifting toward more nuclear family forms in recent centuries, modern societies have been moving away from patriarchy. Although male dominance is still a force to be reckoned with, gone is the systematic exploitation of women, the overt discrimination and repression. Around the world today, nuclear family systems tend to be much less patriarchal than extended family systems.

The evolution of family structure has followed a curvilinear path. The family system in industrialized societies—featuring monogamy and the coresidence of parents in the nuclear family, high husband-wife intimacy, a high divorce rate, and a major contribution by women to subsistence—resembles, in certain respects, that of the simplest gatherer and horticultural societies. After millennia of complex, extended, and often polygynous family forms, modern societies have returned to the more nuclear family form that existed among our early ancestors.[3] We can take some comfort, therefore, in the realization that perhaps we have reattained a more "natural" family form, one that is more in tune with our biological predispositions.

But there is a crucial difference between the nuclear family of modern societies in the late twentieth century and that of our early ancestors—the lack of father involvement today. As evidenced by the !Kung San, the nuclear family form which we think predominated through much of human evolution was one with relatively high father involvement. Moreover, in the cross-cultural studies of father involvement which were reviewed, the few premodern cultures with strictly monogamous and nuclear families also tend to have high father involvement.

The "alternative" family system that is emerging in late modernism is thus unique and unprecedented. Nothing like it can be found in the evolutionary and historical record. This is not surprising. The family is very much a product of the environmental and cultural conditions within which it exists, and the conditions of modern society are almost totally dissimilar to those of our early ancestral environment.

What we are witnessing is the creation of a "postnuclear" family form, a step beyond the so-called modern nuclear family of recent centuries. The latter is distinguished from its predecessors by a distinct separation from relatives and from the surrounding community; mother and father and children live in a separate household and act independently of others. The burden and responsibility of childrearing falls exclusively on parents. With this kind of burden and responsibility, it is more important than ever that mothers and fathers remain together, and devoted to the task. The postnuclear family still has this full burden of childrearing; it is ever more isolated from relatives and from the surrounding community. *But the father is missing.*

The disturbing reality is that this unique postnuclear family form appears to be inherently unstable. With other relatives already out of the family picture, women cannot be expected to do the job of childrearing all by themselves. The state can help economically but not socially.

Without fathers, parental investments—the sine qua non of good child-rearing—are in ever shorter supply. Moreover, the men who are released from family responsibilities have a high propensity for antisocial behavior and violence. Far from being a social improvement, then, as some observers have suggested, the new alternative family forms should be a focus of serious concern.

The Past 250 Years

Up until the last third of the twentieth century, as indicated in chapters 3 and 4, the social conditions for children in America had continuously improved. In late preindustrial times both fathers and mothers were actively involved at home in both childrearing and productive labor. Yet life was a constant struggle, and the childrearing regime was punitive and harsh. Then, in what has been called "one of the most significant transformations that has ever taken place," the modern nuclear family arose.[4] Breadwinning became a specialized, full-time male role outside the home, and women took over homemaking and child care on a full-time basis.

In its time, the modern nuclear family was a very successful system. Women and children were able to thrive on the man's "outside income." Children, especially, benefited enormously from having a full-time mother. And men, even though they were away from home during the day, remained committed to their children as providers and protectors. They had a valued role in society and, in large numbers, acted with social responsibility.

Over the course of the twentieth century, married women began to take over the provider role. But men, having left childrearing for full-time breadwinning, were reluctant to move back into domestic activities. And a changing economy meant that it was financially more disadvantageous for men to do so even if they wanted to. This left a wide parenting gap within the home. Beginning in the 1960s, the time parents spent caring for their children dropped; many children were left untended.

The situation of children deteriorated further when male commitment to children dramatically declined in the late 1960s and 1970s. Not only did men resist movement toward domestic pursuits, but many men abandoned their children entirely. A culture of committed paternity gave way to a culture of casual paternity. In the terms of evolutionary psychology, more and more men abandoned the "dad" strategy of their fathers and grandfathers, whereby men have a few children and invest heavily in them, and adopted the "cad" approach to fatherhood, whereby men spread their seeds more widely, make limited child investments, and depend on others for successful child outcomes.

Cultural Breakdown

To the faithful readers of this book, the underlying biological and cultural mechanics of what has happened to fatherhood should now be clear. Men have a biological capacity for fathering; they are not inherently sex-addicted, utterly promiscuous cads. But the male capacity for fathering must be guided and enforced through culture. Cultural sanctions concerning male behavior are necessary if paternal investments are to be maximized. Unfortunately, such cultural sanctions, because they are dependent for their existence on widely accepted understandings about the meaning and importance of fatherhood, are far more perishable than the biological tendencies they govern.

Today the cultural sanction of male fathering behavior has diminished sharply. Gone are the omnipresent controls provided by close-knit kinship groups in premodern societies, groups with an enormous stake in the life outcomes of their biological offspring. Disappearing are the religiously based cultural controls, the internalized "virtues" of Victorian society. Even our laws have gone soft; instant divorce is now available to men in most states merely for the asking.

Modern cultures are in the process of declaring obsolete the age-old cultural understandings about the importance of fatherhood and the necessity for sanctions against casual paternity. This can be seen most clearly in what has happened to marriage, the key social institution, found in every known society, that has held men to the responsibilities of fatherhood. Not so long ago, America was probably the most marrying society in the world. As recently as 1990, 94 percent of middle-aged men (forty-five to fifty-four years old) either were or had been married. Today marriage is a rapidly weakening social institution. The marriage rate has reached an all-time low; in just two decades, from 1970 to 1990, the percentage of married adults decreased from 72 percent to 62 percent.[5] At the same time, nonmarital birth and nonmarital cohabitation rates have reached all-time highs.

RESTORING SOME CULTURAL PROPOSITIONS

While the future of fatherhood looks very grim indeed, the seeds of change and renewal lie waiting in that invisible but powerful realm called culture—the realm of values, attitudes, and beliefs. Culture, unlike biology, is a human creation—it is somewhat intentional, volitional, and subject to human intervention.[6] Just as cultural forms can be discarded, dismantled, and declared obsolete, so can they be reinvented. There is always the prospect, therefore, that marriage and other cultural guidelines for men can be reclaimed and reinforced.

In order to restore marriage and reinstate fathers into the lives of their children, we are somehow going to have to undo the cultural shift toward radical individualism and get people thinking again in terms of social purposes. Specifically, we are going to have to reembrace some cultural propositions or understandings that throughout history have been universally accepted but which today have become unpopular, if not in fact rejected outright.

What follows is my list of cultural propositions to be restored, with an immediate action implication for each. In part, these cultural propositions consist of moral principles. And because moral principles have some basis in human nature—the inborn biological predispositions of human beings—I believe that these propositions have universal moral validity. Many moral principles are not simply social constructs that vary widely from culture to culture, as James Q. Wilson has recently documented in his important book *The Moral Sense*.[7] Even though the conditions of human societies have radically altered, human nature remains much the same.

These propositions were once intrinsic components of a "cultural wisdom" based on experience, the product of continual, cumulative observations of what humans are like and what works best for the social order. Modern societies are skeptical of all such revealed wisdom; they want hard data. It is important to emphasize, therefore, that each of these propositions is now supported by a substantial and growing body of scientific evidence, much of which has been reviewed in this book.

1. Fathers have a unique and irreplaceable role to play in child development. Fathers are not merely would-be mothers. The two sexes are different to the core, and each is necessary—culturally as well as biologically—for the optimal development of a human being.

Action implication: We should recognize and act on the reality that most children benefit in numerous ways from having a present and involved father and that fatherless children can be seriously disadvantaged in life. This means that we should seek to diminish nonmarital, father-absent births and discourage movements such as Single Mothers by Choice. We should disavow the notion that "mommies can make good daddies," just as we should disavow the popular notion of radical feminists that "daddies can make good mommies." We should deeply respect and support the institution of fatherhood.

2. More than just needing their fathers, children need a committed male and female couple—a mother and a father in a joint partnership—to provide them with dependable and enduring love and attention at least during their growing-up years.

Action implication: We should recognize and act on the reality that children with two cooperating parents tend to be more successful in life than children with just one parent and that, in today's society, if a mother gets no help from the child's father, she may get no help from any other male. This means that we should be promoting not just fatherhood but parenthood—by a man and a woman who live and work together within a nuclear family for their children's benefit.

3. For men, more than for women, marriage and parenthood are strongly interlinked. Men need cultural pressure to stay engaged with their children, and that cultural pressure has long been called marriage.

Action implication: We must reinvigorate and relegitimize marriage as an important social institution. Currently marriage is an institution that is quietly fading away. We should address seriously the growth of unmarried couples with children; a man's chances of staying with the mother are considerably lower when he is not formally married. We should increase social, cultural, and economic supports to help couples stay married.

4. The most important and enduring dimension of fathering has to do with a child's feelings. Children need to feel recognized and accepted by their fathers; they need to feel that they are special.

Action implication: Fathers today should be taught that fathering is more than merely providing food, clothing, and shelter to children and letting mothers take care of the rest. Fathers should become fully engaged in their children's social and psychological development from day one and provide their children with continuing reassurance of their love and devotion.

5. Biological fathers are more likely to be committed to the upbringing of their own children than are nonbiological fathers. Human beings have evolved to invest more readily in genetically related persons than in nonrelated persons. Being a father is much more than merely playing a social role. Engaged biological fathers care profoundly and selflessly about their own children, and such fatherly love is not something that can be transferred easily or learned from a script.

Action implication: We should recognize the negative consequences of the dramatic increase of biological-father substitutes, ranging from temporary boyfriends to stepfathers. We should seek to reduce the necessity for father substitutes with a renewed commitment to marriage and the discouragement of divorce.

We can condense these action implications into two key issues, areas in which social and cultural change must take place if fatherhood is to be reclaimed. First, marriage must be reestablished as a strong social institution. Without marriage, men are less likely to remain involved with their children, there will be few joint partnerships, and surrogate fathers will continue to increase in number.

Second, the father's role must be redefined. Upon entering a marriage, a man needs have an unambiguous set of role expectations for being a father. In redefining the father's role we can learn from historical models. But the father's redefined role must relate to the unique attributes of modern societies, to the new roles for women, and to the special qualities that men bring to childrearing. It must be concerned, above all, with a child's feelings.

REESTABLISHING MARRIAGE

There is no magic ingredient for reestablishing the ideal of marital permanence and reaffirming marriage as the preeminent environment for children. No one sector of society is responsible for the decline of marriage. We are all part of the problem. The remedy will require substantial changes in both cultural values and public policy. It will require resolute action by millions of citizens.

Such changes are by no means impossible. Witness the massive cultural changes of recent decades—the civil rights movement, the women's liberation movement, the environmental movement, the end of communism, even the steep decline of smoking and of driving while drunk. What is necessary is for large numbers of adults, and especially our cultural and intellectual leaders, to decide unequivocally that out-of-wedlock childbearing carries serious negative consequences for children and society, that our divorce rate is far too high, and that every child deserves a father—and then do whatever it takes to convince the younger generation of the importance of these convictions.

The Council on Families in America, a national nonpartisan group of scholars and family experts of which I am cochairman, last year issued a widely discussed document entitled *Marriage in America: A Report to the Nation.*[8] Among the suggestions made to individual sectors of society, with the goal of promoting marriage, are the following:

• *To employers:* Create personnel policies and work environments that respect and favor the marital commitment. Reduce the practice of uprooting and relocating married couples with children; provide generous parental leave, and encourage the use of it by employees; experiment with job sharing; and develop opportunities for compressed workweeks, career breaks, and working at home.

• *To religious leaders and organizations:* Reclaim moral ground from the culture of divorce and nonmarriage. Avoid equating concepts such as "committed relationships" with marriage. Establish new educational and pastoral programs designed to promote commitment to marriage, prepare young people for parenthood, and uphold the ideal of marital permanence; establish and strengthen premarital counseling and marital enrichment programs.

• *To social-work, health-care, and other human-service professionals*: Within the limits of good clinical practice, promote a culture of family formation and treat individuals as much as possible in the context of families. Examine ways in which current policies and models of service delivery either explicitly or implicitly undermine marriage formation and marriage stability. Reassess professional-training and continuing-education curricula, seeking to increase professional knowledge of the benefits and responsibilities of marriage and the most effective support and treatment programs available to married couples.

• *To marriage counselors, family therapists, and family-life educators*: Begin with a bias in favor of marriage. Stress the needs of the marriage at least as much as the needs of the client. Help couples identify the likely pressure points in a marriage, such as the birth of the first child, and guide them toward steps that can help their marriage to thrive.

• *To pregnancy health-care providers and counselors*: Tell young people unequivocally that every child deserves to grow up with two married parents. For every pregnancy, insist upon paternal identification—not simply for purposes of child-support payments but also for purposes of fatherhood and, whenever possible, marriage.

• *To teachers, principals, and leaders in education*: Eliminate the implicit and frequently explicit antimarriage bias currently prevalent in many school curricula. Promote education for successful marriage as a regular part of school curricula. Include understanding of the historical roots of marriage, its desirability as an environment for childrearing, and its psychological, moral, legal, and economic requirements.

• *To family scholars*: Rewrite educational textbooks and family-life education curricula so marriage with children is portrayed as a social good rather than just one of many equally viable lifestyle alternatives. Undertake rigorous new research in the structure and experience of marriage—what makes it work, what makes it vulnerable, how it can be strengthened.

• *To the entertainment industry*: Don't glamorize unwed motherhood, marital infidelity, alternative lifestyles, and sexual promiscuity. Imagine depicting divorce and unwed childbearing as frequently and as approvingly as you currently depict smoking and littering. Examine the ramifications of what happens every day on almost all daytime television talk shows regarding issues of sexuality and marriage. Do these sensational-istic stories accurately reflect the consequences of the behavior being described? Regarding music for young people that celebrates sexual vio-lence and is steeped in a predatory view of the male-female relation-ship, balance commercial success with a sense of responsibility to the wider community of which you are a part.

• *To print and broadcast media journalists and editors:* Encourage jour-nalism on marriage and family life as a professional specialty and as a track for advancement. Guard against widely circulated statistics which distort the realities of the marital institution and family life. For editors of popular magazines aimed at teenage boys and girls, realize that many teenagers are intensely interested in thinking about the kind of person they might marry and that they would enjoy and benefit from good articles about marriage.

• *To civic leaders and community organizers:* Form grass-roots social movements designed to protect marriage and family life, not unlike movements today that seek to protect the natural environment. Dis-seminate information—for example, in schools, religious organizations, libraries, health clinics, and local media—about the personal and social value of marriage. Develop economic strategies aimed at providing more job opportunities for young males, especially poorly educated mi-nority males. Strive to develop neighborhoods which are stable and supportive of family life.

In all, the council made fifty-eight recommendations to fourteen major societal sectors. Other sectors addressed were family-law attor-neys and judges, children's advocates, foundation executives and phil-anthropic leaders, and local, state, and federal legislators.

Individual Measures

The report's final recommendation may be the most crucial: "All of us need to consider ways in which we as individuals, on a daily basis, can demonstrate support for the marriages in which we are involved, as spouse, parent, child, and other relative." It is in our personal lives where most of us have the greatest chance to have a dramatic impact on the lives and futures of those we love and thereby to be a force for good.

There are a number of actions that each person can take to enhance the likelihood of having a successful marriage and family life, actions that are strongly linked by empirical data to greater marital success in the population as a whole. First and foremost among these is to marry relatively late in life. Age at marriage has proven to be one of the single most important predictors of eventual divorce, with the highest divorce rates found among those who marry in their teenage years.[9] Teenage marriages end in divorce at twice the rate of nonteenage marriages, and marriages in the early twenties have a higher breakup rate than those in the late twenties. Young adults, therefore, should be encouraged to marry later in life than is common now, with an average age at time of marriage in the late twenties or early thirties (the average ages currently are twenty-six for men and twenty-four for women). Even later might be better for men, but at older ages than this for women who want children, the "biological clock" becomes a growing problem.[10]

The advantage of marrying later in life is that people are more mature, know better what they want in a mate, and are more established in their jobs or careers. Men have begun to "settle down" sexually (partly due to a biological diminution of their sex drive). Studies have shown that older men are more nurturant and involved with their children than younger men.[11] Another reason for marrying late is that both women and men want to have some time, when they are young and single, to enjoy the many opportunities for personal expression and fulfillment that modern, affluent societies are able to provide.

Second, it is always worth remembering that marriage partners should be selected with head as much as with heart. While love is the basis of modern marriage, love is not enough. The problem is that, especially for short-term sexual partners, opposites often attract. Yet sexual attraction, while certainly important to a marriage, is only a small part of the equation. Ideally, one is marrying not only a sexual partner but a best friend. All of the evidence on long-term marital success suggests that partners should be selected mainly on grounds of mutual compatibility and shared attitudes, values, and beliefs, grounds which extend far beyond sexual attraction. Men and women are different enough as it is; adding still more differences is generally inadvisable.

Third, to insure compatibility, a long acquaintance period prior to marrying is essential. The longer one has known a partner before marrying, the greater the chances of marital success. A short acquaintance provides insufficient time to screen out incompatible partners and to experience troublesome differences that could become serious long-run problems. According to the statistics, "quickie marriages" have a high probability of failure.

Nonmarital Cohabitation

With people marrying at older ages, we have to anticipate that some of the years of young adulthood will be spent in nonmarital cohabitation. The fact is, unpleasant though it may be to some, nonmarital cohabitation is a living arrangement that often makes more practical sense than the alternatives to it, such as early marriage, living alone, or continuing to live with one's family of origin. Because of this fact, it is an arrangement that is probably going to become increasingly common.

According to current statistical data, people who cohabit before marriage lower their chances of later marital success.[12] However, because this is the first generation which has cohabitated in large numbers, the statistical association between nonmarital cohabitation and eventual divorce may be ephemeral. There is a strong "selection factor"; the young tradition challengers who cohabit are the same people who are likely to divorce. Nonmarital cohabitation is becoming widely accepted as a responsible phase of the normal life course, and it is likely that the association between cohabitation and divorce will weaken or vanish as more and more young people cohabit.

There are many reasons for cohabiting before marriage, some desirable and some not. When it involves the clear understanding of being an acquaintance period with the strong possibility of marriage in the future, limited premarital cohabitation seems a worthwhile accommodation to enable postponement of marriage, which may be desirable for any number of reasons in addition to those noted above. I am not implying here, much less advocating, sexual promiscuity but rather serious, caring relationships which involve cohabitation. Moreover, when children are planned, nonmarital cohabitation should immediately give way to committed marriage.

On the negative side, as is commonly known, the system can easily be misused by men who do not have marriage in mind but who instead use cohabitation as a substitute for marriage and permanent commitment. Thus, women especially must be extremely cautious when entering into such a relationship.

For reestablishing marriage, the disadvantage of the growth of nonmarital cohabitation (and of late age at marriage) is that young people live for a decade or more in a nonfamily, "singles" environment. This circumstance may, in turn, reinforce their personal drive for expressive individualism and reduce any impulse toward carrying out eventual family obligations, thereby making the transition from adolescence to responsible marriage and childrearing more difficult.[13] To help overcome the antifamily impact of these years, therefore, it is vital that we find ways to promote among young unmarried adults the kind of long-range thinking that places an eventual marriage and family at the forefront.[14]

Keep in mind that the more powerful and significant statistical association is that between later marriage and marital success. Getting people to select mates wisely and to marry and have children only when they feel ready are two of the best possible antidotes to fatherlessness.

It is hard to see how these actions can be accomplished without some nonmarital cohabitation. The challenge is to keep the nonmarital cohabitation limited and responsible.

Premarital Sexuality

Although the postponement of sexual activity until marriage is still a very worthy alternative, the acceptance of limited nonmarital cohabitation means, of course, that the traditional proscription against all premarital sexuality must be relaxed (as if it weren't already). This relaxation may seem in opposition to the fundamental necessity of curtailing the sex revolution so as to restore, among other things, paternity confidence. But we must be realistic. If we are asking people to wait until their late twenties or early thirties to get married, it is unreasonable to ask them at the same time never to live together or have sex. Although Victorian men tried hard to do it, even they were not terribly successful. And they were not living, as we are today, in a society saturated with sex from childhood on.

What must continue to be morally outlawed is promiscuity. Premarital sexuality should occur only in loving relationships that involve responsibility, commitment, and sharing. This may seem a moral fine line, but there is a profound difference between sleeping with one and only one person in a nonmarital cohabiting relationship for a year and sleeping with many people in that year with whom one has virtually no relationship whatsoever.

At the same time that the moral prohibition against all premarital sex is relaxed so as to permit limited nonmarital cohabitation, however, there is a paramount need for reinstituting a strong prohibition against premarital sexuality in the teenage years. We need to reestablish the simple moral code that young people should wait until adulthood before beginning a sexually active life. This normally means through adolescence and the high school years, at least until age eighteen.

Teenage sex out of wedlock was once almost unanimously considered to be immoral and out of bounds. Today, it is commonly thought to be inevitable, even a positive experience under the right circumstances, and certainly not to be condemned. From many quarters, we are being told "to accept the reality of young people's lives." Rather than take a moral stand, we are urged "to concentrate on giving teenagers the information, guidance, and services they need . . . to have healthy, responsible and mutually protective relationships when they do become sexually active."[15]

But the "safe sex" approach to adolescent sexuality sends precisely the wrong message. Why? Because there is no such thing as safe sex among fourteen- and fifteen-year-olds. More than merely a physical act, sex is an emotional relationship which very few adolescents are mature enough to handle. And even when sex is "safe," few teenagers are prepared for the many personal consequences of sexual activity.

The soft approach to teenage sexuality appeals to most liberals, including those, for example, who are associated with the Sexuality Information and Education Council of the United States (SIECUS) and Planned Parenthood. It is commonly found in Europe, especially in the Scandinavian nations. There, social norms—flexible but widely held and reinforced by community and society—encourage young people to refrain from sex until they feel truly mature enough and then to limit sexual activity—always with the use of contraceptives—to a single partner with whom they have established a strong relationship. This approach accepts the inevitability and even desirability of teen sex. It recognizes that individuals mature at a different rate, that any set age of maturity is artificial, and that a teenager should have increasing say over his or her own body as adulthood is approached.

The liberal strategy seems to work well in many parts of Europe. Sweden, for example, has one of the world's lowest rates of teenage pregnancy. For two reasons, however, it fails in the United States. First, we are surrounded by a remarkably oversexualized culture that continuously pulls young people into sexuality before they are ready. Second, the kind of norms operating in Scandinavia seem difficult if not impossible to establish, given the great diversity of most American communities and the presence of large, undereducated, and disadvantaged population groups. Teenagers are adrift in a sea of diverse values, many of which are extreme or conflict with one another. Under such circumstances, moral codes for teenagers, if they are to be effective, must be relatively simple and clear-cut.

The simple moral proposition of "no sex before adulthood" is a middle ground between the traditional proscription against sexual intercourse before marriage and the seeming free-for-all of today's popular culture. It emphasizes that, in our increasingly complex society, adolescence should be a time for learning and maturing and becoming fully civilized, not for sexuality. Yet it acknowledges that most young people will not be virgins when they marry. It accepts the liberal approach to human sexuality but limits it to adults only.

In the sense that it stands against the powerful thrust of the sexual revolution and that teenage sexuality seems impossible to curtail, this moral proposition may appear naive to some. Actually, it has surprisingly widespread support, not only among religious bodies but among parents and teachers and even teenagers themselves. In a recent survey commissioned by *USA Weekend,* seven in ten adults and teens nationwide agreed with "the teenage abstinence message."[16] And in a recent telephone survey of 503 teenagers in grades nine through twelve, when asked their opinion about the right age to start having sexual intercourse, the high schoolers, on average, said eighteen years old; those who had already had sex said seventeen, while virgins said nineteen.[17]

Holding Marriages Together

Marriage brings with it the attendant need to keep the marriage ongoing and satisfying. Hundreds of books have been written on the topic, and many fads and nostrums ("learn to let out your anger, don't hold it in"; "seek to equalize the costs you are incurring in the marriage with the rewards you are getting from it") have come and gone. Marriage is an extraordinarily complex human institution in psychological terms, and no easy answers are available. One thing is clear: Every successful marriage involves hard work.

Some characteristics of happy and enduring marriages that often turn up in the studies are the following:[18]

1. Ability to change and tolerate change (flexibility)
2. Ability to live with the unchangeable (know when to seek change and when to look away)
3. Assumption of permanence; commitment; determination that "this marriage will last"
4. Trust, which is the basis of real love and intimacy
5. Balance of dependencies (or of power)
6. Enjoyment of each other; especially sharing a sense of humor
7. A shared history that is cherished
8. Luck

Two points are particularly worthy of note because they are often overlooked. One is the assumption of permanence. There is no doubt that the attitude one brings to a marriage is influential for the success of that marriage. If one assumes going into a marriage that "this is it," this attitude alone leads to actions that favor marital permanence. On the other hand, if one goes into the marriage feeling that it will last only "so long as I am feeling happy and fulfilled," this is a ticket for failure. I am reminded of the comment once made by a famous divorce lawyer who recommended that every couple should have a prenuptial agreement in case of a later divorce: "I have never known a couple with a prenuptial agreement," he said, "whose marriage actually survived!"

Second, marriage and family life must be built around much more than the romantic feelings between two people, if for no other reason than that these feelings fluctuate over time. It is essential that, as soon as possible, the marriage become "a little social institution" with its own subculture and family values and special ways of doing things—a shared history that is cherished. The family should have its own rituals, customs, and traditions, its own sense of humor, even its own language and vocabulary, leading to a strong sense of family identity and feelings of family pride.

The more that can be done to build a sense of family solidarity—us apart from the rest of the world—the better. As a part of such solidarity, it is important to establish strong linkages with persons outside the family, especially close relatives and friends on both sides. They should all have the understanding that this is a unique and important social unit; and they should have the expectation that it is incumbent upon them to help the family prevail.

All successful marriages, of course, have been through tough times. Their success comes from the manner in which the tough times are overcome and, perhaps, forgotten. Someone reportedly answered, when asked what makes a happy marriage, "A bad memory."

"A lasting marriage results from a couple's ability to resolve the conflicts that are inevitable in any relationship," concludes the social psychologist John Gottman, who has studied more than two thousand married couples over two decades. "Marriage lives and dies by what you might loosely call its arguments, by how well disagreements and grievances are aired." "The key is how you argue—whether your style escalates tension or leads to a feeling of resolution."[19]

Gottman suggests three essentials for successfully overcoming disagreements: calm yourself so as not to be flooded by negativity; speak and listen nondefensively so that your discussions and disagreements will be more productive; and continually validate each other and your relationship even when the going gets tough. Some people do these things naturally; almost everyone else can learn or be taught to do them.

In one of the few recent in-depth studies of happy marriages, social psychologist Judith S. Wallerstein and science writer Sandra Blakeslee find that "a good marriage is a process of continual change . . . [and] is built on a series of sequential psychological tasks that the man and the woman address together." These tasks, or life challenges, include separating from the families of childhood, becoming parents, maintaining a rich sexual relationship, and keeping alive the early romantic ideal. "If the issues represented by each psychological task are not addressed," they report, "the marriage is likely to fail."[20]

The greatest psychological task faced by most young couples today is the birth of their first child. Following the baby's arrival, gender roles change, family relationships are altered, sexual patterns are shifted, and the family group is transformed from two persons to three persons.

Husbands lose the exclusive relationship with their wives, and wives encounter new responsibilities for which neither they nor their husbands are prepared. Many studies have found this to be the least happy time in the life course of a marriage.[21]

In many cases today, neither husband nor wife has had much if any experience with infants. Rarely are relatives and friends available to lend a hand. The stress and strains in marriages at this time can linger and fester, leading to eventual divorce. Although the chances are not so high that a husband will depart an infant-tending wife, it has become common for husbands to leave their marriages when their children reach school age in response to marital stresses generated years earlier.

Again, how to deal with the psychological challenges that occur over the course of a marriage is something that can be learned and taught. If people understand in advance what is coming, they can anticipate problems and take steps to resolve them. They can learn to envision the marriage over the long term, to realize that times of stress are followed by times of happiness and that the eventual return from a successful marriage is enormous.

Education and Counseling for Marriage and Parenthood

Young people are hard pressed to find happily married role models in our current divorce culture. Absent of such role models, courses in marriage preparation and premarital counseling are ever more important. Many helpful strategies for gaining success in marriage can be taught, and it is a tragedy that formal education for marriage in America is so deficient.

Marriage preparation should be included in the curriculum of every high school in the land. Is there anything more important that could be taught to students this age? One innovative curriculum, aimed at grades seven to twelve, is sponsored by the Dibble Fund for Marital Enhancement of Kensington, California. Entitled "Keys to Success in Marriage and Other Important Relationships," it focuses on developing in students an appreciation of the need to be caring of others; ways to communicate effectively; and the importance of commitment to their partners, their offspring, and themselves. Throughout, students are oriented toward their future marriages, and the curriculum concludes with a lesson that teaches how to choose a good marital partner, the factors involved in marital success, and ways to avoid walking away from a marriage.

Another model curriculum is that devised by, of all people, the nation's divorce lawyers—the Family Law Section of the American Bar Association. Called "Partners for Students," it is an interactive televised course designed to teach junior and senior high school students the relationship skills that can maintain marriage. It focuses on choosing a mate, effective communication and negotiation, and managing stress in relationships, drawing on the knowledge of thirteen thousand lawyers who, as the promotional literature states, "are in a position to have special knowledge about why couples divorce and the incentives that might keep couples together." "People blame financial pressures, job problems, childcare challenges. But the real problem isn't stress. It's how a couple handles it—what they expect from each other, how they communicate, how they resolve conflicts."[22]

Recently, one of the most prominent cultural messages of the past three decades apparently has lost ground. That oft-heard advice is: "Staying in an unhappy marriage is psychologically damaging, and staying only for the children's sake is ultimately not in your interest or anyone else's."[23] This message has been promulgated from, above all, the therapeutic world of psychologists, therapists, counselors, and mental health workers. Many of these professionals have said to their clients, in essence, "Do what's best for yourself, and the children will be fine." Today, fortunately, a number of influential therapists are finally rethinking this message, thanks partly to an acknowledgement of the devastating effects of divorce on the clients they serve and the families of those clients. A good example is the recent book by University of Minnesota family therapist William Doherty entitled *Soul Searching: Why Psychotherapy Must Promote Moral Responsibility.*[24]

Also, there is a new realization that most conflict-ridden marriages can be saved if the spouses are interested in saving them and that salvaging the marriage is usually the better course for each of those involved. The noted marriage counselor Michele Weiner-Davis, author of *Divorce Busting,* estimates that only 15 percent of the couples with whom she has contact should, in her opinion, pursue divorce; these couples face such serious problems as physical abuse, drug addiction, and philandering.[25] The great majority of couples, she believes, would achieve greater happiness in life by staying together.

It is of such modest insights that cultural revolutions can be made.

REDEFINING THE FATHER'S ROLE

Getting and holding men to marriage is one thing; figuring out what they should do as fathers is something else entirely. Marriage is a necessary but by no means sufficient basis of good fathering.

Most societies have had a definitive cultural statement about the ideal behavior expected of fathers. The answer to the question, "what should fathers do?" at one time was unequivocal, but today, in modern societies, it is highly ambiguous; indeed, marital role ambiguity has become one of the defining cultural features of our age. Some still believe in the efficacy of traditional marital roles as we have known them for the past 150 years, while others assert that fathers and mothers should now fulfill almost identical roles. Most are caught somewhere in the middle between these two polar positions.

In light of the changed conditions of modern society, the father's role surely needs to be redefined. We can no longer maintain the traditional marital roles of the modern nuclear family. But in the redefining process we need to be careful not to drift too far in the direction of parental androgyny. Fathers and mothers are by no means the same; they bring to their children a different parenting style, and that difference is important to child development.

Why We Cannot Go Back

The marital roles within the modern nuclear family—woman as housewife and man as breadwinner—worked well in their own time, especially for children. Indeed, the past 150 years in the Anglo-American nations may well have been a golden age of childrearing. But by the late 1940s the Bureau of Labor Statistics listed nearly half of all American women as "essentially idle."[26] These women were defined as not having children under eighteen, not working in the labor force, and not being aged or infirm.[27] Today, owing mainly to steeply falling fertility and ever-increasing longevity, only about one third of the adult years of the average married woman will be spent as the mother of at-home children. This is the end result of a giant historical shift from the days when adult womanhood and motherhood were virtually equivalent.

Because motherhood no longer takes up more than a portion of a woman's adult years, she is freed to pursue gainful employment. In fact, because of the decline of marriage, a woman may well spend half to two thirds of her adulthood not only without children but also without a husband to care for and to rely on economically, forcing her to depend on her own resources. And of course, opportunities for the gainful employment of women are greater than ever before, owing in part to the civil rights laws and efforts of the women's movement, which resulted in the removal of legal barriers to education and jobs.

There is now nearly universal agreement that girls as well as boys should be trained according to their abilities for a socially useful paid job or career. It is important for women to be able to achieve the economic, social, and psychic rewards of the workplace that have long been reserved for men. And society benefits when all adult members make some work contribution during the course of their lives.

Obviously, a full-time working woman cannot at the same time be a full-time mother/homemaker. Yet even if she seeks successfully to combine work with family life—still the goal of almost all women—the traditional marital roles of male-breadwinner and female-homemaker are cast asunder. For best results in a work career, as demographers Kingsley Davis and Pietronella van den Oever have noted, women "must choose an occupation early in order to get the necessary training, and they must enter employment while young and remain employed consistently in order to build up experience, seniority, reputation, and whatever other cumulative benefit comes from occupational commitment."[28] Wealthy working mothers can hire full-time nannies or afford optimum commercial child-care arrangements; a few women will be lucky enough to have that dear relative, such as a mother, available as a recycled parent. Most women, however, if they are to maintain a foot in the work sector and if their children are to be well cared for, will require that their husbands do what few men ever before have had to do—engage in the day-to-day care of their children from birth onward.

The New Father

There is now general agreement, even among men, that fathers should expect to become more nurturing than men have traditionally been in the past and plan to spend more time in domestic pursuits. The father's work should include not only the traditional care of the house as a physical structure and of the yard and car but in many cases cooking, cleaning, laundry, and child care, the exact distribution of such activities depending upon the individual skills, talents, and time of each parent.

Parenting should be a cooperative activity, a true partnership, between husband and wife. Fathers should have an "equivalent parenting role" with mothers; they should commit to carrying "an equitable share" of parenting responsibilities over the course of childhood. Paternal disinterest in infant and child care should never be accepted, or expected, even among high-achieving men.

Having an equivalent parenting role, however, does not mean that fathers and mothers should play the same roles. Social androgyny undoubtedly has been successful in the workplace. No longer are men and women thought of as so different that they should play different work roles. Yet unlike the workplace, family organization is necessarily based to some extent on incontestable biological differences between the sexes. The idea of parental androgyny, notes the famous pediatrician Penelope Leach, "is as poor a fit with scientific facts and personal feelings as the old sexual stereotypes . . . instead of promoting the mutual respect between men and women which is a precondition for ending sexism, it is producing considerable confusion concerning parental roles, responsibilities and rights."[29]

Parental androgyny is not what children need. Males and females bring different qualities to children. "Differences between women and men in parenting," Leach stresses, "are not just inevitable; they are positively desirable."[30] Mothers tend to be "responsive" and fathers "firm"; mothers stress emotional security and relationships, and fathers stress competition and risk taking; mothers express more concern for the child's immediate well-being, while fathers are typically more active and arousing in their nurturing activities, fostering certain physical skills and emphasizing autonomy and independence. Males and females need not be straightjacketed by these gender-typed traits. But, as the eminent social psychologist Willard W. Hartup has concluded, "The importance of fathers . . . may be in the degree to which their interactions with their children do not duplicate the mother's and in the degree to which they support maternal caregiving rather than replicate it."[31]

Just as androgyny is not beneficial for children, neither does it seem to provide a good basis for a lasting marriage. Virtually nothing is more important for children than holding a marriage together. There is some evidence that parental androgyny, and especially role reversal, generates marital breakup.[32] And among couples who share similar gender-role and family attitudes, traditional couples have been found to be more satisfied with their marriages than nontraditional couples.[33]

Fathers and Mothers in Childrearing

How, then, should men and women divide the childrearing tasks? Recognizing that a one-size-fits-all pattern will have to be adapted in individual cases to fit the tremendous diversity of conditions found in marriages today, not to mention human diversity, some general guidelines can be put forth.

In light of all that we now know about child development, women as a general rule should be the primary caretakers of infants during at least the first year to eighteen months of life. One reason for this is breast-feeding. This practice has enormous physical and psychological advantages for the infant and also positive value for most women. A second and equally important reason is that through evolutionary adaptation women are inherently more sensitive to the needs of the nonverbal infant. At birthing time, women have already developed a relationship with their babies in utero that is unlike anything available to fathers. And as Alice Rossi has noted, based on a rapidly accumulating body of evidence, "In caring for a nonverbal, fragile infant, women have a head start in reading an infant's facial expressions, smoothness of body motions, ease in handling a tiny creature with tactile gentleness, and soothing through a high, soft, rhythmic use of the voice."[34]

Surely men can be taught some of these things, as many scholars have pointed out, especially if they are well motivated.[35] But with all the other unresolved problems in this world, it is resolutely silly to think of embarking on a mass reeducation campaign just so that men can do halfheartedly what women can do better. Moreover, the overwhelming majority of women want to care for infants; they receive enormous satisfaction from it.

The father's parenting role with infants should have two primary goals. First is to enhance a home environment that permits a strong mother-child attachment. Such attachment depends heavily on help from the father. He should be prepared to assist in every way possible, to the degree that time permits, in day-to-day child-care activities. This includes help with feeding, dressing, bathing, play, and putting the children to bed. And he should be prepared regularly to spell the mother as primary caretaker so that she can attend to other needs and activities.

The second main parenting goal for the father of infants is to secure and maintain a strong emotional attachment between himself and his children. In his relationship with his children, the father should seek to be warm, affectionate, and fully accepting. As Harvard pediatrician T. Berry Brazelton has pointed out, "All of the studies that measure increasing involvement of fathers in their babies' caretaking point to the gains in the babies' development."[36]

Among other important benefits, the involvement of men in child care, starting in early infancy, accomplishes through psychological means what was once accomplished through social means. Men in close contact with young children become emotionally attached to them, and this attachment causes men to be more willing to make continuing parental investments, even in the absence of the traditional controls of culture and kin group. Close male attachment to infants also appears to have beneficial effects in suppressing sexual abuse (see chapter 2).

After infancy, the desirable division of labor between fathers and mothers in childrearing will vary in terms of a variety of personal and social characteristics, plus the age of the child. Children are able to verbalize fairly well when they are about eighteen months old. By this age, because a wide range of senses is no longer so important, it seems more appropriate for fathers to become primary caretakers.[37] This is the time when mothers can reasonably return to work part-time. As children grow older, it becomes ever more reasonable for either parent to take the leading hand in childrearing. Yet even with older children, the father's style of parenting is not interchangeable with that of the mother's, nor should it be.

Two other father roles are more subtle, but nonetheless immensely important. The first is to help manage family tensions, especially those which arise between the mother and child. A prime value of the two-parent family is that each partner can help to qualify and control the unconsidered, impulsive, or idiosyncratic reactions of the other. The second is to provide a "protective presence," not necessarily physical protection (although that, too, may sometimes be necessary) but reassurance to the mother that she has a strong and reliable ally by her side.

We have already discussed the fact that the period following childbirth and the early years of childhood have proven to be, in modern societies, a time of great stress in many marriages. The quality of the husband-wife relationship is critical for the mother's well-being and for her ability to be a competent parent; the relationship contributes as well to the father's desire to be involved with childrearing.[38] In addition to helping his wife with child care, then, it is very important during this period for the husband to work hard on maintaining a strong marriage.

All of the evidence suggests that the father's traditional role of cold and detached disciplinarian is to be avoided. He should seek to instill discipline through teaching rather than through coercion and punishment. For older children the best discipline, that which teaches prosocial behavior, involves reasoning with the child and pointing out the consequences of his or her actions.[39] This takes time and patience. Also of great importance in disciplining children is that fathers and mothers agree on what they consider proper standards of behavior and that they be good role models for their children.

The use of nonfamily child care has so far not been mentioned. What does the empirical evidence show? It shows that by far the best environment for childrearing is in the home and under the care of the biological parents. The more both parents can be in close contact with the child in the early years, the better. It also indicates that every infant needs one special person to whom he or she can become attached, a person who cares about the child beyond reason.[40] That person typically has been the biological mother, the person most highly motivated for the task.

Out-of-home child care normally should be limited to not more than ten to twenty hours per week for at least the first year of life; a number of studies have found negative effects on child development when out-of-home child care exceeds this amount.[41] After age three there is little evidence that high-quality day care has negative effects on children, and the amount of time spent in day care and preschool activities can increase. Indeed, most children by that age enjoy and benefit from being part of a close-knit peer group, having intimate contact with nonfamily adults, and exploring the wider opportunities of the out-of-home world.

With any reasonable division of labor in childrearing, there is no getting around that fact that, in the short run at least, mothers suffer a greater loss of work status than fathers. To help compensate for this discrepancy, work life needs to be much more accommodating to mothers (and fathers as well). Some government programs can also help, such as family leave and a "Parental Bill of Rights," discussed below. It should be noted that there is some balancing out of domestic and paid-work roles between women and men over the course of life. In later life "role switching" often occurs, presumably caused in part by hormonal changes, in which women become more work oriented and men become more domestic.[42] And husbands, being normally older than their wives, often retire while their wives are still working.

MARRIAGE, FATHERHOOD, AND MALE WELL-BEING

One of the best ways to reestablish marriage and promote fatherhood is to make widely known to men of all ages what is now verified by a substantial body of social research: Marriage and fatherhood are enormously beneficial to the well-being of men. In general, married men are better off than single men in social and psychological terms. They are more effective on the job, and they have a higher level of personal well-being, that pervasive sense that life is good.

Marriage and Male Well-Being

The main cause of happiness among people in general is no longer much in doubt. It is not, as many Americans believe, simply having money and material possessions. The average American is twice as rich today as in the 1950s, yet the percentage of Americans saying they are "very happy" remains virtually unchanged (although youth are less happy than they were at mid-century, and the elderly are more happy).[43] Many surveys have shown that happiness or a sense of well-being is only modestly related to being economically well-off; indeed, the correlation between income and happiness in the United States has dropped nearly to zero. "Actual income doesn't much influence happiness," reports social psychologist David G. Myers; "how *satisfied* we are with our income does."[44] "Once beyond poverty, further economic growth does not appreciably improve human morale."[45]

If not money, then what? The main source of happiness is having close, warm, and enduring relationships. And the main generator of such relationships is marriage and the family. Many studies of marriage and happiness have been conducted over the years, and they invariably find a strong, positive association. In social surveys, fewer than 25 percent of unmarried adults but nearly 40 percent of married adults report being "very happy." Indeed, satisfaction with marriage and family life is the strongest single overall predictor of personal well-being.[46]

Although both men and women are made happier through a good marriage, there is an advantage for men. In the words of the late social psychologist Angus Campbell, "Men appear to suffer more from the absence of a wife than women do from the absence of a husband."[47] The underlying reason is that women, in general, are better at social relationships than men; it is the female sex that provides most of the nurturing and caring on which strong relationships are based. Both men and women, for example, report their friendships with women "to be more intimate, enjoyable, and nurturing."[48]

For a man, the woman who provides the intimate friendship is likely to be his wife. Men are much more likely than women to say that their best friend is their spouse. If a man does not have a wife (or girlfriend), he is not likely to get the emotional sustenance he needs from other men or other women. Women, on the other hand, can more easily turn to other women for intimate friendship. Indeed, four in five women say their best friend is another woman![49]

The marriage relationship tends to be strongly beneficial not only for men's psychological well-being but also for their physical health and longevity. Recent evidence shows that married men are much healthier than single, divorced, or widowed men; they live longer, too. And the longer they have been married, the more they benefit.[50] Unmarried men engage more heavily in negative health behaviors. They drink more, fight more, and have more accidents. Based on the estimated days of life expectancy lost to various causes, being unmarried is a much more dangerous risk factor than being overweight, smoking cigarettes, or even having cancer or heart disease![51]

Health and well-being, of course, are closely related. Both are affected strongly by the quality of social relationships, by the feeling that one is liked, affirmed, encouraged, and looked after. As with psychological well-being, men physically benefit from marriage more than women and probably for the same reason—men are not as able as women to find strong social relationships outside of marriage.[52]

A frequently asked question is, aren't these observed marital benefits merely due to the fact that already superior men are more likely to get married? In other words, marriage may not be the cause of these benefits at all. This issue has been carefully studied, and the results show a strong marriage effect independent of the "selectivity factor." As sociologist Catherine E. Ross recently reported in the *Journal of Marriage and the Family,* "The positive effect of marriage on well-being is strong and consistent, and the selection of the psychologically healthy into marriage or the psychologically unhealthy out of marriage cannot explain the effect."[53]

Only a few studies have looked at the relationship between marriage and male job success. One recent study by economists found that white male married workers, compared to their single counterparts, received higher performance ratings from their supervisors, and these higher ratings, in turn, increased their promotion chances and led to higher wages. Controlling for education, job grade, precompany experience, and a host of others factors, marriage increased by almost 50 percent the probability that a recent hire would receive one of the top two performance ratings. The selection of men into marriage on the basis of their already high wages found no statistical support in this study; the wage rises occurred after the marriages took place.[54]

Putting the lie to the glories of singledom, studies reveal that married men even have better sex lives than unmarried men. The 1992 National Health and Social Life Survey found that married men have twice as much sex per month as single men. Not only that, but the sex married men have is of higher quality, in that married men report higher levels of physical and emotional satisfaction with their sex lives.[55]

Fathering and Male Well-Being

Just as marriage promotes male well-being, so does fathering. Almost all men want to father in order to gain that genetic link to posterity. Unfortunately, not all realize that being an active and engaged father is one of the most deeply satisfying and meaningful of life's endeavors. As longtime fatherhood expert Ross D. Parke concluded, based on all the evidence at his disposal, "Fathering [is] good for men as well as for children."[56]

Few men get accolades from their peers for being a good father. Yet for the internal life of men, fatherhood has no competitors. And the more a man puts into fathering, the more he gets back. In general, children give men a perspective on what is really important in life, as well as the important sense of interpersonal connectedness across the generations. They enhance in men the virtues that are in increasingly short supply—patience, kindness, generosity, compassion—and help prevent the ever more pervasive preoccupation with the self.[57]

One of the most important recent studies of the effects over time of being a father is John Snarey's *How Fathers Care for the Next Generation: A Four Decade Study* (1993).[58] The book compares the life outcomes of two groups of men: those who were highly involved with their children and those who were not very involved.[59] After controlling for many background variables, Snarey concluded that fathering does make a very significant difference—not only for the children who were well fathered but for the fathers themselves in later life. Fathers who had participated actively in rearing their children were somewhat more successful in occupational terms and more successful in their own marriages. In addition, and this is especially important, they demonstrated "a clear capacity for establishing, guiding, or caring for the next generation through sustained responsibility for the growth, well-being, or leadership of younger adults or of the larger society." They were, in words borrowed from the famous psychologist Erik Erikson, "societally generative."[60]

Several studies have corroborated that at older ages, parents on the whole are "better off" and more satisfied with life than childless adults.[61] In their twilight years people who have successfully raised children not only have those children to rely on, a very fortunate situation indeed, but also the realization that they have accomplished one of life's most meaningful missions.[62]

Among men this long-term beneficial effect seems particularly to be true. The happiest and most satisfied with life of all men are those living in the "empty nest"—fathers of grown children who are still married to their wives. They have a consistently high level of perceived well-being.[63] At the opposite extreme is the growing army of males who live apart from their children and are detached from family life. They show the lowest level of well-being. And the worst may be yet to come. Who is going to comfort them in their old age? Who, if anyone, is going to be visiting them in the nursing home?

GOVERNMENT ACTION

Government policies have not been a major focus of this book. Because the causes for the decline of marriage and fatherhood lie mainly in the moral, behavioral, and even spiritual realms, the decline is mostly resistant to public-policy and government cures. The fact is that, regardless of governmental system and political persuasion, marriage decline and fatherlessness have occurred in all industrialized societies in the West as these societies have become more affluent. Marriage decline is almost as great in Sweden, the West's most accomplished welfare state, as it is in the United States, the most laissez-faire of the industrialized nations.

Nevertheless, government policies do make some contribution to family behavior, both in their presence and their absence; and while serious consideration of the role of government is beyond the confines of this book, I would be remiss if I did not suggest some guidelines for government action. Government action, of course, is the focus of partisan politics, and the following guidelines come with this caution: We must not let partisan bickering over government programs weaken our resolve to restore married fatherhood to America. Whether one advocates the welfare state or a laissez-faire economy, big government or small government, liberalism or conservatism, the realization must prevail that strong, intact nuclear families are absolutely essential for a stable democratic social order.

To rebuild a family-oriented culture based on enduring marital relationships and active fathering, I suggest the following as a major, measurable goal of government programs: *to increase the proportion of children who are living with and cared for by their married, biological fathers and decrease the proportion of children who are not.* With this goal in mind, all relevant government programs should undergo at least an informal "family-impact assessment." Records should be maintained that allow measurement of the degree to which this goal is achieved. As a first rule, of course, government programs should seek to do no harm.

The Economy

As indicated in earlier chapters, there is little doubt that male wages in real dollars have been dropping since the early 1970s (almost at the same rate that female wages have increased) and that this has had some effect on marriage rates and marriage stability. Some men clearly have decided to forgo marriage because they are unemployed or don't make enough money to support a family, especially in the inner-city black community where there is a lack of unskilled jobs. Other men will leave a marriage when the economic going gets tough. Many marriages suffer, as do the children, when both parents must be in the labor market full-time out of economic necessity.

While the statistical relationship of economic cycles to marriage and divorce is not robust, low wages, unemployment, and poverty have never been big supporters of marriage. A strong and growing economy is generally good for marriage, as we found out in the 1950s. The generation of a stable and well-paid employment base for all Americans, therefore, should obviously remain a government policy goal of the highest priority.

Economic Support for Childrearing Families

It used to be the case that almost all marriages and the great majority of households involved children; children thus benefited directly from the income of most working adults. Now only a minority of households, less than a third, contain children. A large economic gap has arisen between childrearing families and other families, with childrearing families—owing to their greater need for resources—falling ever farther behind in the struggle for economic survival.

Children are a national asset; they represent the future of our society. That we all should be helping with their economic support is an attitude that prevailed for generations with regard to primary and secondary education, libraries, playgrounds, child health, and tax policy. Unfortunately, government programs in support of children have been falling behind other areas of government spending for a long time. Americans have decided to socialize much of the cost of growing old, for example, but less of the cost of raising children. Peter Peterson and Neil Howe have estimated that eleven times more benefit dollars per capita go to those over sixty-five than to those under eighteen.[64] Our sense of priorities has become distorted. At the very least we should strive for generational equity.

Married couples with children have incurred much larger tax increases than other groups of Americans in recent decades. We should return to the earlier, more favorable tax treatment of families with children. This involves either significantly increasing the current personal exemption for dependent children or replacing it with a substantial child tax credit for all children through age eighteen. In addition, the federal tax code should be revised to eliminate the "marriage penalty," which in some cases requires married couples to pay dramatically higher taxes than unmarried cohabiting couples.

More than anything else, parents need time to be with their children. With most mothers now in the labor force, it is imperative that the United States expand its family leave policy, which permits one parent some time off from work for child care (while maintaining benefits and the right to resume employment.) The current twelve weeks of unpaid leave is in the right direction, but it is woefully inadequate; it is also far out of line with the practice in most other industrialized nations. Our family leave policy should be extended to at least twelve months and with partial pay.

We also should consider providing educational credits or vouchers to parents who leave the paid labor force for extended periods of time to care for their young children. Along the lines of the G.I. Bill for World War II veterans, these credits or vouchers could be provided for high school, vocational, college, graduate, or postgraduate education. As presented by economists Richard T. Gill and T. Grandon Gill at a meeting of the Council on Families in America, the premise of this Parental Bill of Rights is that "parents who raise their own children perform an important social service and that in doing so, they may imperil their long-run career prospects. In return for making this sacrifice for a socially desirable end, society will compensate them by subsidizing their further education so that they can more effectively re-enter the labor force or initiate a long-run career path."[65]

Welfare Reform

Welfare reform should be high on the political agenda, an opinion that fortunately is now held by both political parties. The empirical evidence largely supports the proposition that means-tested welfare programs, those with income-based limits on program eligibility, have weakened the marriage bond and promoted fatherlessness among welfare recipients. While means-tested welfare programs affect only a small segment of the American population, their single-parent and child recipients are overrepresented on all indices of health, social, and criminal problems. We should be concerned, however, that the welfare recipient not become a whipping boy for the much larger problems of fatherlessness and divorce which are pervasive in all strata of our society.

The basic dilemma that welfare programs face is an inherent and long-noted one in public policy: What is subsidized is likely to increase, and what is taxed is likely to decrease. Families on welfare are, in effect, rewarded with public supports when they fail to look after themselves and penalized by losing public supports when they take care of themselves. Marriage has traditionally been an economic partnership as well as a social commitment, one that was favored by the government. Yet in welfare programs the economic incentive for couples to stay together is diminished and, if and when couples break up, the negative economic consequences of the action are rendered relatively benign through public subsidies. Over time, as the family economic partnership is gradually replaced by dependence on government, the interdependencies and reciprocal obligations of family life diminish.

We must learn to strike a better balance in our welfare programs between collective compassion and individual responsibility. Clearly, as President Clinton stated in his 1994 State of the Union address: "If we value strong families, we can't perpetuate a system that actually penalizes those who stay together."[66] Or in the words of social scientist Christopher Jencks, "If we want to promote virtue, we have to reward it."[67]

In addition to providing a safety net that insures adequate food, shelter, and medical care for the destitute, welfare programs should be designed to promote marriage, cultivate family self-sufficiency, reward productive behavior, and require parental responsibility. They should seek to place all able-bodied welfare recipients other than persons caring for infants and young children in paid employment, preferably in the private sector, but if such work is unavailable, in community services and public programs. The identification of fathers prior to the receipt of welfare benefits should be mandatory, and the child-support obligations of noncustodial parents should be vigorously enforced.

Promarriage Values

As we can see in the case of welfare, government programs and tax policies should be formulated to *privilege* married, childrearing couples rather than be neutral toward them (for fear of stigmatizing "alternative lifestyles"), much less economically penalize them. We should acknowledge alternative lifestyles, but that does not mean we have to affirm them as equivalent to marriage. And it should not mean that we are prohibited from favoring childrearing couples who stick together for the sake of the children. Such couples provide society with an enormous increase in social capital.

That the federal government cannot take a position on such family matters because sensitive "moral issues" are involved, as is sometimes argued, is unjustifiable. The government is regularly taking moral positions on a whole range of issues, such as the rights of women, income equality, and race relations. A government position on the right of children to have two committed parents during their formative years is both morally appropriate and socially necessary.

Divorce Reform

A reinstated legal *prohibition* of divorce certainly would be an unreasonable intrusion on personal liberty. Especially when children are not involved, as is the case in many marriages today, there is little social benefit in trying to keep two people together who are miserable in each other's company. With intimacy and companionship now the main basis for marriage, couples without children should have the clear right to move on when these are no longer obtainable, and present divorce laws serve them well.

With 50 to 60 percent of parental unions dissolving through divorce, however, we must be alarmed for children, for families, and for society itself. Making divorce involving children somewhat more difficult to accomplish in legal terms may provide one solution. Laws, after all, do shape behavior, not only through creating rules and incentives but by conveying cultural messages about the institutions they are set up to regulate. Current divorce laws, unfortunately, send the message that marriage is not a socially important relationship that involves a legally binding commitment.

We should consider a two-tier system of divorce law: Marriages without minor children would be relatively easy to dissolve, but marriages with children would be dissolvable only by mutual agreement or on grounds that clearly involve a wrong by one party against the other, such as desertion, repeated adultery, chronic alcoholism and gambling, and physical abuse. Longer waiting periods for divorcing couples with children might also be called for, combined with some form of mandatory marriage counseling or marital education.

Rebuilding Local Communities

There is much truth to the proposition that family life can only be as strong as the community that supports it. Just as the child is dependent on the family, the family is dependent on the surrounding community. Childrearing was once a community affair where the whole community was geared to the task. Today families are becoming ever more isolated from their communities, and the communities are becoming ever less supportive of children. There has been a widespread decline of what has come to be called "civil society." Many of the communities in which American children are growing up today are saturated with crime, materialism, and the loss of neighborliness, leading parents to despair. Nothing could be worse for marriage, children, and fatherhood. It is time for a radical shift in how we think about our communities and how we build them.

Here are some community-building guidelines designed to promote marriage and family life:[68]

• *Foster residential stability.* The constant changing of residence wreaks havoc with family life, especially when the move is to a different community. Moreover, the longer one lives in a community, the more publicly attached to it one becomes, and people who are strongly attached to their communities are more likely to support a rich and sustaining community life.[69] Families ordinarily move away from a local community for two reasons: jobs and housing. To minimize such moves, it is obviously important to maintain high levels of local employment. Less obviously, each community should be encouraged to provide a broad mix of housing types so as to lessen the likelihood that residents will leave simply because they need more appropriate dwelling space.

• *Revitalize community moral standards.* As a nation, we have become utterly preoccupied with individual rights. To be strong and family-supportive, local residential communities must necessarily be moral communities, and the assumptions that all rights rest with the individual and that local government should be morally neutral are antithetical to the continued existence of such communities. Without violating the Bill of Rights, local communities should have more autonomy in establishing and enforcing their own values and moral standards.

• *Provide more public facilities and services.* For family life, and especially for children, the best communities are those with a rich measure of facilities and services available to all. This includes schools, hospitals, libraries, parks and playgrounds, youth centers, museums, and public transportation. One can understand the nation's current antitax mood, but program cuts should not come at the expense of facilities and services that serve children. We must not let our nation's social infrastructure weaken.

• *Favor the development of smaller cities and towns.* Most people say they would prefer to live in a place smaller than that in which they currently live, provided they have reasonable access to jobs and public services; it is the search for community that drives their preference.[70] Small cities and towns, because they are closer to the "human scale," have measurable community-giving and family-supporting advantages over large urban agglomerations.

• *Support local political autonomy.* To the extent possible, political decision making should be decentralized so that local communities have more autonomy. Political autonomy and social autonomy are linked; one enhances the other. The subsidiarity principle should be followed: No political function or social task should be assigned to a unit that is larger than necessary to do the job.

• *Promote comprehensive communities that have functional balance.* Metropolitan conditions have fostered a tremendous overspecialization of local areas, with people living in one place, working at another, shopping at a third, and recreating at a fourth. A negative social consequence of this is that there is little overlap in the social attachments made in the four places; friends made at work are seldom neighbors, for example, and neighbors are seldom coworkers. Friendships and family attachments in metropolitan settings are fragile enough without these kinds of impediments. Also, the ever-increasing length and number of automobile trips made necessary by current metropolitan development are disastrous for both family and community life.

• *Protect and promote family-oriented neighborhoods.* Most people strongly prefer to live next door to others with whom they feel comfortable and can form close friendships.[71] For childrearing families, living in a neighborhood where the residents share similar values and have a similar lifestyle can be an enormous advantage. Provided that laws prohibiting discrimination are not violated, homogeneous neighborhoods made up of families with children, possibly up to the size necessary to support neighborhood schools, should be protected and encouraged.

WINDOWS OF HOPE

How likely is it that the kind of cultural and policy changes outlined in this chapter could ever occur, changes that could help to rebuild a family-oriented culture based on enduring marital relationships and active fathering? If enough people agree that they should, such changes can of course occur. By the same token, they certainly will not occur if people believe that change is impossible or improbable and thereby are deterred from speaking out or acting within their own local environment or sphere of influence.

There are grounds for optimism. A few current trends and conditions, suggested below, provide hope that the kind of changes I am suggesting are possible. Each positive trend or condition, however, comes with a caveat. Counterforces exist that are working, or may work, in an opposing direction. We should consider these counterforces as challenges, obstacles to be overcome.

1. The Baby-Boom Factor. The huge population cohort called the baby boomers, which was instrumental in bringing us the divorce revolution, has reached middle age. As people grow older, their lifestyles and values become more familistic. We are seeing evidence for this familistic shift all around us—more babies, more books and articles on parenting, more concern about antifamily themes in the movies and popular music, more unwillingness to be transferred to a new work location when young children are involved, more women staying at home with their infants and very young children. The boomer group is so large that it will remain highly influential.

Caveat: The boomers could eventually become self-absorbed, "greedy geezers" rather than virtue-oriented and civic-minded citizens. We must find ways to help this generation become more deeply involved in the development of a humane, family-oriented society.

2. The Cultural Dialectic Factor. Cultural change is often dialectical and cyclical, and some cycles of change are patterned in generational terms. They occur over a thirty-year period, the length of one generation. Not all cultural values can simultaneously be maximized, and one generation comes to appreciate, because they have less of it, what their parents' generation rejected. Cultures are thus to some degree self-correcting.

Such a cyclical shift may be occurring today, a shift away from individualism and choice toward family and other social bonds. In their frantic pursuit of expressive individualism, the young baby boomers took marriage and the family for granted. The generations that have followed, the so-called generation X and the baby-boom-echo children, cannot do so; indeed, many within these generations insist that they don't want their children to go through what their parents put them through. There is some evidence that many in the younger generations are rather desperately looking for more stable marriages and family life and stronger social bonds.

Caveat: Many in the younger generation have lacked, in their families of origin, positive marital and parental role models, and some have suffered, because of unstable childhoods, in their ability to form strong, enduring personal relationships. Some have also become the captives of a culture of rampant individualism and consumerism. As a result, they may wish to prevent marital problems by avoiding marriage altogether, remaining free agents in the realm of personal relationships. We must help them to realize that marriage and personal happiness are closely related; that a good marriage and good fathering require a great deal of personal effort but are well worth it because they lead more surely to good prospects for health, prosperity, and the self-confidence that permits—ironically—more individual expression, freedom, and creativity.

3. The Reason Factor. Massive evidence on the relationship of marriage decline and fatherlessness to the deterioration of child well-being has become available. The highlights have been presented in this book. Americans are a reasonable people. They want to see the evidence, and when they see it, they often follow its dictates. This has certainly been the case, for example, with smoking.

Caveat: The evidence is never conclusive; there is always room for doubt. Also, some behavior can be very hard to change, despite the evidence. Take our knowledge about AIDS and how little it has actually changed sexual behavior in America. The social and behavioral sciences need to gather more and better evidence about the effects of marriage decline and fatherlessness and make sure—in conjunction with the media—that it is disseminated widely.

4. The Government Factor. In a perverse and paradoxical way, some government welfare programs have been the enemy of marriage and fatherhood. In the process of helping those in need, they have, in effect, rewarded those who choose not to live in marriage-based, father-headed families and, for the destitute, made unwed single-parenthood not only a viable but a preferable life choice. We now realize this, and concern about marriage and family life and fatherhood has come back into government thinking within both political parties. Corrective policy actions will be taken.

Caveat: Poverty is also the enemy of marriage. We must be careful to design government programs that strike a good balance between the necessity for individual responsibility and people's material needs. While government policies need to deter, not encourage, unwed single-parenthood, they should aim to provide better life options for potential unwed parents.

5. *The Affluence Factor.* Much of the marriage decline and fatherlessness of the past few decades has come about through "sudden affluence," which has engendered social disengagement and permitted highly individualistic forms of self-fulfillment (the decadence of the rich, if you will). Today we are settling into our new affluence, and there is no longer such a constant upsurge of wealth; for many families there has even been an economic downturn. We are realizing that we have to rely more on our families, and not just on the market, for economic and other kinds of support.

Caveat: Unemployment, economic downturns, and depressions are hardly the answer to our problems of marriage and fatherhood. Maintaining a strong economy is important. And we must find better ways to protect people from family-damaging market forces, such as those requiring incessant residential mobility, and from the mesmerizing qualities of late twentieth-century consumption-driven materialism.

6. *The Religious Factor.* There are signs today that secularization may have run its course; people are longing for a more spiritual dimension to life, for religious wisdom. Religion has long been a supporter of marriage and strong families.

Caveat: We may turn, as have many in Hollywood, toward an individualistic, self-centered, new-age style religion that is silent or even negative about marriage and family life, to say nothing of fatherhood.

7. *The Biological Factor.* Recent investigations, reviewed in this book, have indicated that much of marital and nuclear family behavior has a biological basis. No matter what the postmodern world throws at us, human nature and human psychology have probably not changed much from the millions of years we lived as hunter-gatherers in our ancestral environment. We still are mostly monogamous and have a need for stable, intimate attachments and reliance on close relatives. We still have a built-in love for our children. Fathers are still essential.

Caveat: There is no indication that we, men especially, are biologically well-suited to being monogamous for life. That's what modern marriage systems were established to achieve, however.

In view of all these factors, I believe that the cultural revitalization of marriage and the consequent reclaiming of fatherhood is achievable. But there are many obstacles to be overcome. Much human effort lies ahead.

We are at a major fork in the road in America. It is imperative that we take one path—the path that requires a shift of direction—and not the other. For in the words of an ancient Chinese proverb: "Unless we change direction, we're likely to end up where we're headed." And that would be a social disaster—for our children, our families, and our society.

The act of being a good father, now so cavalierly discounted, is an essential building block of every successful society. Just as a multitude of personal failings becomes a major public crisis, so does a multitude of personal contributions add up to an enormous public gain. In the final analysis, every father counts.

Notes

Introduction

1. *New York Times,* Sept. 25, 1986, p. C7.
2. U.S. Department of Health and Human Services. *Vital Statistics of the United States, 1991.* Vol. 1, *Natality.* Washington, DC: GPO, 1993. Among blacks, the increase has been from 23% to 68%.
3. Congressional testimony of Lee Rainwater, Harvard University. Cited in William J. Bennett. 1994. *The Index of Leading Cultural Indicators.* New York: Simon and Schuster, p. 47.
4. It should be noted that social science evidence is never conclusive, on this or any other matter we will be taking up in this book. The world is too complex; the scientific method can only imperfectly be applied to the study of human beings; researchers have biases; and people may not always be telling investigators the truth. These are but a few of the many problems endemic to the social sciences. The best use of the social science evidence is to help confirm or disconfirm. Does the evidence generally support a proposition or not? If it does, fine; if it does not, one had better have a good explanation as to why that proposition may still be true.
5. Sara S. McLanahan. 1994. "The Consequences of Single Motherhood." *The American Prospect,* 18:48–58, esp. 49. Article is drawn from Sara McLanahan and Gary Sandefur. 1994. *Growing Up with a Single Parent.* Cambridge, MA: Harvard University Press.
6. McLanahan. *Consequences,* p. 52.
7. Elaine Ciulla Kamark and William A. Galston. 1990. *Putting Children First: A Progressive Family Policy for the 1990s.* Washington, DC: Progressive Policy Institute, pp. 14–15.
8. See Henry B. Biller. 1993. *Fathers and Families: Paternal Factors in Child Development.* Westport, CT: Auburn House.
9. McLanahan. *Consequences,* p. 51.
10. Biller. *Fathers and Families.*
11. January 20, 1993.
12. Alice Rossi. 1987. "Parenthood in Transition: From Lineage to Child to Self-Orientation." Pp. 31–81 in Jane B. Lancaster, Jeanne Altmann, Alice Rossi, and Lonnie R. Sherrod, eds., *Parenting Across the Life Span: Biosocial Dimensions.* New York, NY: Aldine de Gruyter, p. 64.
13. Eleanor E. Maccoby and Carol N. Jacklin. 1974. *The Psychology of Sex Differences.* Palo Alto, CA: Stanford University Press. J. Archer and B. Lloyd. 1985. *Sex and Gender.* New York: Cambridge University Press. Robert Pool. 1994. *Eve's Rib: Searching for the Biological Roots of Sex Differences.* New York: Crown.

14. Anne Moir and David Jessel. 1991. *Brain Sex.* New York: Lyle Stuart, p. 17.
15. Rossi. *Parenthood,* p. 69.
16. M. W. Yogman. 1982. "Development of the Father-Infant Relationship." Pp. 221–280 in H. E. Fitzgerald, B. M. Lester, and M. W. Yogman, eds., *Theory and Research in Behavioral Pediatrics 1.* New York: Plenum Press; J. L. Roopnarine and N. S. Mounts. 1985. "Mother-Child and Father-Child Play." *Early Child Development Care* 20:157–169.
17. Emile Durkheim. 1951. *Suicide: A Study in Sociology.* New York: Free Press.
18. Arthur Kraus and Abraham Lilienfeld. 1959. "Some Epidemiologic Aspects of the High Mortality Rate in the Young Widowed Group." *Journal of Chronic Diseases* 10:207–217. Walter Gove. 1973. "Sex, Marital Status, and Mortality." *American Journal of Sociology* 79:45–67.
19. Two general books on this topic are: James Lincoln Collier. 1991. *The Rise of Selfishness in America.* New York: Oxford University Press; and Art Carey. 1991. *The United States of Incompetence.* Boston: Houghton Mifflin. See also: Louis Harris. 1987. *Inside America.* New York: Vintage Books; and William J. Bennett. 1994. *The Index of Leading Cultural Indicators.* New York: Simon & Schuster. In the light of such changes, some observers have called into question the very idea of social progress itself. See Christopher Lasch. 1991. *The True and Only Heaven.* New York: W. W. Norton.
20. Mary Ann Glendon. 1991. *Rights Talk: The Impoverishment of Political Discourse.* New York: Free Press.
21. Robert A. Nisbet. 1966. *The Sociological Tradition.* New York: Basic Books.

Chapter 1. The Remarkable Decline of Fatherhood and Marriage

1. In 1990, 57.7% of American children under age 18 lived with both their biological parents, 21.6% lived with their mother only, 11.3% lived with two parents married to each other, one of whom was their stepparent, 3.1% lived with their father only, and the remaining 6.3% lived with neither parent or were "unknown or unaccounted for." U.S. Bureau of the Census. 1992. "Marriage, Divorce, and Remarriage in the 1990s (Current Population Reports, P23–180)." Washington, DC: GPO. Tables M and N.
2. Donald J. Hernandez. 1993. *America's Children.* New York: Russell Sage Foundation, p. 71
3. See E. Thomson and U. Colella. 1992. "Cohabitation and Marital Stability." *Journal of Marriage and the Family* 54:259–267.
4. D. B. Rutman and A. H. Rutman. 1984. *A Place in Time: Middlesex County, Virginia, 1650–1750.* New York: Norton.
5. Rutman and Rutman. *A Place in Time;* Hernandez. *America's Children,* p. 69.
6. The average expectation of life for a male born at the turn of the century was only 48 years, compared to 71.5 years in 1988 (much of that difference is accounted for by steeply dropping infant mortality rates). Judith Treas and Ramon Torrecilha. 1995. "The Older Population." Pp. 47–92 in Reynolds Farley, ed., *State of the Union: America in the 1990s.* New York: Russell Sage Foundation, p. 62.
7. See Andrew J. Cherlin. 1992. *Marriage, Divorce, and Remarriage.* Cambridge, MA: Harvard University Press, pp. 20–27.
8. Linda Gordon and Sara McLanahan. 1991. "Single Parenthood in 1900." *Journal of Family History* 16(2):97–116. In 1900, 83% of children living with their fathers and 77% of children living with their mothers lived with a widowed parent.

9. Christopher Jencks and Barbara Boyle Torrey. 1988. "Beyond Income and Poverty: Trends in Social Welfare and Among Children and the Elderly Since 1960." Pp. 229–273 in John L. Palmer, T. Smeeding, and B. B. Torrey, eds., *The Vulnerable.* Washington, DC: Urban Institute.

10. Andrew Cherlin and Frank F. Furstenberg, Jr. 1988. "The Changing European Family: Lessons for the American Reader." *Journal of Family Issues* 9(3):291–297, esp. 294. John Modell, Frank F. Furstenberg, Jr., and Douglas Strong. 1978. "The Timing of Marriage in the Transition to Adulthood: Continuity and Change, 1860–1975." *American Journal of Sociology* 84:S120–S150.

11. Larry L. Bumpass and James A. Sweet. 1989. "Children's Experience in Single-Parent Families: Implications of Cohabitation and Marital Transitions." *Family Planning Perspectives* 6:256–260.

12. Lawrence Stone. 1989. "The Road to Polygamy." *New York Review,* March 2, pp. 12–15 (p. 14).

13. Bumpass and Sweet. "Children's Experience." Paul C. Glick. 1984. "Marriage, Divorce, and Living Arrangements: Prospective Changes." *Journal of Family Issues* 5(1):7–26.

14. Sandra L. Hofferth. 1985. "Updating Children's Life Course." *Journal of Marriage and the Family* 47:93–115.

15. An overlooked fact is that, earlier in this century, many more single-parent families were headed by fathers than is the case today. This is because the parental death rate, unlike today, was gender neutral. Almost as often as not at the turn of the twentieth century, it was the child's mother who died (10.7% of children lost a mother and 11.9% lost a father), and with the death of the mother, the children were typically left in the care of their father. This meant that overall in 1900, a surprising 27% of the single-parent children lived with their fathers. (It is also worth noting that 20% of the single-parent children in 1900 were living with their single parent as part of a larger household of people, something which is less common today.) Yet following divorce, in contrast, most children end up with their mothers. So by 1960, as parental divorce had overtaken parental death, only about 10% of single-parent children were living with their fathers.

    The same effect can be seen with teenagers over the first six decades of the century. The percentage of teenagers living with father only and with father and stepmother (and also other relatives) substantially decreased and the percentage living with mother only and with mother and stepfather increased. Christopher Jencks and Barbara Boyle Torrey. 1988. "Beyond Income and Poverty: Trends in Social Welfare and Among Children and the Elderly Since 1960." Pp. 229–273 in John L. Palmer, T. Smeeding, and B. B. Torrey, eds., *The Vulnerable.* Washington, DC: Urban Institute. The main reason, again, is that death was replaced by divorce as the leading cause of family breakup. Fewer mothers were dying young, leaving fewer widowers; if both parents were still alive following a marriage breakup, the children would normally go to the mother. Also, improved job opportunities and general affluence made it easier for single mothers to keep their children. In recent years, however, this trend seems to have reversed, and the percentage of father-headed single-parent families has been on the increase.

16. Hofferth. "Updating." Another way to look statistically at the family turmoil of the past three decades is in terms of the family structure of all American children at a single point in time. In 1960, 88% of all children lived with two parents. By 1990 that figure had dropped to 73% (60% with both biological parents, 11% with a

stepparent, and 2% with adoptive parents). In 1960, 9% of children in America lived in single-parent families; by 1990, the percentage had increased to 24%.

17. Arlene F. Saluter. 1993. "Marital Status and Living Arrangements: March, 1993." *Current Population Reports* P20–478. Washington, DC: U.S. Bureau of the Census. Table G, p. xii.

18. The replacement of death by divorce as the leading cause of marital breakup has had a marked effect on the marital life course of men over the course of the twentieth century. Let us compare the marital life course of a typical male born during the period 1888–1892 and thus coming of age during the first decade of this century, with the projected marital life course of a male born in 1980 and thus coming of age in the 1990s. Of those who reached age fifteen, about the same proportion in each era would marry sometime during their lives—a little below 90%. And they would marry at about the same average age—a little over twenty-six years. Thus, both the marriage rate and the average age at marriage today have returned to roughly what they were at the turn of the twentieth century. There, however, the marital life course similarities end. For every ten marriages in the earlier era, 0.54 would be ended by the death of the man, 0.28 by the death of his wife, and only 0.18 by divorce. For every ten marriages in the later era, only 0.38 would end by the man's death, only 0.17 would end by the wife's death, and 0.45—or nearly half—would end by divorce. Robert Schoen, William Urton, Karen Woodrow, and John Baj. 1985. "Marriage and Divorce in Twentieth Century American Cohorts." *Demography* 22(1):101–114.

19. Peter Uhlenberg. 1992. "Population Aging and Social Policy." In Judith Blake and John Hagan, eds., *Annual Review of Sociology* 18. Palo Alto, CA: Annual Reviews, pp. 449–474, esp. 459.

20. Thomas J. Espenshade. 1985. "The Recent Decline of American Marriage." Pp. 53–90 in Kingsley Davis, ed., *Contemporary Marriage*. New York: Russell Sage Foundation.

21. Kingsley Davis. 1985. "The Meaning and Significance of Marriage in Contemporary Society." Pp. 1–21 in Kingsley Davis, ed., *Contemporary Marriage,* p. 21.

22. Dennis A. Ahlburg and Carol J. De Vita. 1992. "New Realities of the American Family." *Population Bulletin* 47(2):12.

23. Arlene F. Saluter. 1994. "Marital Status and Living Arrangements: March 1993." *Current Population Reports.* P20–478. Washington, DC: U.S. Bureau of the Census. Table C.

24. T. C. Martin and L. L. Bumpass. 1989. "Recent Trends in Marital Disruption." *Demography* 26:37–51.

25. Norval D. Glenn. 1991. "The Recent Trend in Marital Success in the United States." *Journal of Marriage and the Family* 53:261–270. N. D. Glenn and C. N. Weaver. 1988. "The Changing Relationship of Marital Status to Reported Happiness." *Journal of Marriage and the Family* 50:317–324.

26. Daniel Yankelovich. 1994. "How Changes in the Economy Are Reshaping American Values." Pp. 16–53 in Henry J. Aaron, Thomas Mann, and Timothy Taylor, eds., *Values and Public Policy.* Washington, DC: Brookings Institution, p. 37.

27. Sara McLanahan and L. Bumpass. 1988. "Intergenerational Consequences of Family Disruption." *American Journal of Sociology* 94:130–152.

28. Jay Belsky, Lise Youngblade, Michael Rovine, and Brenda Volling. 1991. "Patterns of Marital Change and Parent-Child Interaction." *Journal of Marriage and the Family* 53(2):487–498.

29. Joseph Veroff, Elizabeth Douvan, and Richard A. Kulka. 1981. *The Inner American: A Self-Portrait from 1957 to 1976.* New York: Basic Books, chapter 5.

30. Tamar Lewin. 1994. "Poll of Teen-Agers Finds Boys Prefer Traditional Family." *New York Times,* July 7, p. B7.

31. Frank Furstenberg, Jr. 1988. "Good Dads–Bad Dads: Two Faces of Fatherhood." Pp. 193–218 in Andrew Cherlin, ed., *The Changing American Family and Public Policy.* Washington, DC: Urban Institute, pp. 201–202.

32. David Eggebeen and Peter Uhlenberg. 1985. "Changes in the Organization of Men's Lives: 1960–1980." *Family Relations* 34:251–257.

33. The drop in years spent in families with young children was greater still—43%— and the drop was greatest for the more educated men.

34. Calculations from data provided by the Fertility Statistics Branch and the Marriage and Family Statistics Branch, U.S. Bureau of the Census, Washington, DC.

35. Judith A. Seltzer. 1994. "Consequences of Marital Dissolution for Children." *Annual Review of Sociology* 20:235–266 (p. 237).

36. Larry L Bumpass. 1990. "What's Happening to the Family? Interactions Between Demographic and Institutional Change." *Demography* 27(4):483–498.

37. Craig A. Everett and Sandra Volgy Everett. 1994. *Healthy Divorce.* San Francisco: Jossey-Bass. Quote is from publisher's advertising circular.

38. William J. Goode. 1993. *World Changes in Divorce Patterns.* New Haven, CT: Yale University Press, p. 345.

39. Frank Furstenberg, Jr., and Andrew J. Cherlin. 1991. *Divided Families: What Happens to Children When Parents Part.* Cambridge, MA: Harvard University Press, p. 105.

40. Alisa Burns and Cath Scott. 1994. *Mother-Headed Families and Why They Have Increased.* Hillsdale, NJ: Lawrence Erlbaum Associates, p. 1.

41. Herbert Jacob. 1988. *Silent Revolution: The Transformation of Divorce Law in the United States.* Chicago: University of Chicago Press. On this topic see also Stephen D. Sugarman and Herma Hill Kay. 1990. *Divorce Reform at the Crossroads.* New Haven, CT: Yale University Press; and Mary Ann Glendon. 1987. *Abortion and Divorce in Western Law.* Cambridge, MA: Harvard University Press.

42. See David M. Wagner. 1994. "Taming the Divorce Monster." *Family Policy* (April).

43. John Modell. 1989. *Into One's Own: From Youth to Adulthood in the United States, 1920–1975.* Berkeley, CA: University of California Press, pp. 62–63.

44. Bumpass. "What's Happening?"

45. Tim B. Heaton. 1990. "Marital Stability Throughout the Child-Rearing Years." *Demography* 27(1):55–63. S. Philip Morgan, Diane Lye, and Gretchen Condran. 1988. "Sons, Daughters, and the Risk of Marital Disruption." *American Journal of Sociology* 94(1):110–129. Linda Waite and Lee A. Lillard. 1991. "Children and Marital Disruption." *American Journal of Sociology* 96(4):930–953.

46. Arland Thornton. 1989. "Changing Attitudes Toward Family Issues in the United States." *Journal of Marriage and the Family* 51(4):873–893.

47. Judith A. Seltzer. 1991. "Relationships Between Fathers and Children Who Live Apart: The Father's Role After Separation." *Journal of Marriage and the Family* 53:79–101.

48. Frank Furstenberg, Jr., and Christine W. Nord. 1985. "Parenting Apart: Patterns of Childbearing After Marital Disruption." *Journal of Marriage and the Family* 47(4):893–905. Frank Furstenberg, Jr., Christine W. Nord, James L. Peterson, and Nicholas Zill. 1983. "The Life Course of Children of Divorce: Marital Disruption and Parental Contact." *American Sociological Review* 48(2):656–658. A similarly low

level of father-child contact was found by Judith A. Seltzer and Susan M. Bianchi. 1988. "Children's Contact with Absent Parents." *Journal of Marriage and the Family* 50:663–677. See also Frank L. Mott. 1990. "When Is a Father Really Gone? Paternal-Child Contact in Father-Absent Homes." *Demography* 27(4):499–517. Using 1979–1986 data from the National Longitudinal Survey of Labor Market Experience of Youth, Mott determined that about 60% of youth who did not have a resident biological father "had access to a male figure either in or out of the home who may potentially be considered a father or father substitute." He was unable to determine, however, how many of these men actually fill the various father roles.

49. Furstenberg and Cherlin. "Divided Families," p. 36. Some portion of the lack of contact, of course, is no doubt due to mothers' resistance to the fathers playing a larger role.

50. Ibid.

51. Frank Furstenberg, Jr. 1990. "Divorce and the American Family." Pp. 379–403 in W. Richard Scott and Judith Blake, eds., *Annual Review of Sociology* 16. Palo Alto, CA: Annual Reviews, pp. 387–388.

52. Larry Hugick. 1989. "Mirror of America." *Gallup Report* 286 (July): 28.

53. Judith A. Seltzer. 1994. "Consequences of Marital Dissolution for Children." *Annual Review of Sociology* 20:235–266 (p. 246).

54. Office of Child Support Enforcement. 1988. "Twelfth Annual Report to Congress for the Period Ending September 30, 1987." Washington, DC: GPO.

55. Reported in Linda Jacobsen and Brad Edmondson. 1993. "Father Figures." *American Demographics* (August): 27.

56. U.S. Bureau of the Census. 1987. "Child Support and Alimony, 1985." *Current Population Reports,* series P-23, no. 152 (August).

57. Jay D. Teachman. 1991. "Contributions to Children by Divorced Fathers." *Social Problems* 38(3):358–371 (p. 368). The level of support is higher in joint-custody arrangements, but these make up only about 10% of all divorce arrangements. See Judith A. Seltzer. 1991. "Legal Custody Arrangements and Children's Economic Welfare." *American Journal of Sociology* 96(4):895–929.

58. Estimated from U.S. Bureau of the Census (1992) and Hernandez (1993). Estimates for 1960 from personal communication with Hernandez, September 1993.

59. Frank F. Furstenberg, Jr. 1988. "Child Care After Divorce and Remarriage." Pp. 245–261 in E. Mavis Hetherington and Josephine D. Arasteh. *Impact of Divorce, Single Parenting, and Stepparenting on Children.* Hillsdale, NJ: Erlbaum.

60. William R. Beer. 1989. *Strangers in the House: The World of Stepsiblings and Half-Siblings.* New Brunswick, NJ: Transaction, p. 134.

61. Frank F. Furstenberg, Jr., Christine W. Nord, James L. Peterson, and Nicholas Zill. 1983. "The Life Course of Children of Divorce: Marital Disruption and Parental Contact." *American Sociological Review* 48(2):656–658. Frank F. Furstenberg, Jr., and Christine W. Nord. 1985. "Parenting Apart: Patterns of Childbearing After Marital Disruption." *Journal of Marriage and the Family* 47(4):893–905. Frank L. Mott. 1990. "When Is a Father Really Gone? Paternal-Child Contact in Father Absent Homes." *Demography* 27(4):499–517. Judith A. Seltzer and Susan M. Bianchi. 1988. "Children's Contact with Absent Parents." *Journal of Marriage and the Family* 50:663–677. Lynn White. 1994. "Stepfamilies over the Life Course: Social Support." Pp. 109–137 in Alan Booth and Judy Dunn, eds., *Stepfamilies: Who Benefits? Who Does Not?* Hillsdale, NJ: Erlbaum.

62. James H. Bray. 1988. "Children's Development During Early Remarriage." Pp.

279–298 in E. M. Hetherington and J. D. Arasteh, eds., *Impact of Divorce, Single Parenting, and Stepparenting on Children.* Hillsdale, NJ: Lawrence Erlbaum. E. Mavis Hetherington. 1987. "Family Relations Six Years After Divorce." Pp. 185–205 in K. Pasley and M. Ihinger-Tollman, eds., *Remarriage and Stepparenting Today: Current Research and Theory.* New York: Guilford Press. Lynn White. "Stepfamilies Over the Life Course."

63. E. Mavis Hetherington, Margaret Stanley-Hagan, and Edward R. Anderson. 1989. "Marital Transitions: A Child's Perspective." *American Psychologist* 44(2):303–312.

64. E. Mavis Hetherington and Kathleen M Jodl. 1994. "Stepfamilies as Settings for Child Development." Pp. 55–79 in Alan Booth and Judy Dunn, eds., *Stepfamilies: Who Benefits? Who Does Not?*, p. 66.

65. Lynn K. White and Alan Booth. 1985. "The Quality and Stability of Remarriages: The Role of Stepchildren." *American Sociological Review* 50(5):689–698.

66. Frank F. Furstenberg, Jr. 1990. "Divorce and the American Family." *Annual Review of Sociology* 16:379–403 (p. 384).

67. From Anne Bernstein (1988). Cited in Andrew J. Cherlin and Frank F. Furstenberg, Jr. 1994. "Stepfamilies in the United States: A Reconsideration." *Annual Review of Sociology* 20:359–381 (p. 365).

68. "Shuttle Diplomacy." *Psychology Today* 26(4) (July/August 1993): 15.

69. Roger A. Wojtkiewicz, Sara S. McLanahan, and Irwin Garfinkel. 1990. "The Growth of Families Headed by Women: 1950–1980." *Demography* 27(1):19–30.

70. Nicholas Zill and Carolyn C. Rogers. 1988. "Recent Trends in the Well-Being of Children in the United States and Their Implications for Public Policy." Pp. 31–115 in Andrew Cherlin, ed., *The Changing American Family and Public Policy.* Washington, DC: Urban Institute, p. 81. See also Martin O'Connell and Carolyn C. Rogers. 1984. "Out of Wedlock Births, Premarital Pregnancies, and Their Effect on Family Formation and Dissolution." *Family Planning Perspectives* 16(4):157–162.

71. For the 1970–1984 period, among non-Hispanic whites, 10% of all births were nonmarital and of these, 29% were to cohabiting parents. Of all births to blacks, 55% were nonmarital and 18% of these were to cohabiting couples. Among Mexican Americans, 25% of births were nonmarital and of these, 40% were to cohabiting parents. Bumpass and Sweet. 1989.

72. Bumpass and Sweet. "Children's Experience in Single-Parent Families."

73. Hofferth. "Updating Children's Life Course," p. 107. Frank Furstenberg, Jr. reports, however, that "matrimony confers little advantage in maintaining bonds between noncustodial fathers and their offspring" because support by and contact with never-married fathers are almost as high as with men who were once wed to the mothers. Frank Furstenberg, Jr. 1988. "Good Dads–Bad Dads: Two Faces of Fatherhood." Pp. 193–218 in Andrew Cherlin, ed., *The Changing American Family and Public Policy.* Washington, DC: Urban Institute, p. 203.

74. Daniel Yankelovich. 1981. *New Rules: Searching for Self-Fulfillment in a World Turned Upside Down.* New York: Random House.

75. Sharon Schlegel. 1994. "Thoughts on Dads for Women." *Trenton* (NJ) *Times*, p. A2.

76. Bronislaw Malinowski. 1930. *Sex, Culture and Myth.*

77. Data from Office of Technology Assessment. Cited in John A. Robertson. 1994. *Children of Choice: Freedom and the New Reproductive Technologies.* Princeton, NJ: Princeton University Press.

78. Andrea Engber. 1994. "Choosing Motherhood Through Donor Insemination." *Trenton* (NJ) *Times*, October 9, p. A5.

79. "Dad's Love for the Five Kids He'll Never Know." *National Inquirer,* November 11, 1993, p. 38.

80. Written testimony by Alison Ward, quoted in Ruth Macklin. 1991. "Artificial Means of Reproduction and Our Understanding of the Family." *Hastings Center Report* (January-February), p. 11.

81. Quoted in Gloria Hochman. 1994. "The New Facts of Life." *Philadelphia Inquirer Magazine,* July 17, p. 20.

82. Kingsley Davis. 1985. "The Meaning and Significance of Marriage in Contemporary Society." Pp. 1–21 in Kingsley Davis, ed., *Contemporary Marriage.* New York: Russell Sage Foundation, pp. 7–8.

83. Susan Cotts Watkins, Jane A. Menken, and John Bongaarts. 1987. "Demographic Foundations of Family Change." *American Sociological Review* 52(3):346–358.

84. For example, Stephanie Coontz. 1992. *The Way We Never Were: American Families and the Nostalgia Trap.* New York: Basic Books. See also Elaine Tyler May. 1988. *Homeward Bound: American Families in the Cold War Era.* New York: Basic Books.

85. In developing this historical sequence, I am indebted to the work of Dirk J. van de Kaa. 1987. "Europe's Second Demographic Transition." *Population Bulletin* 42(1):1–57.

86. "Only a fifth of young adults now disapprove of premarital sex, even for 18-year-olds." Larry Bumpass. "What's Happening?" 486.

87. J. Gordon Melton, ed., 1991. *The Churches Speak On: Sex and Family Life.* Detroit, MI: Gale Research, Inc., pp. 71–81. This statement was eventually rejected by the New Jersey Diocese of the Episcopal Church, but it reflects the thinking of many religious liberals.

88. See Frances K. Goldscheider and Calvin Goldscheider. 1993. *Leaving Home Before Marriage: Ethnicity, Familism, and Generational Relationships.* Madison, WI: University of Wisconsin Press.

89. Sara McLanahan and Lynne Casper. 1995. "Growing Diversity and Inequality in the American Family." Pp. 1–45 in Reynolds Farley, ed., *State of the Union: America in the 1990s.* Vol. 2.

90. Linda J. Waite. 1995. "Does Marriage Matter?" Presidential Address to the Population Association of America. Chicago: Department of Sociology, University of Chicago. Unpublished.

91. Bumpass. "What's Happening?" 483–498 (p. 486).

92. Ronald R. Rindfuss and Audry VandenHeuvel. 1992. "Cohabitation: A Precursor to Marriage or an Alternative to Being Single?" Pp. 118–142 in Scott J. South and Stewart E. Tolnay, eds., *The Changing American Family: Sociological and Demographic Perspectives.* Boulder, CO: Westview Press. James A. Sweet and Larry L. Bumpass. 1992. "Young Adults' Views of Marriage, Cohabitation, and Family." Pp. 143–170 in Scott J. South and Stewart E. Tolnay, eds., *The Changing American Family: Sociological and Demographic Perspectives.*

93. Larry L. Bumpass, J. A. Sweet, and A. Cherlin. 1991. "The Role of Cohabitation in Declining Marriage Rates." *Journal of Marriage and the Family* 53:913–927.

94. Alan Booth and D. Johnson. 1988. "Premarital Cohabitation and Marital Success." *Journal of Family Issues* 9:255–272; A. J. DeMaris and K. V. Rao. 1992. "Premarital Cohabitation and Subsequent Marital Stability in the United States: A Reassessment." *Journal of Marriage and the Family* 54:178–190; E. Thomson and U. Colella. 1992. "Cohabitation and Marital Stability." *Journal of Marriage and the Family* 54:259–267.

95. The most authoritative advocate of this perspective is Gary S. Becker. 1991. *A Treatise on the Family.* Cambridge, MA: Harvard University Press.

96. This is reviewed in Andrew Cherlin. 1992. *Marriage, Divorce, Remarriage.* Cambridge, MA: Harvard University Press, chapter 2. See also McLanahan and Casper. "Growing Diversity and Inequality." For a skeptical view of the evidence, see Valerie Kincade Oppenheimer. 1994. "Women's Rising Employment and the Future of the Family in Industrial Societies." *Population and Development Review* 20(2):293–342.

97. For a review of this position, see Oppenheimer. "Women's Rising Employment."

98. In the spring of 1995, this gained national press attention through the release of the 1995 *Kids Count Data Book* (Baltimore: Annie E. Casey Foundation), which focused on the topic. According to this source, the median earned income of all men aged 25 to 34 has fallen since 1972 by 26% in inflation-adjusted dollars; for high school dropouts the decrease has been even greater.

99. William Julius Wilson. 1987. *The Truly Disadvantaged: The Inner City, The Underclass, and Public Policy.* Chicago: University of Chicago Press; William Julius Wilson. 1980. *The Declining Significance of Race: Blacks and Changing American Institutions.* Chicago: University of Chicago Press.

100. On the special situation of African Americans, see M. Belinda Tucker and Claudia Mitchell-Kernan, eds., 1995. *The Decline of Marriage Among African Americans.* New York: Russell Sage Foundation.

101. Robert D. Mare and Christopher Winship. 1991. "Socioeconomic Change and the Decline of Marriage for Blacks and Whites." Pp. 175–202 in Christopher Jencks and Paul E. Peterson, eds., *The Urban Underclass.* Washington, DC: Brookings Institution.

102. William A. Galston. 1993. "Beyond the Murphy Brown Debate: Ideas for Family Policy." Speech to the Institute for American Values, Family Policy Symposium, New York City. See also Charles Murray. 1993. "Welfare and the Family: The U.S. Experience." *Journal of Labor Economics* 11(1):S224–S262.

103. Irwin Garfinkel and Sara. S. McLanahan. 1986. *Single Mothers and Their Children.* Washington, DC: Urban Institute Press, p. 63.

104. The negative role of government in society as a whole is much more important in the welfare states. See David Popenoe. 1994. "Scandinavian Welfare." *Society* 31(6):78–81; and 1988. *Disturbing the Nest: Family Change and Decline in Modern Societies.* New York: Aldine de Gruyter.

105. Allan C. Carlson. 1987. "Treason of the Professions: The Case of Home Economics." *The Family in America* 1–6, p. 1.

106. Steven Mintz and Susan Kellogg. 1988. *Domestic Revolutions: A Social History of American Family Life.* New York: Free Press, p. 204.

107. The classic work on the new individualism is Robert N. Bellah et al. 1985. *Habits of the Heart: Individualism and Commitment in American Life.* Berkeley, CA: University of California Press.

108. Daniel Yankelovich. 1994. "How Changes in the Economy are Reshaping American Values." Pp. 16–53 in Henry J. Aaron, Thomas Mann, and Timothy Taylor, eds., *Values and Public Policy.* Washington, DC: Brookings Institution.

109. Louis Harris. 1987. *Inside America.* New York: Vintage Books.

110. Louis Roussel. 1989. *La Famille Incertaine.* Paris: Editions Odile Jacob.

111. A point stressed by the first analyst of American individualism, Alexis de Tocqueville. 1956. *Democracy in America.* J. B. Mayer, ed. New York: Harper and Row.

112. Robert D. Putnam. 1995. "Bowling Alone: America's Declining Social Capital." *Journal of Democracy* 6(1):65–78; James S. House. 1986. "Social Support and the Quality of Life." In Frank M. Andrews, ed., *Research on the Quality of Life.* Ann Arbor: University of Michigan Press.

113. Satires I.i.106.
114. For a major theoretical statement of this shift, see Harry C. Triandis. 1990. "Cross-Cultural Studies of Individualism and Collectivism," pp. 41–133 in Nebraska Symposium on Motivation, 1989. Lincoln, NE: University. of Nebraska Press.
115. To be sure, what some have called the decline of "male institutional authoritarianism" has brought social benefits, especially for women and minorities. The legal, sexual, and financial emancipation of women has become a reality as never before. We are a much more inclusive society today—segregation and racism have diminished, and we now accept more African Americans, Hispanics, and other minority groups into the mainstream. Yet all societies depend on social institutions for their very existence, and those institutions that we have torn down have not been replaced.
116. Martin O'Connell and A. Bachu. 1992. "Who's Minding the Kids? Child Care Arrangments: Fall, 1988." *Current Population Reports* P70, no. 30. Washington, DC: U. S. Census Bureau. Martin O'Connell. 1993. "Where's Papa? Fathers' Role in Child Care." Washington, DC: Population Reference Bureau.
117. Furstenburg and Cherlin. "Divided Families," p. 36.
118. Jonathan Gershuny and J. P. Robinson. 1988. "Historical Changes in the Household Divison of Labor." *Demography* 25(4):537–552; Harriet B. Presser. 1989. "Can We Make Time for Children? The Economy, Work Schedules, and Child Care." *Demography* 26(4):523–543; Steven L. Nock and P. W. Kingston. 1988. "Time with Children: The Impact of Couples' Work-Time Commitments." *Social Forces* 67(1):59–85. There has been some increase in father time if calculated on a per child basis, due to smaller family size, and also some increase in the time that fathers spend doing "housework."

Chapter 2. The Human Carnage of Fatherlessness

1. April 12, 1994, p. A1; October 18, 1993, p. B7.
2. Both children and their parents have a higher educational level than they did in 1960; the rate of high school completion has increased, as has the average number of years of education completed. Up until 1980, at least, the economic situation of children improved; the years between 1964 and 1979 saw a 42% increase in the material standard of the average child. This was mainly due to fewer children in each household, children born to older (and thus more financially viable) parents, and the movement of mothers into the work force. Diane J. Macunovich and Richard J. Easterlin. 1990. "How Parents Have Coped: The Effect of Life Cycle Demographic Decisions on the Economic Status of Pre-School Age Children, 1964–87." *Population and Development Review* 16(2):301–325.
Other gains: Children today are in some respects healthier—for example, infant mortality and child death rates have fallen by more than 50% since 1960; a smaller percentage of children are born to teenagers, mainly because the average age of marriage for women has jumped from 20 to over 24. According to what their parents say, fewer children are "unwanted"—20% in 1960 versus 7% today. And there is now a much greater concern for children's rights and the problem of child abuse.
3. Judith Seltzer. 1994. "Consequences of Marital Dissolution for Children." *Annual Review of Sociology* 20:235–266, esp. 244.
4. See "Families on a Treadmill: Work and Income in the 1980s." A Staff Study Prepared for the Use of Members of the Joint Economic Committee of the U.S. Congress, January 17, 1992. Frank Levy and Richard C. Michel. 1991. *The Economic*

Future of American Families: Income and Wealth Trends. Washington, DC: Urban Institute Press. Frank Levy. 1987. *Dollars and Dreams: The Changing American Income Distribution.* New York: Basic Books. Victor R. Fuchs and Diane M. Reklis. 1992. "America's Children: Economic Perspectives and Policy Options." *Science* 255 (January 3):41–46.

5. David J. Eggebeen and Daniel T. Lichter. 1991. "Race, Family Structure, and Changing Poverty Among American Children." *American Sociological Review* 56(6):801–817.

6. Terry Lugaila. 1992. *Households, Families and Children: A Thirty-Year Perspective.* Current Population Reports P23-181. Washington, DC: U.S. Bureau of the Census.

7. Irwin Garfinkel and Sara S. McLanahan. 1986. *Single Mothers and Their Children: A New American Dilemma.* Washington, DC: Urban Institute, p. 13.

8. Stacy Furukawa. 1994. *The Diverse Living Arrangements of Children: Summer 1991.* Current Population Reports P70-38. Washington, DC: U.S. Bureau of the Census.

9. David Elwood. 1988. *Poor Support.* New York: Basic Books, chapters 4–5.

10. See Sara McLanahan and Gary Sandefur. 1994. *Growing Up with a Single Parent.* Cambridge, MA: Harvard University Press.

11. One recent study, for example, found few if any "unique effects of fathering" once family resources are statistically controlled; "The only discernable impact of father-presence on children's well-being appeared to result from the coresident father's economic contribution to the family." Lisa J. Crockett, David J. Eggebeen, and Alan J. Hawkins. 1993. "Father's Presence and Young Children's Behavioral and Cognitive Adjustment." *Journal of Family Issues* 14(3):355–377 (372).

12. McLanahan and Sandefur. *Growing Up with a Single Parent.*

13. Ronald J. Angel and Jacqueline L. Angel. 1993. *Painful Inheritance: Health and the New Generation of Fatherless Families.* Madison, WI: University of Wisconsin Press, p. 119.

14. Nicholas Zill and Charlotte A. Schoenborn. 1990. "Developmental, Learning, and Emotional Problems: Health of Our Nation's Children, United States, 1988." *Advance Data,* National Center for Health Statistics, no. 120, p. 9.

15. Deborah A. Dawson. 1991. "Family Structure and Children's Health and Well-Being: Data from the 1988 National Health Interview Survey on Child Health." *Journal of Marriage and the Family* 53(3):573–584 (573).

16. Sara S. McLanahan and L. Bumpass. 1988. "Intergeneration Consequences of Family Disruption." *American Journal of Sociology* 94(1):130–152 (147). See also Sara S. McLanahan. 1988. "Family Structure and Dependency: Early Transitions to Female Household Headship." *Demography* 25:1–16.

17. John Guidubaldi, Joseph D. Perry, and Bonnie K. Nastasi. 1987. "Growing Up in a Divorced Family: Initial and Long-Term Perspectives on Children's Adjustment." *Applied Social Psychology Annual* 7:202–237.

18. Ibid., 231.

19. Duncan W. G. Timms. 1991. *Family Structure in Childhood and Mental Health in Adolescence.* Research Report, Project Metropolitan. Stockholm, Sweden: Department of Sociology, University of Stockholm, p. 93.

20. Judith S. Wallerstein. 1991. "The Long-Term Effects of Divorce on Children: A Review." *Journal of the American Academy of Child and Adolescent Psychiatry* 30(3)(May 1991):358–359. See also Judith S. Wallerstein and Sandra Blakeslee. 1989. *Second Chances: Men, Women and Children a Decade After Divorce.* New York: Ticknor and Fields. Wallerstein was subjected to lengthy criticism within the scientific community for her methodology, especially the lack of a control group of matched chil-

dren in intact families. Her methodology was not very sophisticated, but she was the first to probe in depth the psyches of a large number of children of divorce. It is likely that the negative criticism was triggered as much by her message as by her research medium.

21. Paul R. Amato. 1991. "Parental Absence During Childhood and Depression in Later Life." *Sociological Quarterly* 32(4):543–556 (p. 553).

22. Norval D. Glenn and Kathryn D. Kramer. 1985. "The Psychological Well-Being of Adult Children of Divorce." *Journal of Marriage and the Family* 47:905–912 (p. 911). See also their 1987 article "The Marriage and Divorces of the Children of Divorce." *Journal of Marriage and the Family* 49:811–825.

23. Tom Krattenmaker. 1994. "Single-Parent Families: Sara McLanahan Strikes a Balance in a Fierce Ideological Debate." Princeton Alumni Weekly, December 7, p. 15.

24. Elizabeth Herzog and Cecelia E. Sudia. 1973. "Children in Fatherless Families." Chapter 3 in B. Caldwell and H. Ricciuti, eds., *Review of Child Development Research* 3, pp. 214, 220–221.

25. Alisa Burns and Cath Scott. 1994. *Mother-Headed Families and Why They Have Increased.* Hillsdale, NJ: Erlbaum, p. 54.

26. John Leo. 1992. "Sneer Not at 'Ozzie and Harriet.'" *U.S. News and World Report,* September 14, p. 24.

27. April 1993.

28. Paul E. Tracy, Marvin E. Wolfgang, and Robert M. Figlio. 1990. *Delinquency Careers in Two Birth Cohorts.* New York: Plenum Press.

29. We do not have the evidence to demonstrate *conclusively* that fatherlessness is a major cause of increased delinquency and violent behavior among adolescents and young adults. (See Marvin D. Free, Jr. 1991. "Clarifying the Relationship between the Broken Home and Delinquency." *Deviant Behavior* 12:109–167.) Neither do we have conclusive evidence about any other single cause of delinquency or violence. Given the complexities of the issue, fully conclusive evidence will probably never exist. Nevertheless, the present evidence is substantial and convincing.

30. L. Edward Wells and Joseph H. Rankin. 1991. "Families and Delinquency: A Meta-Analysis of the Impact of Broken Homes." *Social Problems* 38(1):71–93 (p. 87).

31. David H. Demo and Alan C. Acock. 1988. "The Impact of Divorce on Children." *Journal of Marriage and the Family* 50(3):619–648 (p. 639).

32. The first wave was conducted in 1976–1977 with a national probability sample of households containing children aged 7–11; in all, 2,301 children were interviewed in 1,747 households. The second wave was a follow-up in 1981 of 1,423 of the children, then aged 12–16.

33. James L. Peterson and Nicholas Zill. 1986. "Marital Disruption, Parent-Child Relationships, and Behavior Problems in Children." *Journal of Marriage and the Family* 48(2):295–307 (p. 295).

34. Michael R. Gottfredson and Travis Hirschi. 1990. *A General Theory of Crime.* Stanford, CA: Stanford University Press, p. 103.

35. Ibid., p. 103. See also Robert J. Sampson. "Urban Black Violence: The Effect of Male Joblessness and Family Disruption." *American Journal of Sociology* (1987) 93:348–382.

36. Data provided by the National Fatherhood Initiative.

37. Quoted in Joe Urschel. "Expert Seeks Classroom of Millions." *USA Today,* April 11, 1995, p. 1.

38. Alan Guttmacher Institute. 1994. *Sex and America's Teenagers,* pp. 19–20.

39. Ibid., p. 41.
40. Ibid., p. 45.
41. Ibid., p. 56.
42. Ibid., p. 38.
43. Ibid., pp. 30–31.
44. McLanahan and Sandefur. *Growing Up with a Single Parent,* p. 52.
45. Kathleen E. Kiernan. 1992. "The Impact of Family Disruptions in Childhood on Transitions Made in Young Adult Life." *Population Studies* 46:213–234 (p. 233).
46. Andrew J. Cherlin and Frank F. Furstenberg, Jr. 1994. "Stepfamilies in the United States: A Reconsideration." In *Annual Review of Sociology* 20, pp. 359–381 (p. 374).
47. Most studies show an increase, but the rate can be heavily affected by increased awareness of the problem and greater willingness to detect and disclose. The exact rate of increase is not known. See David Finkelhor. 1994. "Current Information on the Scope and Nature of Child Sexual Abuse." *Future of Children* 4(2):31–53. According to data from the National Incidence Studies, physical abuse increased 58% and sexual abuse increased 300% between 1980 and 1986. National Research Council. 1993. *Understanding Child Abuse and Neglect.* Washington, DC: National Academy Press, p. 81.
48. This is an estimate by David Finkelhor based on the findings of nineteen adult retrospective surveys, together with other information sources. "Current Information," p. 42.
49. In the period 1979 through 1988, some 2000 child deaths (aged 0–17) per year that resulted from abuse and neglect were recorded, and in 1990 alone 160,000 additional cases resulted in serious injuries. National Research Council. 1993. *Understanding Child Abuse and Neglect,* p. 1.
50. U.S. Advisory Board on Child Abuse and Neglect. 1990. *Child Abuse and Neglect: Critical First Steps in Response to a National Emergency.* Washington, DC: GPO.
51. National Center on Child Abuse and Neglect. 1981. *National Study of the Incidence and Severity of Child Abuse and Neglect.* Washington, DC: NCCAN.
52. David Finkelhor, Gerald Hotaling, I. A. Lewis, and Christine Smith. 1990. "Sexual Abuse in a National Survey of Men and Women: Prevalence, Characteristics, and Risk Factors." *Child Abuse and Neglect* 14:19–28. Richard J. Gelles. 1989. "Child Abuse and Violence in Single-Parent Families: Parent Absence and Economic Deprivation." *American Journal of Orthopsychiatry* 59(4):492–501 (p. 495).
53. Finkelhor. "Current Information," p. 46.
54. Ibid., 45–46.
55. Ibid., 48.
56. Leslie Margolin. 1991. "Child Sexual Abuse by Nonrelated Caregivers." *Child Abuse and Neglect* 15:213–221.
57. Fragmentary data which show a disproportionate risk of being abused by a mother's boyfriend can be found in Elizabeth A. Sirles and Colleen F. Lofberg. 1990. "Factors Associated with Divorce in Family Child Sexual Abuse Cases." *Child Abuse and Neglect* 14:165–170. David T. Ballard et al. 1990. "A Comparative Profile of the Incest Perpetrator: Background Characteristics, Abuse History, and Use of Social Skills." Pp. 43–73 in Anne L. Horton et al. *The Incest Perpetrator.* Newbury Park, CA: Sage.
58. James Garbarino and Gwen Gilliam. 1980. *Understanding Abusive Families.* Lexington, MA: D. C. Heath, p. 151.
59. Clive V. J. Welham. 1990. "Incest: An Evolutionary Model." *Ethology and Sociobiology* 11:97–111.

60. Diana E. H. Russell. 1984. "The Prevalence and Seriousness of Incestuous Abuse: Stepfathers vs. Biological Fathers." *Child Abuse and Neglect* 8:15–22.

61. Michael Gordon. 1989. "The Family Environment of Sexual Abuse: A Comparison of Natal and Stepfather Abuse." *Child Abuse and Neglect* 13:121–130.

62. See, e.g., David Finkelhor, Gerald Hotaling, I. A. Lewis, and Christine Smith. 1990. "Sexual Abuse in a National Survey of Men and Women: Prevalence, Characteristics, and Risk Factors." *Child Abuse and Neglect* 14:19–28.

63. Hilda Parker and Seymour Parker. 1986. "Father-Daughter Sexual Abuse." *American Journal of Orthopsychiatry* 56:531–549.

64. Clive V. J. Welham. 1990. "Incest: An Evolutionary Model." *Ethology and Sociobiology* 11:97–111.

65. This difference is modified in adolescence, however, when the physical abuse of boys drops and females recede as abusers, owing mainly to the obvious imbalance of physical strength between mothers and their adolescent sons. James A. Rosenthal. 1988. "Patterns of Reported Child Abuse and Neglect." *Child Abuse and Neglect* 12:263–271.

66. Patricia Y. Hashima and Paul R. Amato. 1994. "Poverty, Social Support, and Parental Behavior." *Child Development* 65:394–403 (p. 400).

67. W. H. Kimball, R. B. Stewart, R. D. Conger, and R. L. Burgess. 1980. "A Comparison of Family Interaction in Single Versus Two Parent Abusive, Neglectful, and Normal Families." In T. Field, S. Goldberg, D. Stern, and A. Shostak, eds., *Interaction of High Risk Infants and Children*. New York: Academic Press.

68. Richard J. Gelles. 1989. "Child Abuse and Violence in Single-Parent Families: Parent Absence and Economic Deprivation." *American Journal of Orthopsychiatry* 59(4):492–501 (p. 496).

69. Leslie Margolin. 1992. "Child Abuse by Mothers' Boyfriends: Why the Overrepresentation?" *Child Abuse and Neglect* 16:541–551 (p. 546).

70. Ibid., 543.

71. Ibid., 542–543.

72. Margo Wilson and Martin Daly. 1987. "Risk of Maltreatment of Children Living with Stepparents." Pp. 215–232 in R. Gelles and J. Lancaster, eds., *Child Abuse and Neglect: Biosocial Dimensions*. New York: Aldine de Gruyter, p. 228.

73. Martin Daly and Margo Wilson. 1988. *Homicide*. New York: Aldine de Gruyter, pp. 87–88. For some evidence to the contrary, see Catharine M. Malkin and Michael E. Lamb. 1994. "Child Maltreatment: A Test of Sociobiological Theory." *Journal of Comparative Family Studies* 25(1):121–133.

74. Lucile Duberman. 1975. *The Reconstituted Family: A Study of Remarried Couples and Their Children*. Chicago, IL: Nelson-Hall.

75. Andrew Cherlin. 1978. "Remarriage as an Incomplete Institution." *American Journal of Sociology* 84:634–650. J. Giles-Sims. 1984. "The Stepparent Role: Expectations, Behavior and Sanctions." *Journal of Family Issues* 5:116–130.

76. Martin Daly and Margo Wilson. 1988. "Evolutionary Social Psychology and Family Homicide." *Science* 242:519–524.

77. Margo Wilson and Martin Daly. 1987. "Risk of Maltreatment of Children Living with Stepparents." Pp. 215–232 in R. Gelles and J. Lancaster, eds., *Child Abuse and Neglect: Biosocial Dimensions*, p. 230.

78. Martin Daly and Margo I. Wilson. 1994. "Some Differential Attributes of Lethal Assaults on Small Children by Stepfathers Versus Genetic Fathers." *Ethology and Sociobiology* 15:207–217 (p. 207).

79. Martin Daly and Margo Wilson. 1991. "A Reply to Gelles: Stepchildren Are Disproportionately Abused, and Diverse Forms of Violence Can Share Causal Factors." *Human Nature* 2(4):419–426 (p. 421).

80. Martin Daly and Margo I. Wilson. 1994. "Some Differential Attributes of Lethal Assaults on Small Children by Stepfathers Versus Genetic Fathers." *Ethology and Sociobiology* 15:207–217.

81. Data from Marianne W. Zawitz et al. 1993. "Highlights from Twenty Years of Surveying Crime Victims." Washington, DC: Bureau of Justice Statistics.

82. Ronet Bachman. 1994. "Violence Against Women." Washington, DC: Bureau of Justice Statistics, p. 6.

83. Caroline Wolf Harlow. 1991. "Female Victims of Violent Crime." Washington, DC: Bureau of Justice Statistics, p. 4.

84. Daly and Wilson. *Homicide*, chapter 9.

85. Ibid.

86. Calculation by David Courtwright. [forthcoming]. *Explaining American Violence.*

87. See Courtwright. *Explaining American Violence.*

88. Carolyn Pape Cowan and P. A. Cowan. 1987. "Men's Involvement in Parenthood: Identifying the Antecedents and Understanding the Barriers." Pp. 145–174 in P. W. Berman and F. A. Pedersen, eds., *Men's Transitions to Parenthood: Longitudinal Studies of Early Family Experience.* Hillsdale, NJ: Lawrence Erlbaum. See also C. P. Cowan and P. A. Cowan. 1992. *When Partners Become Parents.* New York: Basic Books.

89. D. H. Heath. 1978. "What Meaning and Effects Does Fatherhood Have for the Maturing of Professional Men?" *Merrill-Palmer Quarterly* 24(4):265–278. See also D. H. Heath and H. E. Heath. 1991. *Fulfilling Lives: Paths to Maturity and Success.* San Francisco: Jossey-Bass.

90. Reported in *U.S. News and World Report*, February 27, 1995, p. 45.

91. Arne Mastekaasa. 1992. "Marriage and Psychological Well-Being: Some Evidence on Selection into Marriage." *Journal of Marriage and the Family* 54:901–911.

92. Walter R. Gove, Carolyn Briggs Style, and Michael Hughes. 1990. "The Effect of Marriage on the Well-Being of Adults." *Journal of Family Issues* 11(1):4–35; Robert H. Coombs. 1991. "Marital Status and Personal Well-Being: A Literature Review." *Family Relations* 40:97–102.

Chapter 3. Victorian Fathers and the Rise of the Modern Nuclear Family

1. Rev. John S. C. Abbott. 1842. "Paternal Neglect." *Parents' Magazine* (March). Cited in Mark C. Carnes. 1990. "Middle Class Men and the Solace of Fraternal Ritual." Pp. 37–52 in Mark C. Carnes and Clyde Griffen, eds., *Meanings for Manhood.* Chicago: University of Chicago Press, p. 47.

2. Lawrence Stone. 1977. *The Family, Sex and Marriage in England, 1500–1800.* New York: Harper and Row, p. 687.

3. Reith Lectures. 1967. London: British Broadcasting System.

4. Ann Oakley. 1993. "Women and Children First and Last: Parallels and Differences Between Children's and Women's Studies." Pp. 51–69 in Jens Qvortrup, ed., *Childhood as a Social Phenomenon: Lessons from an International Project.* Vienna: European Centre for Social Welfare Policy and Research, p. 55.

5. The first full-length history of American fathers is Robert L. Griswold. 1993. *Fatherhood in America.* New York: Basic Books.

6. John Demos. 1986. *Past, Present, and Personal: The Family and Life Course in American History.* New York: Oxford University Press, p. 42.

7. Richard Wall et al., eds., *Family Forms in Historic Europe.* Cambridge: Cambridge University Press. Jack Goody. 1983. *The Development of Family and Marriage in Europe.* Cambridge: Cambridge University Press. Michael Anderson. 1980. *Approaches to the History of the Western Family, 1500–1914.* London: Macmillan. Michael Mitterauer and Reinhard Sieder. 1983. *The European Family.* Chicago: University of Chicago Press.

8. Alan Macfarlane. 1979. *The Origins of English Individualism.* New York: Cambridge University Press. Alan Macfarlane. 1986. *Marriage and Love in England, 1300–1840.* New York: Basil Blackwell.

9. Mitterauer and Sieder. *The European Family,* p. 38

10. Peter Laslett. 1977. *Family Life and Illicit Love in Earlier Generations.* New York: Cambridge University Press.

11. One interesting and unusual social pattern was that prior to marriage, which occurred at a much later age than in other parts of the world, young people often circulated among households as servants, thereby filling the work roles that relatives play in extended family systems. It was thought that proper discipline and good work habits could be taught more forcefully in the homes of nonrelatives. Perhaps 50% of all adolescents participated in this activity, which has been labeled a "life-cycle servanthood." There was no notion of inferiority connected with the position, unlike other forms of servanthood, and most adolescent servants eventually married and went on to other things. Peter Laslett. *Family Life and Illicit Love,* p. 34.

12. Quoted in C. C. Harris. 1983. *The Family and Industrial Society.* London: Allen and Unwin, p. 137.

13. Mitterauer and Sieder. 1983. *The European Family,* p. 89.

14. D. B. Rutman and A. H. Rutman. 1984. *A Place in Time: Middlesex County, Virginia, 1650–1750.* New York: Norton.

15. These, of course, are broad generalizations that do not do justice to the diversity of the time. American family life and fatherhood in the 1600s differed considerably between the New England colonies and the rest of British North America (to say nothing of the rest of America). Family life in the Chesapeake region, for example, was more unstable than in New England. Many more immigrants to the Chesapeake area came as single, indentured servants, and they typically found a disease-ridden environment that led to early death. Ross W. Beales, Jr. 1991. "The Preindustrial Family: 1600–1815." Pp. 35–82 in Joseph M. Hawes and Elizabeth I. Nybakken, eds., *American Families: A Research Guide and Historical Handbook.* New York: Greenwood Press. Life was tough, households were more scattered, and reliance on the kin group was greater. Yet these two regions grew more alike over time. Less is known about family life in other colonial areas, although it appears to have been particularly stable in the Quaker areas of Pennsylvania and New Jersey. Barry Levy. 1988. *Quakers and the American Family.* New York: Oxford University Press.

16. It is important to note that the experience of families in the American South was substantially different from that of the Puritans and New Englanders in general. See, e.g., James Henretta. 1978. "Families and Farms: Mentality in Pre-Industrial America." *William and Mary Quarterly* 35. Unfortunately, any discussion of the Southern experience lies beyond the confines of this book.

17. John Demos. 1970. *A Little Commonwealth: Family Life in Plymouth Colony.* New York: Oxford University Press.

18. John Demos. 1979. "Images of the American Family, Then and Now." Pp. 43–60 in Virginia Tufte and B. Meyerhoff, eds., *Changing Images of the Family.* New Haven, CT: Yale University Press, pp. 46–48.

19. E. Anthony Rotundo. 1985. "American Fatherhood: A Historical Perspective." *American Behavioral Scientist* 29(1):7–25. Peter N. Stearns. 1991. "Fatherhood in Historical Perspective: The Role of Social Change." Pp. 28–52 in Frederick W. Bozett and Shirley M. H. Hanson, eds., *Fatherhood and Families in Cultural Context.* New York: Springer. Steven Mintz and Susan Kellogg. 1988. *Domestic Revolutions: A Social History of American Family Life.* New York: Free Press, chapter 1.

20. John Demos. 1986. *Past, Present, and Personal: The Family and Life Course in American History.* New York: Oxford University Press.

21. Philip J. Greven, Jr. 1977. *The Protestant Temperament: Patterns of Child-rearing, Religious Experience, and the Self in Early America.* New York: Alfred Knopf.

22. Quoted in Mintz and Kellogg. *Domestic Revolutions,* p. 15.

23. E. Anthony Rotundo. 1993. *American Manhood.* New York: Basic Books.

24. Cited in Mintz and Kellogg. *Domestic Revolutions,* p. 19.

25. David Hackett Fischer. 1981. "Forenames and the Family in New England: An Exercise in Historical Onomastics." *Chronos* 1:76–111.

26. Linda Kerber. 1980. *Women of the Republic: Intellect and Ideology in Revolutionary America.* Chapel Hill: University of North Carolina Press. Mary Beth Norton. 1980. *Liberty's Daughters: The Revolutionary Experience of American Women, 1750–1800.* Boston: Little, Brown.

27. Barry Levy. 1988. *Quakers and the American Family.* New York: Oxford University Press.

28. J. P. Brissot de Warville. *New Travels in the United States of America, 1778,* pp. 172, 312. Quoted in Levy. *Quakers,* p. 15.

29. John Demos. *Past, Present, and Personal,* p. 32.

30. Christopher Lasch. 1977. *Haven in a Heartless World.* New York: Basic Books.

31. The drop in the birthrate over the course of the nineteenth century was enormous. At the beginning of the century, the average number of children in a white native-born American family was 7.04; at the end of the century, the average number of children was only 3.56.

32. Historian Daniel Blake Smith depicts the shift to the modern nuclear family as "a movement away from the well-ordered, father dominated family of the colonial era—with its emphasis on parental control, obedience, and restraint of emotions—toward a strikingly affectionate, self-consciously private family environment in which children became the center of indulgent attention and were expected to marry for reasons of romance and companionship rather than parental design and economic interest." 1982. "The Study of the Family in Early America: Trends, Problems, and Prospects." *William and Mary Quarterly* (3rd ser.) 39:3–28.

33. E. B. Duffey. 1873. *What Women Should Know: A Woman's Book About Women.* Chicago: J. S. Goodman, p. 111. Quoted in Clifford Edward Clark, Jr. 1986. *The American Family Home.* Chapel Hill: University of North Carolina Press, p. 46.

34. Carl N. Degler. 1980. *At Odds: Women and the Family in America from the Revolution to the Present.* Oxford: Oxford University Press, p. 82.

35. Mintz and Kellogg. *Domestic Revolutions,* p. 53.

36. Linda A. Kerber. 1988. "Separate Spheres, Female Worlds, Woman's Place." *Journal of American History* 75:9–39.

37. It is not that love was totally absent from earlier family systems; love was simply not

the basis for marriage. Marriages were contracted largely on economic and other functional considerations, and love was incidental. The absence of love was not a compelling reason for a young person to reject a potential mate who was otherwise suitable, for example, nor was it a reasonable basis for dissolving a marriage.

38. Karen Lystra. 1989. *Searching the Heart: Women, Men and Romantic Love in Nineteenth Century America.* New York: Oxford University Press, p. 6.

39. Ibid., p. 8.

40. Peter N. Stearns and Mark Knapp. 1993. "Men and Romantic Love: Pinpointing a Twentieth-Century Change." *Journal of Social History* 26(4):769–795.

41. Lystra. *Searching the Heart,* p. 85.

42. Cited in E. Anthony Rotundo. *American Manhood,* p. 121.

43. Catherine E. Beecher and Harriet Beecher Stowe. 1869. *The American Woman's Home.* New York: J. B. Ford, p. 203. The first edition of this book, with the title *A Treatise on Domestic Economy,* appeared in 1842 under the sole authorship of Catherine Beecher and established her as the nineteenth-century woman who perhaps did most to define the Victorian domestic sphere. See Kathryn Kish Sklar. 1973. *Catherine E. Beecher: A Study in American Domesticity.* New Haven, CT: Yale University Press.

44. Mintz and Kellogg. *Domestic Revolutions,* p. 52.

45. *The Homes of the New World: Impressions of America.* Quoted in Degler, *At Odds,* p. 27.

46. Alexis de Tocqueville. 1969. *Democracy in America.* (Translated by George Lawrence; edited by J. P. Mayer). New York: Harper and Row, pp. 585, 588.

47. See Mary P. Ryan. 1981. *Cradle of the Middle Class: The Family in Oneida County, New York, 1790–1865.* New York: Cambridge University Press.

48. See Nancy Woloch. 1984. *Women and the American Experience.* New York: Knopf.

49. Often writing under the name of Timothy Titcomb, Holland was the most popular nonministerial writer about family life in the latter half of the nineteenth century. Josiah Gilbert Holland. 1858. *Titcomb's Letters to Young People, Single and Married.* New York: Charles Scribner, pp. 200–201. Quoted in Harvey Green. 1983. *The Light of the Home.* New York: Pantheon, p. 29.

50. Barry Levy. 1988. *Quakers and the American Family.* New York: Oxford University Press.

51. See Mary Ann Mason. 1994. *From Father's Property to Children's Rights.* New York: Columbia University Press, chapter 1.

52. Summing up the new family division of labor, the tender-years doctrine was succinctly stated by the California Supreme Court in 1860: "That a child of the tender age of this could be better served by the mother, with whom she could be almost constantly, than the father, whose necessary avocations would withdraw him, in a great measure, from personal superintendence and care of her, is plain enough." Quoted in Griswold. *Fatherhood in America,* p. 30.

53. Stephen Frank. 1992. "'Their Own Proper Task': The Construction of Meanings for Fatherhood in Nineteenth-Century America." Unpublished MS. Department of History, University of Michigan, Ann Arbor, p. 1.

54. Quoted in Frank. "'Their Own Proper Task,'" p. 13.

55. Mintz and Kellogg. *Domestic Revolutions,* p. 54.

56. A major exception is the work of Gertrude Himmelfarb. See esp. 1995. *The DeMoralization of Society: From Victorian Virtues to Modern Values.* New York: Knopf.

57. Elizabeth Pleck. 1987. *Domestic Tyranny: The Making of American Social Policy*

Against Family Violence from Colonial Times to the Present. New York: Oxford University Press.

58. Jackson Lears. 1994. "The Hidden Persuader." *New Republic*, October 3, p. 35.

59. Stone. *The Family, Sex and Marriage*, p. 679.

60. Lystra. *Searching the Heart*, p. 136.

61. Elaine Tyler May. 1980. *Great Expectations: Marriage and Divorce in Post-Victorian America*. Chicago: University of Chicago Press, p. 157.

62. "Life in the Nineties: Home and Parents." *Harpers* 169 (1934): 278. Quoted in Paula S. Fass. 1979. *The Damned and the Beautiful: American Youth in the 1920s*. New York: Oxford University Press, p. 92.

63. Lystra. *Searching the Heart*, chapter 7.

64. William L. O'Neill. 1967. *Divorce in the Progressive Era*. New Haven, CT: Yale University Press, p. 89.

65. Margaret Marsh. 1990. "Suburban Men and Masculine Domesticity, 1870–1915." Pp. 111–127 in Mark C. Carnes and Clyde Griffen, eds., *Meanings for Manhood*. Chicago: University of Chicago Press, p. 112.

66. Barbara Welter. 1966. "The Cult of True Womanhood: 1800–1860." *American Quarterly* 18:151–175.

67. See Carol Zisowitz Stearns and Peter N. Stearns. 1985. "Victorian Sexuality: Can Historians Do It Better?" *Journal of Social History* (Summer):625–634.

68. Paul C. Glick. 1989. "The Family Life Cycle and Social Change." *Family Relations* 38(2):123–129.

69. Glenna Matthews. 1987. *"Just a Housewife": The Rise and Fall of Domesticity in America*. New York: Oxford University Press, p. 34.

70. Sarah Elbert. 1987. *A Hunger for Home: Louisa May Alcott's Place in American Literature*. New Brunswick, NJ: Rutgers University Press.

71. Robert L. Griswold. 1982. *Family and Divorce in California, 1850–1890: Victorian Illusions and Everyday Realities*. Albany: State University of New York Press.

72. Carl N. Degler. *At Odds*, pp. 8–9.

73. Nancy Cott. 1977. *The Bonds of Womanhood*. New Haven, CT: Yale University Press, p. 197.

74. Robert L. Griswold. 1990. "Divorce and the Legal Redefinition of Victorian Manhood." Pp. 96–110 in Carnes and Griffen, eds., *Meanings for Manhood*, p. 97.

75. Although women were mostly excluded from public life, they were at least treated by men in public with deference and respect, a function, in part, of the belief in their moral superiority. The Frenchman August Carlier, writing of his travels to America in the late 1850s, notes with disapproval the lingering patriarchy of America and the separate sphere exclusion of women from public life (both of which were more extreme in America than in France). But at the same time he says that the American woman is "the object of every attention and regard . . . however inexperienced in life, she may travel alone, and pass through the whole United States, without a man daring to hazard a word or gesture in her presence which could offend her" (Auguste Carlier. 1972 [1867]. *Marriage in the United States*. New York: Arno Press and the *New York Times*, pp. 31, 32). Mark Twain echoed this observation two decades later in his 1880 story "American Manners," writing that, unlike in Europe, "a lady may traverse our streets all day, going and coming as she chooses and she will never be molested by any man" (quoted in Kevin White. 1993. *The First Sexual Revolution: The Emergence of Male Heterosexuality in Modern America*. New York: New York University Press, p. 4).

76. See, e.g., Louise A. Tilly and Joan W. Scott. 1978. *Women, Work, and Family.* New York: Holt, Rinehart and Winston.

77. See, e.g., Joanna Bourke. 1994. "Housewifery in Working-Class England, 1860–1914." *Past and Present* 143:167–197.

78. Clifford E. Clark, Jr. 1986. *The American Family Home: 1800–1960.* Chapel Hill: University of North Carolina Press.

79. Susan Strasser. 1982. *Never Done: A History of American Housework.* New York: Pantheon Books, p. 6.

80. Anne M. Boylan. 1985. "Growing Up Female in America, 1800–1860." Pp. 153–184 in Joseph M. Hawes and N. Ray Hiner, eds., *American Childhood.* Westport, CT: Greenwood Press, p. 157.

81. Sally Allen McNall. 1985. "American Children's Literature, 1880–Present." Pp. 377–413 in Hawes and Hiner, eds., *American Childhood,* p. 377.

82. Carl Degler. *At Odds,* pp. 8–9.

83. Patricia Draper and Henry Harpending. 1987. "Parent Investment and the Child's Environment." Pp. 207–235 in Jane B. Lancaster, Jeanne Altmann, Alice S. Rossi, and Lonnie R. Sherrod, eds., *Parenting Across the Life Span: Biosocial Dimensions.* New York: Aldine de Gruyter.

84. Sheila Ryan Johansson. 1987. "Neglect, Abuse, and Avoidable Death: Parental Investment and the Mortality of Infants and Children in the European Tradition." Pp. 57–93 in Richard J. Gelles and Jane B. Lancaster, eds., *Child Abuse and Neglect: Biosocial Dimensions.* New York: Aldine de Gruyter, p. 68.

85. Draper and Harpending. "Parent Investment."

86. See Marilyn Dell Brady. 1991. "The New Model Middle-Class Family." Chapter 4 in Joseph M. Hawes and Elizabeth I. Nybakken, eds., *American Families: A Research Guide and Historical Handbook.* New York: Greenwood Press.

87. Robert Karen. 1994. *Becoming Attached.* New York: Warner Books.

88. Leonard A. Sagan. 1987. *The Health of Nations.* New York: Basic Books.

89. For a review of the data, see Himmelfarb. *The De-Moralization of Society;* and James Q. Wilson and Richard Herrnstein. 1985. *Crime and Human Nature.* New York: Simon and Schuster, chapter 16.

90. James Lincoln Collier. 1991. *The Rise of Selfishness in America.* New York: Oxford University Press, p. 18.

91. Gertrude Himmelfarb. 1994. "A De-moralized Society: The British American Experience." *Public Interest* 117:57–80 (p. 75).

92. These values are being heavily promoted today by, among other organizations, a burgeoning "Character Counts" coalition.

93. Brigitte Berger and Peter L. Berger. 1983. *The War Over the Family.* Garden City, NY: Anchor Press/Doubleday.

Chapter 4. The Shrinking Father and the Fall of the Nuclear Family

1. David Pivar. 1973. *Purity Crusade: Sexual Morality and Social Control, 1868–1900.* Westport, CT: Greenwood Press.

2. Mark C. Carnes. 1990. "Middle-Class Men and the Solace of Fraternal Ritual." Pp. 37–52 in Mark C. Carnes and Clyde Griffen, eds., *Meanings for Manhood.* Chicago: University of Chicago Press.

3. Stephen Frank. 1992. "'Their Own Proper Task': The Construction of Meanings for Fatherhood in Nineteenth-Century America." Unpublished MS., Department of History, University of Michigan, Ann Arbor.

4. John Demos. 1986. *Past, Present, and Personal: The Family and Life Course in American History.* New York: Oxford University Press, p. 60.

5. John Higham. 1970. "The Reorientation of American Culture in the 1890s." Pp. 73–102 in John Higham, ed., *Writing American History.* Bloomington: Indiana University Press, p. 79.

6. This is suggested by Peter N. Stearns. 1990. *Be a Man! Males in Modern Society.* New York: Holmes and Meier, p. 63.

7. Stearns. *Be a Man!* p. 71.

8. Stephen Frank. "Their Own Proper Task."

9. See E. Anthony Rotundo. 1993. *American Manhood.* New York: Basic Books, p. 55.

10. The new power of youth was strongly in evidence in Middletown in the 1920s. Joseph F. Kett. 1977. *Rites of Passage: Adolescence in America, 1790 to the Present.* New York: Basic Books. John Modell. 1989. *Into One's Own: From Youth to Adulthood in the United States, 1920–1975.* Berkeley: University of California Press.

11. Michael Grossberg. 1985. *Governing the Hearth: Law and Family in Nineteenth-Century America.* Chapel Hill: University of North Carolina Press.

12. David J. Rothman. 1971. *The Discovery of the Asylum.* Boston: Little, Brown.

13. Joe Dubbert. 1979. *A Man's Place: Masculinity in Transition.* Englewood Cliffs, NJ: Prentice-Hall.

14. Robert S. Lynd and Helen Merrell Lynd. 1929. *Middletown: A Study in American Culture.* New York: Harcourt Brace.

15. E. Anthony Rotundo. 1985. "American Fatherhood: A Historical Perspective." *American Behavioral Scientist* 29(1):7–25 (p. 14).

16. Randal D. Day and Wade C. Mackey. 1986. "The Role Image of the American Father." *Journal of Comparative Family Studies* 3:371–388. Peter G. Filene. 1986. *Him/Her/Self: Sex Roles in Modern America.* 2nd ed. Baltimore: Johns Hopkins. Ralph La Rossa, Betty Ann Gordon, Ronald Jay Wilson, Annette Bairan, and Charles Jaret. 1991. "The Fluctuating Image of the Twentieth-Century American Father." *Journal of Marriage and the Family* 53(4):987–997.

17. New York: Thomas Whittaker, p. 7.

18. Nelson Manfred Blake. 1962. *The Road to Reno: A History of Divorce in the United States.* New York: Macmillan, chapter 9.

19. Quote in Steven Mintz and Susan Kellogg. 1988. *Domestic Revolutions: A Social History of American Family Life.* New York: Free Press, p. 108.

20. Carroll D. Wright. 1902. *Outline of Practical Sociology.* 5th ed., rev. New York: Longmans, Green.

21. *Papers and Proceedings.* 1909. Third Annual Meeting of the American Sociological Society, December 28–30, 1908. Chicago: University of Chicago Press, pp. 1–15.

22. One landmark was the establishment by the federal government of the U.S. Children's Bureau in 1912, to investigate and report on "all matters pertaining to the welfare of children and child life among all classes of our people." Joseph M. Hawes. 1991. *The Children's Rights Movement.* Boston: Twayne, p. 47.

23. Arthur W. Calhoun. 1945 [1917–1919]. *A Social History of the American Family.* 3 vols. New York: Barnes and Noble, vol. 3, p. 131.

24. 173:56–77 (p. 73).

25. Karen Lystra. 1989. *Searching the Heart: Women, Men and Romantic Love in Nineteenth-Century America.* New York: Oxford University Press, p. 84.

26. Lystra. *Searching the Heart,* p. 250.

27. Paula S. Fass. 1979. *The Damned and the Beautiful: American Youth in the 1920s.* New York: Oxford University Press, p. 6.

28. Kevin White. 1993. *The First Sexual Revolution: The Emergence of Male Heterosexuality in Modern America*. New York: New York University Press.

29. Ellen K. Rothman. 1984. *Hands and Hearts: A History of Courtship in America*. New York: Basic Books.

30. Lewis Terman. 1938. *Psychological Factors in Marital Happiness*. New York: McGraw-Hill.

31. William Johnson. 1925. "Why Men Won't Marry the New Woman." *Collier's*, March 14, pp. 22–23. Quoted in White. *The First Sexual Revolution*, p. 171.

32. Christopher Lasch. 1977. *Haven in a Heartless World: The Family Besieged*. New York: Basic Books, pp. 35–36.

33. William F. Ogburn and Clarke Tippitts. 1933. "The Family and Its Functions." Chapter 13 in President's Research Committee on Social Trends. *Recent Social Trends*, p. 697.

34. Mary E. Overholt. 1932. "For Fathers Only." *Parents' Magazine* 7 (July):39. Quoted in Robert L. Griswold. 1993. *Fatherhood in America*. New York: Basic Books, p. 95.

35. Griswold. *Fatherhood*, p. 117. He states: "The new fatherhood arose at the historical moment when masculinity and domesticity were both in crisis. Traditional sources of male identity in work, religion, and community had evaporated during the second half of the nineteenth century; consequently, many middle-class men . . . increasingly sought meaning in the private realm" (p. 115).

36. Rotundo. *American Manhood*, Epilogue.

37. Glen H. Elder. 1974. *Children of the Great Depression: Social Change in Life Experience*. Chicago: University of Chicago Press.

38. Elder. *Children of the Great Depression*, pp. 114–115.

39. Winifred D. Wandersee. 1991. "Families Face the Great Depression." Chapter 5 in Joseph M. Hawes and Elizabeth I. Nybakken, eds., *American Families: A Research Guide and Historical Handbook*. New York: Greenwood Press.

40. Cited in Elaine Tyler May. 1988. *Homeward Bound: American Families in the Cold War Era*. New York: Basic Books, p. 49.

41. Ibid., chapter 2.

42. John Modell and Duane Steffey. 1988. "Waging War and Marriage: Military Service and Family Formation, 1940–1950." *Journal of Family History* 13(2):195–218.

43. U. S. Bureau of the Census. *Historical Statistics of the U.S., Colonial Times to 1970*. Bicentennial Edition, Part 1. Washington, DC: GPO. Series D, p. 133.

44. Griswold. *Fatherhood*, pp. 168–172.

45. Charlotte Towle. 1943. "The Effect of the War upon Children." *Social Service Review* 17:154. Cited in Griswold. *Fatherhood*, p. 316.

46. Francis E. Merrill. 1948. *Social Problems on the Home Front: A Study of Wartime Influences*. New York: Harper, chapter 7.

47. Philip Wylie. 1955 [1942)]. *A Generation of Vipers*. New York: Holt, Rinehart and Winston.

48. Andrew J. Cherlin. 1992. *Marriage, Divorce, Remarriage*. Cambridge, MA: Harvard University Press, p. 25.

49. Cited in May. *Homeward Bound*, p. 28.

50. Judith Sealander. 1985. "Families, World War II, and the Baby Boom (1940–1955)." Chapter 6 in Joseph M. Hawes and Elizabeth I. Nybakken, eds., *American Families: A Research Guide and Historical Handbook*. New York: Greenwood Press.

51. "The New Domesticated Male." *Life,* January 4, 1954, pp. 42–45. See also *Parents' Magazine.* 1947.

52. Kyle Pruett. 1987. *The Nurturing Father.* New York: Warner Books, p. 14.

53. Ernest R. Mowrer. Cited in Charles E. Strickland and Andrew M. Ambrose. 1985. "The Changing Worlds of Children, 1945–1963." Pp. 533–585 in Joseph M. Hawes and N. Ray Hiner, eds., *American Childhood.* Westport, CT: Greenwood Press, p. 543.

54. Joseph H. Pleck. 1987. "American Fathering in Historical Perspective." Pp. 83–97 in Michael S. Kimmel, ed., *Changing Men.* Beverly Hills, CA: Sage, p. 90.

55. Cited in Strickland and Ambrose. "Changing Worlds," p. 543.

56. Betty Friedan. 1963. *The Feminine Mystique.* New York: Dell.

57. Barbara Ehrenreich. 1984. *The Hearts of Men: American Dreams and the Flight from Commitment.* Garden City, NY: Anchor Press/Doubleday.

58. Cited in Strickland and Ambrose. "Changing Worlds," p. 558.

59. See David Popenoe. 1977. *The Suburban Environment: Sweden and the United States.* Chicago: University of Chicago Press.

60. Herbert Hendin. 1975. *The Age of Sensation.* New York: McGraw-Hill, p. 317.

Chapter 5. What Do Fathers Do?

1. Urie Bronfenbrenner. 1990. "Discovering What Families Do." In D. Blankenhorn, S. Bayme, and J. B. Elshtain. *Rebuilding the Nest.* Milwaukee, WI: Family Service America, p. 33.

2. James Q. Wilson. 1994. "Culture, Incentives, and the Underclass." Pp. 54–80 in Henry J. Aaron, Thomas E. Mann, and Timothy Taylor, eds., *Values and Public Policy.* Washington, DC: Brookings Institution, pp. 70–71.

3. David M. Buss. 1994. *The Evolution of Desire: Strategies of Human Mating.* New York: Basic Books, pp. 22, 24.

4. Quote attributed to Vice President Albert Gore, Jr., in Randy Rieland. 1995. "Fathers and Sons." *Washingtonian* (June). 56.

5. John Snarey. 1993. *How Fathers Care for the Next Generation.* Cambridge, MA: Harvard University Press, pp. 163–164.

6. See David D. Gilmore. 1990. *Manhood in the Making.* New Haven, CT: Yale University Press.

7. Samuel Osherson. 1986. *Finding Our Fathers: The Unfinished Business of Manhood.* New York: Free Press, p. 4.

8. See Kim A. McDonald. 1995. "The Secrets of Animal Play." *Chronicle of Higher Education,* July 13, pp. A9–A13.

9. M. W. Yogman. 1982. "Development of the Father-Infant Relationship." Pp. 221–280 in H. E. Fitzgerald, B. M. Lester, and M. W. Yogman, eds., *Theory and Research in Behavioral Pediatrics* 1. New York: Plenum Press. J. L. Roopnarine and N. S. Mounts. 1985. "Mother-Child and Father-Child Play." *Early Child Development Care* 20:157–169; S. Ricks. 1985. "Father-Infant Interactions: A Review of Empirical Research." *Family Relations* 34:505–511.

10. K. Allison Clarke-Stewart. 1980. "The Father's Contribution to Children's Cognitive and Social Development in Early Childhood." In F. A. Pedersen, ed., *The Father-Infant Relationship: Observational Studies in the Family Setting.* New York: Praeger.

11. Snarey. *How Fathers Care,* pp. 35–36.

12. Nancy A. Crowell and Ethel M. Leeper, eds. 1994. *America's Fathers and Public Policy.* Washington, DC: National Academy Press, p. 8.

13. Reported in Kim A. McDonald. 1995. "The Secrets of Animal Play." *Chronicle of Higher Education,* July 13, pp. A9–A13.

14. Jerrold Lee Shapiro. 1994. "Letting Dads Be Dads." *Parents* 69 (June): 168.

15. Ibid., 166.

16. Carol Gilligan. 1982. *In a Different Voice.* Cambridge, MA: Harvard University Press; Carol Gilligan, Janie Victoria Ward, and Jill McLean Taylor. 1988. *Mapping the Moral Domain.* Cambridge, MA: Harvard University Press.

17. Jean Piaget. 1965 [1932]. *The Moral Judgment of the Child.* Glencoe, IL: Free Press.

18. Diana Baumrind. 1982. "Are Androgynous Individuals More Effective Persons and Parents?" *Child Development* 53:44–75 (p. 44).

19. Diana Baumrind. 1991. "The Influence of Parenting Style on Adolescent Competence and Substance Use." *Journal of Early Adolescence* 11(1):56–95. See also Frances K. Grossman, William S. Pollack, and Ellen Golding. 1988. "Fathers and Children: Predicting the Quality and Quantity of Fathering." *Developmental Psychology* 24(1):82–92.

20. E. Greenberger. 1984. "Defining Psychosocial Maturity in Adolescence." Pp. 3–39 in P. Karoly and J. J. Steffen, eds., *Adolescent Behavior Disorders: Foundation and Contemporary Concerns.* Lexington, MA: D. C. Heath.

21. The major research findings are reviewed in Snarey, *How Fathers Care,* chapter 6. It should be noted that the research findings are often complex and sometimes contradictory. A few studies have found, e.g., that it is mainly the father's money and not the father per se that makes the difference. See L. J. Crockett, D. J. Eggebeen, and A. J. Hawkins. 1993. "Father's Presence and Young Children's Behavioral and Cognitive Adjustment." *Family Relations* 14:355–377. The study of father involvement is an area in which further research could pay enormous dividends in our increase of knowledge.

22. 1993. Westport, CT: Auburn House, p. 1.

23. E.g., H. S. Goldstein. 1982. "Fathers' Absence and Cognitive Development of 12–17-Year-Olds. *Psychological Reports* 51:843–848.

24. E. Bing. 1963. "The Effect of Child-Rearing Practices on the Development of Differential Cognitive Abilities." *Child Development* 34:631–648.

25. See N. Radin. 1981. "The Role of the Father in Cognitive, Academic and Intellectual Development." Pp. 379–427 in M. E. Lamb, ed., *The Role of the Father in Child Development.* New York: John Wiley. N. Radin. 1986. "The Influence of Fathers on Their Sons and Daughters." *Social Work in Education* 8:77–91. N. Radin and G. Russell. 1983. "Increased Paternal Participation and Childhood Outcomes." Pp. 191–218 in M. E. Lamb and A. Sagi, eds., *Fatherhood and Family Policy.* Hillsdale, NJ: Lawrence Erlbaum.

26. Richard Koestner, Carol Franz, and Joel Weinberger. 1990. "The Family Origins of Empathic Concern: A Twenty-Six-Year Longitudinal Study." *Journal of Personality and Social Psychology.* 58(4):709–717. See also A. Sagi. 1982. "Antecedents and Consequences of Various Degrees of Paternal Involvement in Childrearing: The Israeli Project." In M. E. Lamb, ed., *Nontraditional Families: Parenting and Child Development.* Hillsdale, NJ: Lawrence Erlbaum.

27. E.g., J. Block. 1971. *Lives Through Time.* Berkeley, CA: Bancroft Books. John Snarey. *How Fathers Care.*

28. Carol E. Franz, David C. McClelland, and Joel Weinberger. 1991. "Childhood An-

tecedents of Conventional Social Accomplishment in Midlife Adults: A Thirty-Six-Year Prospective Study." *Journal of Personality and Social Psychology* 60(4):586–595.

29. Paul R. Amato. 1994. "Father-Child Relations, Mother-Child Relations, and Off-spring Psychological Well-Being in Early Adulthood." *Journal of Marriage and the Family* 56:1031–1042.

30. Amanda McCombs Thomas and Rex Forehand. 1993. "The Role of Paternal Variables in Divorced and Married Families: Predictability of Adolescent Adjustment." *American Journal of Orthopsychiatry* 63(1):126–135. R. D. Hess and K. A. Camara. 1979. "Post-Divorce Family Relationships as Mediating Factors in the Consequences of Divorce for Children." *Journal of Social Issues* 35:79–96.

31. Valarie King. 1994. "Nonresident Father Involvement and Child Well-Being: Can Dads Make a Difference?" *Journal of Family Issues* 15(1):78–96. Frank F. Furstenberg, Jr., S. P. Morgan, and P. D. Allison. 1987. "Paternal Participation and Children's Well-Being After Marital Dissolution." *American Sociological Review* 52:695–701.

32. These studies are reviewed in Marvin D. Free, Jr. 1991. "Clarifying the Relationship Between the Broken Home and Juvenile Delinquency: A Critique of the Current Literature." *Deviant Behavior: An Interdisciplinary Journal* 12:109–167 (pp. 121–122). See also R. E. Johnson. 1986. "Family Structure and Delinquency: General Patterns and Gender Differences." *Criminology* 24:65–84.

33. Annette U. Rickel and Thomas S. Langer. 1985. "Short-Term and Long-Term Effects of Marital Disruption on Children." *American Journal of Community Psychology* 13:599–611.

34. James H. Bray, Sandra H. Berger, Carol L. Boethel, Josue R. Maymi, and Gini Touch. 1992. "Longitudinal Changes in Stepfamilies: Impact on Children's Adjustment." Unpublished paper presented at the Annual Meeting of the American Psychological Association, Washington, DC, August 15.

35. Sara McLanahan and Gary Sandefur. 1994. *Growing Up With a Single Parent.* Cambridge, MA: Harvard University Press, p. 29.

36. E. Mavis Hetherington and Kathleen M. Jodl. 1994. "Stepfamilies as Settings for Child Development." Pp. 55–76 in Alan Booth and Judy Dunn, eds., *Stepfamilies: Who Benefits? Who Does Not?* Hillsdale, NJ: Lawrence Erlbaum.

37. David Popenoe. 1994. "The Evolution of Marriage and the Problem of Stepfamilies: A Biosocial Perspective." Pp. 3–27 in Booth and Dunn, eds., *Stepfamilies.*

38. Martin Daly and Margo Wilson. 1988. *Homicide.* New York: Aldine de Gruyter, pp. 87–88 (83).

39. McLanahan and Sandefur, *Growing Up*, pp. 67–68. In these comparisons, other differences in family characteristics are held constant, such as race, parents' education, family size, residential location, and sometimes ability.

40. Ellen B. Berlinsky and Henry B. Biller. 1982. *Parental Death and Psychological Development.* Lexington, MA: D. C. Heath, chapters 3–4.

41. Of course, the circumstances of the death can be a factor, whether illness, accident, homicide, suicide, or war.

42. Robert J. Sampson and John H. Laub. 1992. "Crime and Deviance in the Life Course." *Annual Review of Sociology* 18:63–84.

43. Don Olweus. 1979. "Stability of Aggressive Reaction Patterns in Males: A Review." *Psychological Bulletin* 86:852–875. A. Caspi et al. 1987. "Moving Against the World: Life-Course Patterns of Explosive Children." *Developmental Psychology* 23:308–313.

44. J. White, T. Moffitt, F. Earls, L. Robins, and P. Silva. 1990. "How Early Can We Tell?

Predictors of Childhood Conduct Disorder and Adolescent Delinquency." *Criminology* 28:507–533 (p. 521).

45. Quoted in Sampson and Laub. "Crime and Deviance," p. 68.

46. Ibid. It is extremely difficult in individual cases to predict adult criminality from childhood behaviors. Many positive and negative factors and events can intervene in adolescent and adult lives. Especially important, according to recent evidence, are the social bonds which people develop when they become adults. "The trajectories of crime and deviance are systematically modified by social bonds to adult institutions of informal social control." Robert J. Sampson and John H. Laub. 1990. "Crime and Deviance over the Life Course: The Salience of Adult Social Bonds." *American Sociological Review* 55:609–627 (p. 625). Specifically, the stronger the adult ties to work and to family, the less likely an adult trajectory of antisocial behavior. See L. Robins and M. Rutter, eds., 1990. *Straight and Devious Pathways from Childhood to Adulthood*. Cambridge: Cambridge University Press.

47. See David C. Rowe. 1994. *The Limits of Family Influence: Genes, Experience and Behavior*. New York: Guilford Press. The role of genetic factors has been made clear by studies of identical twins and of adoptees, including a famous study of Danish children adopted at birth that found a much higher relationship between the children's later criminality and the criminality of their birth parents, not their adopted parents who had actually raised them. S. A. Mednick, W. F. Gabrielli, Jr., and B. Hutchings. 1984. "Genetic Influences in Criminal Convictions: Evidence from an Adoption Cohort." *Science* 224:891–894.

48. James Q. Wilson. 1991. *On Character*. Washington, DC: AEI Press, p. 59.

49. Robert J. Sampson and John H. Laub. 1993. *Crime in the Making*. Cambridge, MA: Harvard University Press, p. 247.

50. Albert J. Reiss, Jr., and Jeffrey A. Roth, eds. 1993. *Understanding and Preventing Violence*. Washington, DC: National Academy Press, p. 105.

51. Ibid., p. 368. One study found, for black males only, that it was not only a violent or abusive childhood that led to later violence. "Neglect in childhood without violence was just as likely to lead to an arrest for violence in adulthood as was physical abuse in childhood." C. S. Widom. 1989. "The Cycle of Violence." *Science* 244:160–166.

52. Michael R. Gottfredson and Travis Hirschi. 1990. *A General Theory of Crime*. Stanford, CA: Stanford University Press, p. 90.

53. Ibid., p. 255.

54. Ibid., p. 68.

55. Nancy Eisenberg and Paul H. Mussen. 1989. *The Roots of Prosocial Behavior in Children*. Cambridge: Cambridge University Press. For the development of both self-control and empathy, in addition, it is important for children to be strongly "attached" to their parents, to regard their parents with love and respect, and for the children's parents to be good role models (and especially not be criminals themselves!).

56. Gottfredson and Hirschi. *A General Theory of Crime*, p. 104.

57. Laurence Steinberg. 1987. "Susceptibility of Adolescents to Antisocial Peer Pressure." *Child Development* 58:269–275.

58. Sanford M. Dornbusch, J. M. Carlsmith, S. J. Bushwall, P. L. Ritter, H. Leiderman, A. H. Hastorf, and R. T. Gross. 1985. "Single Parents, Extended Households, and the Control of Adolescents." *Child Development* 56:326–341 (pp. 326, 332).

59. McLanahan and Sandefur. *Growing Up*, p. 75. They explain that their finding may relate to the fact that they studied families with teenagers, whereas those studies that

have found a positive impact for grandmothers were looking at families with younger children. Also, they did not look at effects on juvenile delinquency and violence.

60. P. L. Chase-Lansdale, J. Brooks-Gunn, and E. S. Zamsky. [forthcoming]. "Young African American Multigenerational Families in Poverty: Quality of Mothering and Grandmothering." *Child Development.*

61. Another factor is that single mothers living with their mothers are, in the first place, more dependent and immature than those who have been able to establish themselves apart from their families of origin and hence are less effective parents.

62. Lawrence Steinberg. 1987. "Single Parents, Step-Parents and the Susceptibility of Adolescents to Antisocial Peer Pressure." *Child Development* 58:269–275. This is based on a sample of 865 adolescents in grades 5, 6, 8, and 9; Madison, WI, school district.

63. Henry B. Biller. 1993. *Fathers and Families: Paternal Factors in Child Development.* Westport, CT: Auburn House, pp. 1, 2.

64. See Beatrice Whiting. 1965. "Sex Identity Conflict and Physical Violence." *American Anthropologist* 67:123–140.

65. B. B. Whiting and J. W. M. Whiting. 1975. *Children of Six Cultures: A Psychocultural Analysis.* Cambridge, MA: Harvard University Press.

66. E.g., Robert L. Munroe and Ruth L. Munroe. 1992. "Fathers in Children's Environments: A Four Culture Study." Pp. 213–229 in Barry S. Hewlett, ed., *Father-Child Relations: Cultural and Biosocial Contexts.* New York: Aldine De Gruyter.

67. Patricia Draper and Henry Harpending. 1982. "Father Absence and Reproductive Strategy: An Evolutionary Perspective." *Journal of Anthropological Research* 38(3):255–273 (p. 257).

68. Patricia Draper and Henry Harpending. 1988. "A Sociobiological Perspective on the Development of Human Reproductive Strategies." Pp. 340–372 in Kevin B. MacDonald, ed., *Sociobiological Perspectives on Human Development.* New York: Springer-Verlag, p. 353.

69. Cited in Tamar Lewin. 1995. "Creating Fathers out of Men with Children." *New York Times.* June 18, p. A1.

70. E. Mavis Hetherington. 1972. "Effects of Father Absence on Personality Development in Adolescent Daughters." *Developmental Psychology* 7(3):313–326.

71. One of the positive effects of girls living with their fathers rather than their mothers in single-parent households is a lower rate of teen pregnancy. See Brian Powell and Douglas B. Downey. Unpublished MS. "Adolescents' Well-Being in Single-Parent Households: The Case of the Same-Sex Hypothesis." Indiana University, Bloomington.

72. N. Radin and G. Russell. 1983. "Increased Paternal Participation and Childhood Outcomes." Pp. 191–218 in M. E. Lamb and A. Sagi, eds., *Fatherhood and Family Policy.* Hillsdale, NJ: Lawrence Erlbaum.

73. Patricia Draper and Henry Harpending. 1982. "Father Absence and Reproductive Strategy: An Evolutionary Perspective." *Journal of Anthropological Research* 38(3):255–273 (p. 258).

74. Jenny Blain and Jerome Barkow. 1988. "Father Involvement, Reproductive Strategies, and the Sensitive Period." Pp. 373–396 in Kevin B. MacDonald, ed., *Sociobiological Perspectives on Human Development.* New York: Springer-Verlag, p. 380.

75. Jay Belsky, Laurence Steinberg, and Patricia Draper. 1991. "Childhood Experience, Interpersonal Development, and Reproductive Strategy: An Evolutionary Theory of Socialization." *Child Development* 62:647–670. See also Patricia Draper and Jay

Belsky. 1990. "Personality Development in Evolutionary Perspective." *Journal of Personality* 58(1):141–161.

76. See, e.g., Shere Hite. 1994. *The Hite Report on the Family: Growing Up Under Patriarchy.* New York: Grove Press.

77. Scott Coltrane. 1988. "Father-Child Relationships and the Status of Women: A Cross-Cultural Study." *American Journal of Sociology* 93(5):1060–1095 (p. 1060).

78. See, e.g., Charles W. Meuller, Sarosh Kuruvilla, and Roderick D. Iverson. 1994. "Swedish Professionals and Gender Inequalities." *Social Forces* 73(2):555–572.

79. Coltrane. "Father-Child Relationships," p. 1088.

80. New York: Morrow. Quoted in Coltrane. "Father-Child Relationships," p. 1062.

81. Admittedly, some circularity is involved in the relationship between childhood socialization and adult male attitudes. The public participation of women contributes, in a reverse causal flow, to increased paternal involvement in domestic tasks.

82. Nancy Chodorow. 1978. *The Reproduction of Mothering.* Berkeley: University of California Press.

83. See N. Radin and G. Russell. 1983. "Increased Father Participation and Child Development Outcomes." Pp. 191–218 in M. Lamb and A. Sagi, eds., *Fatherhood and Family Policy.* Hillsdale, NJ: Lawrence Erlbaum.

Chapter 6. The Essential Father

1. Three recent books provide excellent overviews of this topic: Robert Wright. 1994. *The Moral Animal.* New York: Pantheon. Adam Kuper. 1994. *The Chosen Primate: Human Nature and Cultural Diversity.* Cambridge, MA: Harvard University Press. Matt Ridley. 1993. *The Red Queen: Sex and the Evolution of Human Nature.* New York: Macmillan.

2. For a similar conclusion, see Wade C. Mackey. 1985. *Fathering Behaviors: The Dynamics of the Man-Child Bond.* New York: Plenum. In the positing of a "human nature" we must, of course, be careful. The use of the phrase is not meant to imply that biology *determines* social behavior, for that is never the case. Consider the sex drive. It is about as inborn to our beings as anything can be, yet one can find subcultures that practice celibacy, others that practice promiscuity. In other words, the biological sex drive is culturally patterned in precisely opposite ways. It is also important to stress that what is biologically inherent in human nature—or "natural"—is not necessarily "good." Men are aggressive, for example, but that does not make inappropriate male aggression morally right. The good and the right are cultural concepts, designed to guide human behavior in ways that benefit society as a whole. Every society carefully restricts aggression, notably the right to kill. Indeed, imbedded in the very concept of human civilization is the idea that humankind has evolved by following cultural and moral principles, not just those that govern animal behavior.

3. Quoted in Martin Daly and Margo Wilson. 1983. *Sex, Evolution, and Behavior.* 2nd ed. Belmont, CA: Wadsworth, p. iii.

4. R. J. Britten. 1986. "Rates of DNA Sequence Evolution Differ Between Taxonomic Groups." *Science* 23:1393–1398. Discussed in Jared Diamond. 1992. *The Third Chimpanzee: The Evolution and Future of the Human Animal.* New York: HarperCollins.

5. Katharine M. Noonan. 1987. "Evolution: A Primer for Psychologists." Pp. 31–60

in Charles Crawford, Martin Smith, and Dennis Krebs, eds., *Sociobiology and Psychology*. Hillsdale, NJ: Lawrence Erlbaum, p. 42.

6. William D. Hamilton. 1964. "The Genetic Evolution of Social Behavior I, II. *Journal of Theoretical Biology* 7:7–52.

7. Robert J. Blumenshine and John A. Cavallo. 1992. "Scavenging and Human Evolution." *Scientific American* 267 (October):4.

8. This is the recent position of Richard Leakey. See Richard Leakey and Roger Lewin. 1992. *Origins Reconsidered: In Search of What Makes Us Human*. New York: Doubleday, chapters 8–9.

9. There is evidence that to this day "we enjoy being in savannah vegetation, prefer to avoid both closed forests and open plains, will pay more for land giving us the impression of being a savannah, mold recreational environments to be more like savannahs, and develop varieties of ornamental plants that converge on the shapes typical of tropical savannahs." Gordon H. Orians. 1980. "Habitat Selection: General Theory and Applications to Human Behavior." In J. S. Lockard, ed., *The Evolution of Human Social Behavior*. New York: Elsevier, p. 64. Quoted in Donald Symons. 1985. "Darwinism and Contemporary Marriage." Pp. 133–155 in Kingsley Davis, ed., *Contemporary Marriage*. New York: Russell Sage Foundation, p. 137. See also Gordon H. Orians and Judith H. Heerwagen. 1992. "Evolved Responses to Landscapes." Pp. 555–579 in Jerome H. Barkow, Leda Cosmides, and John Tooby, eds., *The Adapted Mind: Evolutionary Psychology and the Generation of Culture*. New York: Oxford University Press.

10. For a general-interest discussion of early human bands, see Leakey and Lewin, *Origins Reconsidered*.

11. John Paul Scott. 1989. *The Evolution of Social Systems*. New York: Gordon and Breach. C. R. Hallpike. 1986. *The Principles of Social Evolution*. New York and Oxford: Clarendon Press.

12. Jane B. Lancaster. 1985. "Evolutionary Perspectives on Sex Differences in the Higher Primates." Pp. 3–27 in Alice S. Rossi, ed., *Gender and the Life Course*. New York: Aldine de Gruyter.

13. Doreen Kimura. 1992. "Sex Differences in the Brain." *Scientific American* (September):119–125. Anne Moir and David Jessel. 1991. *Brain Sex*. New York: Lyle Stuart. Jill B. Becker, S. Marc Breedlove, and David Crews, eds., 1992. *Behavioral Endocrinology*. Cambridge, MA: MIT Press/Bradford Books.

14. Alice S. Rossi. 1985. "Gender and Parenthood." Pp. 161–191 in Rossi, ed., *Gender and the Life Course*.

15. Reported in Mary Maxwell Katz and Melvin J. Konner. 1981. "The Role of the Father in Anthropological Perspective." Pp. 155–185 in Michael E. Lamb, ed., *The Role of the Father in Child Development*. New York: John Wiley, p. 164.

16. Kyle D. Pruett. 1987. *The Nurturing Father*. New York: Warner Books. Ross D. Parke. 1981. *Fathers*. Cambridge, MA: Harvard University Press. Michael E. Lamb, Joseph H. Pleck, Eric L. Charnov, and James A. Levine. 1987. "A Biosocial Perspective on Paternal Behavior and Involvement." Pp. 111–142 in Jane B. Lancaster et al., *Parenting Across the Life Span: Biosocial Dimensions*. New York: Aldine de Gruyter.

17. C. Owen Lovejoy. 1981. "The Origin of Man." *Science* 211(4480):341–350. See also William J. Hamilton III. 1984. "Significance of Paternal Investment by Primates to the Evolution of Adult Male-Female Associations." Pp. 309–335 in David M. Taub, ed., *Primate Paternalism*. New York: Van Nostrand Reinhold.

18. Helen E. Fisher. 1992. *Anatomy of Love.* New York: W. W. Norton.
19. Jane B. Lancaster and Chet S. Lancaster. 1987. "The Watershed: Change in Parental-Investment and Family Formation Strategies in the Course of Human Evolution." Pp. 187–205 in Lancaster et al., *Parenting Across the Life Span,* p. 189.
20. Ibid., p. 192.
21. Monogamy is most common among birds; 90% of bird species are monogamous. High rates of avian monogamy are found because nestling birds are so helpless and avian mothers (who don't lactate) are commonly no better suited to parenting tasks than fathers. Douglas W. Mock and Masahiro Fujioka. 1990. "Monogamy and Long-Term Pair Bonding in Vertebrates." *Trends in Ecology and Evolution* 5(2):39–43.
22. Leakey and Lewin. *Origins Reconsidered,* pp. 56–57.
23. See discussion in Fisher. *Anatomy of Love,* p. 334.
24. Pierre L. van den Berghe. 1988. "The Family and the Biological Base of Human Sociality." Pp. 39–60 in Erik E. Filsinger, *Biosocial Perspectives on the Family.* Newbury Park, CA: Sage, p. 43.
25. See, e.g., R. D. Alexander. 1979. *Darwinism and Human Affairs.* Seattle: University of Washington Press.
26. See Paul W. Turke. 1988. "Concealed Ovulation, Menstrual Synchrony, and Paternal Investment." Pp. 119–136 in Filsinger, *Biosocial Perspectives on the Family.* For a critical view of this theory, see R. D. Martin. 1992. "Female Cycles in Relation to Paternity in Primate Societies." Pp. 238–274 in R. D. Martin, A. F. Dixson, and E. J. Wickings, eds., *Paternity in Primates: Genetic Tests and Theories.* Basel: Karger.
27. See Robert A. Hinde. 1987. *Individuals, Relationships and Culture: Links Between Ethology and the Social Sciences.* Cambridge: Cambridge University Press. Anthony Walsh. 1991. *The Science of Love.* Buffalo, NY: Prometheus Books.
28. Donald Symons. "Darwinism," p. 151.
29. Quoted in Daly and Wilson. *Sex, Evolution, and Behavior,* p. 281.
30. Robert L. Trivers. 1972. "Parental Investment and Sexual Selection." In B. Campbell, ed., *Sexual Selection and the Descent of Man.* Chicago: Aldine. David Buss. 1994. *The Evolution of Desire.* New York: Basic Books.
31. Daly and Wilson. *Sex, Evolution, and Behavior,* p. 280.
32. Robert A. Hinde. *Individuals, Relationships, and Culture,* pp. 119–122; G. P. Murdock and D. R. White. 1969. "Standard Cross-Cultural Sample." *Ethnology* 8:329–369.
33. Quoted in Lawrence Stone. 1990. *Road to Divorce: England, 1530–1987.* New York: Oxford University Press, p. 7.
34. Joel R. Peck and Marcus W. Feldman. 1988. "Kin Selection and the Evolution of Monogamy." *Science* 240:1672–1674.
35. Steven Gaulin and Alice Schlegel. 1980. "Paternal Confidence and Paternal Investment: A Cross-Cultural Test of a Sociobiological Hypothesis." *Ethology and Sociobiology* 1:301–309 (308).
36. Mark V. Flinn. 1992. "Paternal Care in a Caribbean Village." Pp. 57–84 in Barry S. Hewlett, ed., *Father-Child Relations: Cultural and Biosocial Contexts.* New York: Aldine de Gruyter, p. 80.
37. Patricia Draper and Henry Harpending. 1982. "Father Absence and Reproductive Strategy: An Evolutionary Perspective." *Journal of Anthropological Research* 38(3):255–273.
38. See Buss. *Evolution of Desire.*

39. Martin Daly and Margo Wilson. 1988. *Homicide*. New York: Aldine de Gruyter, p. 294.
40. Laura Betzig. 1986. *Despotism and Differential Reproduction: A Darwinian View of History*. New York: Aldine de Gruyter.
41. Devra G. Kleiman and James R. Malcolm. 1981. "The Evolution of Male Parental Investment in Mammals." Pp. 347–387 in D. J. Gubernick and P. H. Klopfer, eds., *Paternal Care in Mammals*. New York: Plenum.
42. This relies heavily on the discussion in Barry S. Hewlett. 1991. *Intimate Fathers*. Ann Arbor: University of Michigan Press, chapter 8.
43. Katz and Konner. "Role of the Father."
44. Marshall Sahlins. 1972. *Stone Age Economics*. Chicago: Aldine.
45. Katz and Konner. "Role of the Father," p. 167.
46. See R. B. Lee. 1979. *The !Kung San: Men, Women, and Work in a Foraging Society*. Cambridge: Cambridge University Press.
47. Katz and Konner. "Role of the Father," p. 167.
48. See Jacqueline S. Solway and Richard B. Lee. 1990. "Foragers, Genuine or Spurious?" (with following commentary). *Current Anthropology* 31(2):109–146; Edwin N. Wilmsen and James R. Denbow. 1990. "Paradigmatic History of San-speaking Peoples and Current Attempts at Revision"(with following commentary). *Current Anthropology* 31(5):489–524.
49. For an overview of these changes, see Daniel Chirot. 1994. *How Societies Change*. Thousand Oaks, CA: Pine Forge Press; and Gerhard Lenski, Jean Lenski, and Patrick Nolan. 1991. *Human Societies*. 6th ed. New York: McGraw-Hill.
50. Jane B. Lancaster and Chet S. Lancaster. 1987.
51. Martin King Whyte. 1978. *The Status of Women in Preindustrial Societies*. Princeton, NJ: Princeton University Press, p. 172.
52. For an intriguing perspective that the rise of complex, culturally based societies represents a "social cage" that has produced tensions with our primate biological legacy, see Alexandra Maryanski and Jonathan H. Turner. 1993. *The Social Cage: Human Nature and the Evolution of Society*. Stanford, CA: Stanford University Press. See also Riane Eisler. 1987. *The Chalice and the Blade*. San Francisco: Harper and Row. It persuasively argues that gender "partnership" societies were replaced by male "dominator" societies.
53. Jane B. Lancaster. 1985. "Evolutionary Perspectives in Sex Differences in the Higher Primates." Pp. 3–27 in Alice S. Rossi, ed., *Gender and the Life Course*. New York: Aldine de Gruyter.
54. Herbert Barry and L. M. Paxson. 1971. "Infancy and Early Childhood: Cross-Cultural Codes." *Ethnology* 10:467–508.
55. Ibid.
56. Reported in Barry Hewlett. *Intimate Fathers*, p. 158.
57. Barry and Paxson. "Infancy and Early Childhood."
58. Suzanne Frayser. 1985. *Varieties of Sexual Experience: An Anthropological Perspective on Human Sexuality*. New Haven, CT: HRAF Press, p. 248.
59. Margaret Mead. 1949. *Male and Female*. New York: Dell.
60. Fisher. *Anatomy of Love*.
61. The divorce rate among the !Kung is estimated to be about as high as that of modern societies. Nancy Howell. 1979. *Demography of the Dobe !Kung*. New York: Academic Press.
62. Roderick Phillips. 1988. *Putting Asunder: A History of Divorce in Western Society*.

Cambridge: Cambridge University Press; William J. Goode. 1993. *World Changes in Divorce Patterns.* Cambridge, MA: Harvard University Press.

63. Laura Betzig. 1989. "Causes of Conjugal Dissolution: A Cross-Cultural Study." *Current Anthropology.* 30:654–676.

64. E.g., Gary R. Lee and Les B. Whitbeck. 1990. "Economic Systems and Rates of Polygyny." *Journal of Comparative Family Studies* 21(1):13–24.

65. See Hewlett. *Father-Child Relations.*

66. E.g., Barry S. Hewlett. 1992. "Husband-Wife Reciprocity and Father-Infant Relationship Among Aka Pygmies." Pp. 153–176 in Hewlett, *Father-Child Relations.*

Chapter 7. Reclaiming Fatherhood and Marriage

1. *The Hite Report on the Family: Growing Up under Patriarchy.* New York: Grove Press, 1994. Quote is from book excerpt in "Bringing Democracy Home." *Ms.,* March/April 1995, p. 56.

2. *Ms.,* p. 57

3. In the words of sociologist Pierre van den Berghe: "Advanced industrial societies have recreated, through a long evolutionary path, much the same kind of mobile, seminomadic, nuclear, bilateral family, minimally restricted by collateral relatives [and] by extended kin obligations . . . as existed in the simplest, smallest societies." Pierre van den Berghe. 1979. *Human Family Systems: An Evolutionary View.* Prospect Heights, IL: Waveland Press, p. 132.

4. Lawrence Stone. 1977. *The Family, Sex and Marriage in England, 1500–1800.* New York: Harper and Row, p. 687.

5. Dennis A. Ahlburg and Carol J. DeVita. 1992. "New Realities of the American Family." *Population Bulletin* 47(2).

6. Of course, genetic engineering and other biotechnological interventions threaten to diminish the difference.

7. James Q. Wilson. 1993. *The Moral Sense.* New York: Free Press.

8. Available for $10. from the Institute for American Values, 1841 Broadway, Suite 211, New York, NY 10023.

9. Teresa Castro Martin and Larry L. Bumpass. 1989. "Recent Trends in Marital Disruption." *Demography* 26(1):37–51. The effect of age of marriage on divorce seems to diminish and eventually becomes negligible after the late twenties.

10. The late age of marriage is one of the many ways in which this marriage pattern differs significantly from that of the fifties; in 1957 the average woman who married was still a teenager!

11. See, e.g., L. E. Troll and V. L. Bengston. 1982. "Intergenerational Relations Through the Life Span." Pp. 890–911 in B. B. Wolman, ed., *Handbook of Developmental Psychology.* Englewood Cliffs, NJ: Prentice-Hall.

12. See discussion and sources in chapter 1.

13. "More difficult" may be an understatement. As Leon R. Kass has noted (personal communication), "People will enter into [marriage] only after multiple disappointments, with massive experience of impermanence, withheld commitments, and loss of trust. We will have fully formed, self-seeking individuals wedded to work and the habits of the single life. We will have individuals who have been indulged in a prolonged functional immaturity with respect to the emotional requirements necessary for stable marriages. Marriages will be looked upon more as a contract, a deal, a settling, entered into with calculation and caution, and not following falling

in love." For empirical analysis of this problem, see Alice S. Rossi. 1980. "Life Span Theories and Women's Lives." *Signs: Journal of Women in Culture and Society* 6:4–32; Linda J. Waite, Frances K. Goldscheider, and Christina Witsberger. 1986. "Nonfamily Living and the Erosion of Traditional Family Orientations Among Young Adults." *American Sociological Review* 51(4):541–554.

14. For example, it might be useful public policy to provide incentives to unmarried adults to save a substantial portion of their income in a "family fund," with an eye toward eventually offsetting the temporary loss of one spouse's income after marriage and childbirth.

15. Allan Guttmacher Institute. 1994. *Sex and America's Teenagers.* New York: Allan Guttmacher Institute, p. 8.

16. *USA Weekend,* March 25–27, 1994, p. 4.

17. Rolonda/Siecus Survey Conducted by Roper Starch Worldwide, Inc. Reported in the *New York Times,* May 18, 1994, p. A20.

18. From Francine Klagsbrun. 1985. *Married People.* New York: Bantam Doubleday Dell.

19. John Gottman. 1994. *Why Marriages Succeed or Fail.* New York: Simon and Schuster, pp. 28, 173.

20. Judith Wallerstein and Sandra Blakeslee. 1995. *The Good Marriage.* New York: Houghton Mifflin, pp. 26, 331.

21. Carolyn Pape Cowan and Philip A. Cowan. 1992. *When Partners Become Parents: The Big Life Change for Couples.* New York: Basic Books. Wallerstein and Blakeslee. *The Good Marriage.*

22. Contact the ABA's Family Law Section at 750 Lake Shore Drive, Chicago, IL 60611.

23. Pepper Schwartz. 1995. "When Staying Is Worth the Pain." *New York Times,* April 4, C1.

24. 1995. New York: Basic Books

25. 1992. New York: Summit Books. Estimate is from a television conversation with Dr. Weiner-Davis.

26. Reported in "American Woman's Dilemma." *Life,* June 16, 1947, pp. 101–116.

27. More often than not, of course, they cared for the elderly and infirm who today would be consigned to nursing homes; were expected to take care of every aspect of their husband's life outside of his work; often served as unpaid labor enhancing their husband's career (typing, writing, entertaining); and through their volunteer work and unheralded neighborly help, held together the social fabric of a community with few or no government welfare programs.

28. Kingsley Davis and Pietronella van den Oever. 1982. "Demographic Foundations of New Sex Roles." *Population and Development Review* 8(3):495–511 (p. 508).

29. Penelope Leach. 1994. *Children First.* New York: Alfred A. Knopf, p. 47.

30. Leach. *Children First,* p. 38.

31. Willard W. Hartup. 1989. "Social Relationships and Their Developmental Significance." *American Psychologist* (February):120–126 (p. 122).

32. Graeme Russell. 1983. *The Changing Role of Fathers?* New York: University of Queensland Press. Philip Blumstein and Pepper Schwartz. 1983. *American Couples.* New York: Pocket Books. Despite their hopes, Russell found that shared caregiving couples had marriages of "significantly lower quality" than traditional couples, and Blumstein and Schwartz concluded that "when roles are reversed, with men doing housework and women taking over as provider, couples become dreadfully un-

happy" (p. 324). An additional problem is that when a divorce comes to a shared caregiving couple, it is much more likely for a child-custody battle to ensue, since the man wishes to keep the children as much as the woman does.

33. Diane N. Lye and Timothy J. Biblarz. 1993. "The Effects of Attitudes Toward Family Life and Gender Roles on Marital Satisfaction." *Journal of Family Issues* 14(2):157–188.

34. Alice S. Rossi. 1987. "Parenthood in Transition: From Lineage to Child to Self-Orientation." Pp. 31–81 in Jane B. Lancaster, Jeanne Altmann, Alice S. Rossi, and Lonnie R. Sherrod, eds., *Parenting Across the Life Span*. New York: Aldine de Gruyter, p. 69.

35. Kyle D. Pruett. 1987. *The Nurturing Father*. New York: Warner Books.

36. T. Berry Brazelton. 1992. *Touchpoints*. Reading, MA: Addison Wesley, p. 423.

37. Alice Rossi. "Parenthood in Transition," pp. 57–61.

38. Jay Belsky, Lise Youngblade, Michael Rovine, and Brenda Volling. 1991. "Patterns of Marital Change and Parent-Child Interaction." *Journal of Marriage and the Family* 53(2):487–498.

39. Nancy Eisenberg and Paul H. Mussen. 1989. *The Roots of Prosocial Behavior in Children*. Cambridge: Cambridge University Press.

40. The evidence is reviewed in Robert Karen. 1994. *Becoming Attached*. New York: Warner Books.

41. See Jay Belsky. 1988. "Infant Day Care and Socio-Emotional Development: The United States." *Journal of Child Psychology and Psychiatry* 29(4):397–406; Penelope Leach. *Children First*, chapter 4.

42. See David Gutmann. 1994. *Reclaimed Powers: Men and Women in Later Life*. Evanston, IL: Northwestern University Press.

43. Angus Campbell. 1981. *The Sense of Well-Being in America*. New York: McGraw-Hill, pp. 202–203.

44. David G. Myers. 1992. *The Pursuit of Happiness*. New York: William Morrow, p. 39. Based on Angus Campbell. 1981. *The Sense of Well-Being in America*. New York: McGraw-Hill.

45. David G. Myers. *Pursuit of Happiness*, p. 44.

46. Norval D. Glenn. 1991. "The Family Values of Americans." Working Paper, Institute for American Values, New York. The "satisfaction" component should be stressed; marriage quality is very important (see Myers, *Pursuit of Happiness*, pp. 156–158). People who say their marriage is satisfying rarely report being unhappy, discontented with life, or depressed, while the unhappily married are among the least happy. A bad marriage may be worse for happiness than having no marriage at all.

Unfortunately, the satisfaction of people with their marriages has declined some in recent decades. People in today's surviving marriages are less likely to describe their marriages as "very happy" than they were several decades ago; the percentage had dropped from 68% in 1973 to 61% in 1989, with larger drops in selected age groups (a surprising finding, perhaps, in view of the fact that the "bad" marriages were supposed to have been cleared out through easy access to divorce.) See Norval D. Glenn. 1993. "What's Happening to American Marriage?" *USA Today*, May 27–28; Norval D. Glenn. 1991. "The Recent Trend in Marital Success in the United States." *Journal of Marriage and the Family* 53:261–270; G. R. Lee, K. Seccombe, and C. L. Shehan. 1991. "Marital Status and Personal Happiness: An Analysis of Trend Data." *Journal of Marriage and the Family* 53:839–844. Norval D.

Glenn and Charles N. Weaver. 1988. "The Changing Relationship of Marital Status to Reported Happiness." *Journal of Marriage and the Family* 50:317–324.

47. Campbell. *Sense of Well-Being,* p. 197.
48. Myers. *Pursuit of Happiness,* p. 83.
49. Ibid., p. 84. Apparently, however, the percentage of people who report that their spouse is their best friend has been dropping. See Linda DiStefano. 1990. "Pressures of Modern Life Bring Increased Importance to Friendship." *Gallup Poll Monthly* 294 (March):24–33.
50. Lee A Lillard and Linda J. Waite. 1995. "'Til Death Do Us Part: Marital Disruption and Mortality." *American Journal of Sociology* 100(5):1131–1156.
51. Bernard L. Cohen and I-Sing Lee. 1979. "A Catalog of Risks." *Health Physics* 36:707–722. Cited in Linda J. Waite. 1995. "Does Marriage Matter?" University of Chicago. Unpublished presidential address to the Population Association of America.
52. James S. House, Karl R. Landis, and Debra Umberson. 1988. "Social Relationships and Health." *Science* 241:540–545 (p. 542).
53. Catherine E. Ross. 1995. "Reconceptualizing Marital Status as a Continuum of Social Attachment." *Journal of Marriage and the Family* 57(1):129–140. Quoted in Waite. "Does Marriage Matter?"
54. Sanders Korenman and David Neumark. 1990. "Does Marriage Really Make Men More Productive?" *Journal of Human Resources* 26(2):282–307.
55. Edward O. Laumann, John H. Gagnon, Robert T. Michael, and Stuart Michaels. 1994. *The Social Organization of Sexuality: Sexual Practices in the United States.* Chicago: University of Chicago Press.
56. Ross D. Parke. 1981. *Fathers.* Cambridge, MA: Harvard University Press, p. 11.
57. See Aaron Hass. 1994. *The Gift of Fatherhood: How Men's Lives Are Transformed by Their Children.* New York: Simon and Schuster. Michael E. Lamb, Joseph H. Pleck, and James A. Levine. 1986. "The Effects of Paternal Involvement on Fathers and Mothers." In Robert A. Lewis and Marvin B. Sussman, eds., *Men's Changing Roles in the Family.* New York: Haworth.
58. Cambridge, MA: Harvard University Press.
59. He used a most interesting data set drawn from the Gluecks' comparative study of 500 delinquent boys and a matched control group of 500 nondelinquent boys from lower- and working-class families in the Boston area. Snarey reinterviewed the available members *of the control group* who went on to marry and father children, some 240 men born during the 1920s and 1930s. The interviews included not only the fathering behaviors and general adult outcomes of these men but also the childhood experiences and adult outcomes of their firstborn children (both sons and daughters), most of whom were born during the baby boom 1950s.
60. P. 98. Erik Erikson considered "generativity"—active concern for others beyond the confines of the nuclear family, for future generations, and for the nature of the society in which those generations will live—to be an important mark of maturity in middle age. He suggested that people who do not develop generativity fall into a state of self-absorption in which their personal needs and comforts become their main concerns; they become self-centered and narcissistic. Snarey's work provides strong support for Erikson's views.
61. Discussed in Sara McLanahan and Julia Adams. 1987. "Parenthood and Psychological Well-Being." *Annual Review of Sociology* 13:237–257 (p. 247).
62. Among the general population, surveys show that being married is more critical to positive feelings of well-being than having children (Angus Campbell. *Sense of Well-*

Being, p. 203). Adults with young children living at home report somewhat lower levels of happiness and less satisfaction with their marriages, friends, and leisure activities than adults not living with children. Moreover, there has been a decline in recent decades in the well-being of adults with children, and the well-being gap between parents and nonparents has slightly increased (Sara McLanahan and Julia Adams. 1989. "The Effects of Children on Adults' Psychological Well-Being, 1957–1976." *Social Forces* 68(1):124–146; McLanahan and Adams. "Parenthood"). Yet much of the decline of satisfaction that comes from having children relates to the changing family conditions of recent years, and it mainly involves women. Single mothers and working mothers, for example, have lower levels of satisfaction than do other mothers, and the steepest declines in satisfaction have been among working mothers.

63. Angus Campbell. *Sense of Well-Being*, p. 231.
64. 1988. *On Borrowed Time: How the Growth in Entitlement Spending Threatens America's Future*. San Francisco: ICS Press.
65. *Family Affairs* (Winter 1994):1,2 (p. 2).
66. *New York Times*, January 16, 1994.
67. Christopher Jencks. 1992. *Rethinking Social Policy: Race, Poverty, and the Underclass*. Cambridge, MA: Harvard University Press, p. 88.
68. See David Popenoe. 1995. "The Roots of Declining Social Virtue: Family, Community, and the Need for a 'Natural Communities Policy.'" Pp. 71–104 in Mary Ann Glendon and David Blankenhorn, eds., *Seedbeds of Virtue: Sources of Competence, Character, and Citizenship in American Society*. Lanham, MD: Madison Books (from which these community guidelines are adapted).
69. John Kasarda and M. Janowitz. 1974. "Community Attachment in Mass Society." *American Sociological Review* 39:328–339. Robert J. Sampson. 1988. "Local Friendship Ties and Community Attachment in Mass Society: A Multilevel Systemic Model." *American Sociological Review* 53(5):766–779.
70. Studies have found that "the larger the community a person lives in, the less likely he or she is to say that it is 'a good place to live' . . . and to be fully satisfied with their immediate neighborhood." Angus Campbell. *Sense of Well-Being*, p. 150.
71. See Oscar Newman. 1980. *Community of Interest*. Garden City, NY: Anchor Press/Doubleday. Clark, William A.V. 1992. "Residential Preferences and Residential Choices in a Multiethnic Context." *Demography* 29(3):451–466.

Index